TWENTY-SIXTH, OR CAMERONIAN REGIMENT 1866

HISTORICAL RECORD

OF

THE TWENTY-SIXTH,

OR

CAMERONIAN REGIMENT.

EDITED BY

THOMAS CARTER,

ADJUTANT-GENERAL'S OFFICE, HORSE GUARDS;

AUTHOR OF "CURIOSITIES OF WAR," "MEDALS OF THE BRITISH ARMY," &c.

"The lyart veteran heard the word of God
By Cameron thundered."
          "Their deeds,
These on tradition's tongue still live, these shall
On history's honest page be pictured bright
To latest times."   *Grahame.*

WITH ILLUSTRATIONS.

The Naval & Military Press Ltd

Published by

The Naval & Military Press Ltd
Unit 10 Ridgewood Industrial Park,
Uckfield, East Sussex,
TN22 5QE England

Tel: +44 (0) 1825 749494
Fax: +44 (0) 1825 765701

www.naval-military-press.com
www.military-genealogy.com
www.militarymaproom.com

In reprinting in facsimile from the original, any imperfections are inevitably reproduced and the quality may fall short of modern type and cartographic standards.

THE TWENTY-SIXTH,

OR

CAMERONIAN REGIMENT,

BEARS ON THE REGIMENTAL COLOUR

"EGYPT,"   "THE SPHINX,"

"CORUNNA,"

"CHINA,"   "THE DRAGON."

PREFACE.

THE official publication of the Historical Records of the Regiments of the British Army was authorised by the following General Orders, dated Horse Guards, 1st January, 1836:—

HIS MAJESTY has been pleased to command that, with the view of doing the fullest justice to Regiments, as well as to Individuals who have distinguished themselves by their Bravery in Action with the Enemy, an Account of the Services of every Regiment in the British Army, shall be published under the superintendence and direction of the Adjutant-General; and that this Account shall contain the following particulars, viz.:—

—— The Period and Circumstances of the Original Formation of the Regiment; The Stations at which it has been from time to time employed; The Battles, Sieges, and other Military Operations in which it has been engaged, particularly specifying any Achievement it may have performed, and the Colours, Trophies, &c., it may have captured from the Enemy.

—— The Names of the Officers, and the Number of Non-Commissioned Officers and Privates Killed or Wounded by the Enemy, specifying the Place and Date of the Action.

—— The Names of those Officers who, in consideration of their Gallant Services and Meritorious conduct in Engagements with the Enemy, have been distinguished with Titles, Medals, or other Marks of His Majesty's gracious favour.

—— The Names of all such Officers, Non-Commissioned Officers, and Privates, as may have specially signalized themselves in Action.

And,

—— The Badges and Devices which the Regiment may have been permitted to bear, and the Causes on account of which such Badges or Devices, or any other Marks of Distinction, have been granted.

By Command of the Right Honourable

GENERAL LORD HILL,
Commanding-in-Chief.

JOHN MACDONALD,
Adjutant-General.

Several regimental histories were in consequence compiled by the late Mr. Richard Cannon, when Principal Clerk of the Adjutant-General's Office, and published, in the first instance, under the patronage of KING WILLIAM THE FOURTH, and afterwards of HER MAJESTY THE QUEEN. Upon Mr. Cannon's retirement, after a lengthened official career of upwards of half a century, the Adjutant-General, in consequence of my having assisted that gentleman in preparing these Records, recommended me to the Lords Commissioners of the Treasury as the future Editor, but it was decided that they should not be continued.

Although the present History is not, therefore,

published by authority, yet I have endeavoured by fresh research, suggested by increased experience, to make it as complete as possible; and to keep up that desirable feeling of *esprit-de-corps* which the publication of Regimental Records, under such distinguished patronage, was specially designed to encourage, these pages are now submitted to the Army and to the Public, in the hope that they will not prove altogether unacceptable; while, at the same time, they are intended to afford pleasure to those who have served, are serving, or who have had relatives and friends, in the fine old TWENTY-SIXTH, or CAMERONIAN REGIMENT.

T. C.

THE TWENTY-SIXTH,
OR
CAMERONIAN REGIMENT.

CONTENTS
OF THE
HISTORICAL RECORD.

YEAR		PAGE
1688	INTRODUCTION	1
1689	Formation of the Regiment	3
——	The Earl of Angus appointed its Colonel . .	—
——	Names of Officers	5
——	Terms of agreement on which the Cameronians were embodied	6
——	Action at Dunkeld	9
——	Death and services of Colonel Cleland . . .	10
——	Remodelling of the Regiment	15
1690	Names of Officers	16
1691	The Regiment embarked for Flanders . . .	17
1692	Battle of Steinkirk	19
——	Death of the Earl of Angus	21
——	Lieut.-Colonel Andrew Monro promoted Colonel of the Regiment	22
1693	Battle of Landen, or Neer-Winden . . .	23
——	Lieut.-Colonel James Ferguson promoted Colonel of the Regiment	24
1694	Operations of the Campaign	25
1695	Attack on Fort Kenoque	—
——	Capture of Namur	26
1696	Reviewed by King William III. . . .	28
1697	Peace of Ryswick	—
1700	The Regiment proceeded to Scotland . . .	—
1701	War of the Spanish Succession	29

CONTENTS OF THE HISTORICAL RECORD.

Year		Page
1702	The Regiment embarked for Flanders	29
	Siege of Kaiserwært	—
	Capture of Venloo, Stevenswaert, Ruremond, and Liege	31
1703	Reviewed by the Duke of Marlborough	32
	Sieges of Bonn, Limburg, and Guelders	33
1704	Action at Donawert	35
	Capture of Rain and Aicha	37
	Occupation of Friedburg	—
	Battle of Blenheim	39
	Landau invested	42
	Occupation of Lauterburg	—
	Surrender of Landau	43
1705	Relief of Liege	44
	Recapture of Huy	—
	Forcing the lines at Hildesheim	—
	Surrender of Louvain	45
	Passage of the Dyle	—
	Siege of Sandvliet	46
	Colonel John Borthwick appointed Colonel of the Regiment	48
1706	Exchanged with Colonel Lord John Dalrymple, afterwards Earl of Stair	—
	Battle of Ramillies	49
	Lieut.-Colonel George Preston promoted Colonel of the Regiment	50
	Sieges of Ostend, Dendermond, and Aeth	—
1707	Operations of the Campaign	52
1708	Battle of Oudenarde	53
	Siege of Lisle	54
	Action at Wynendale	56
	Capture of Lisle	59
	Siege of Ghent	60
1709	Capitulation of Tournay	61
	Siege of Mons	62
	Battle of Malplaquet	—
	Reduction of Mons	65
1710	Passage of the lines at Pont à Vendin	66

CONTENTS OF THE HISTORICAL RECORD. xi

Year		Page
1710	Investment of Douay	66
——	Siege of Bethune	69
1711	Passage of the lines on the Scheldt	71
——	Siege and capture of Bouchain	72
——	Services of Colonel Blackader	73
1712	The Duke of Marlborough succeeded by the Duke of Ormond	75
——	Bombardment of Arras	—
——	Siege of Quesnoy	76
——	Suspension of Arms	—
1713	Treaty of Utrecht	—
——	The Regiment embarked for Ireland	77
1715	Ordered to England, on account of the Rebellion in favour of the Pretender	—
——	Action at Preston, Lancashire	78
1716	Additional services, and death of Colonel Blackader	81
——	The Regiment returned to Ireland	—
1720	Lieut.-Colonel Philip Anstruther appointed Colonel of the Regiment	—
1727	The Regiment embarked for Gibraltar	82
——	Defence of Gibraltar	—
1738	The Regiment embarked for Minorca	83
1748	The Regiment returned to Ireland	—
1751	Royal Warrant regulating the clothing, standards, facings, number, and rank of Regiments	—
1754	The Regiment proceeded to Scotland	—
1757	Returned to Ireland	—
1760	Colonel Edward Sandford appointed Colonel of the Regiment	—
1763	Colonel John Scott appointed Colonel of the Regiment	—
1767	The Regiment embarked for North America	—
1775	War with the American Colonists	—
——	Services of the Regiment at Fort Ticonderoga, Crown Point, St. John's, and Fort Chambly	85
——	Defence of Quebec	87
——	Major-General Lord Adam Gordon appointed Colonel of the Regiment	88

CONTENTS OF THE HISTORICAL RECORD.

Year		Page
1776	The Regiment removed to New York . . .	89
——	Action near Elizabeth Town Point . . .	—
1777	Attack on Forts Montgomery and Clinton . .	90
1778	Evacuation of Philadelphia	91
——	Declaration of War by France	—
1779	Remains of the Regiment embarked for England .	92
1780	Ordered to Tamworth to recruit	93
1781	Marched to Shrewsbury	—
1782	Arrived at Tynemouth	—
——	Major-General Sir William Erskine, Bart., appointed Colonel of the Regiment	—
1783	The Regiment proceeded to Scotland . . .	—
——	Embarked for Ireland	—
1786	Authorised to revive the title of "Cameronian" .	—
1787	Embarked for Canada	94
1793	Inspected by His Royal Highness the Duke of Kent	95
1795	Major-General the Honourable Sir Charles Stuart, K.B., appointed Colonel of the Regiment . .	96
1800	The Regiment proceeded from Canada to Nova Scotia	97
——	Embarked for England	—
1801	Lieut.-General Andrew Gordon appointed Colonel of the Regiment	—
——	The Regiment proceeded to Egypt . . .	—
——	Action near Alexandria	99
——	Surrender of Alexandria	—
——	The Regiment returned to England . . .	100
——	Authorised to bear the word "Egypt," with the "Sphinx"	—
——	Medal conferred by the Sultan	101
——	Names of Recipients	—
1802	The Regiment proceeded to Scotland . . .	103
1803	Formation of the Second Battalion . . .	104
——	The First Battalion embarked for Ireland . .	—
——	Demonstration of national feeling at Maybole by the Mayor and Corporation	—
——	The Second Battalion proceeded to Ireland . .	—
1804	Both Battalions encamped on the Curragh . .	—

CONTENTS OF THE HISTORICAL RECORD. xiii

YEAR		PAGE
1805	The First Battalion embarked for Germany	108
——	Wreck of the "Maria" and "Aurora" transports	—
——	Officers and men lost therein	109
——	Return home of the remainder of the Battalion	—
1806	Major-General Lord Elphinstone appointed Colonel of the Regiment	110
——	The First Battalion embarked for Ireland	111
1807	The Second Battalion proceeded from Ireland to North Britain	112
1808	The First Battalion encamped on the Curragh	114
——	Embarked for Corunna	—
——	Names of Officers who proceeded to Spain	115
——	Subsequent operations	116
1809	Retreat on, and Battle at, Corunna	126
——	Authorised to bear the word "CORUNNA"	127
——	The Battalion embarked for England	128
——	Encamped near Portsmouth	131
——	The First Battalion embarked for Walcheren	132
——	Names of Officers who proceeded therewith	—
——	Operations after the landing	133
——	Fearful casualties from Fever	135
——	Return home of the Expedition	—
1810	The First Battalion ordered to proceed to the neighbourhood of London, on the occasion of the Riots, when Sir Francis Burdett was sent to the Tower	137
——	The First Battalion embarked for Jersey	—
1811	Ordered to Portugal	—
——	Names of Officers embarked	—
——	Blockade of Ciudad Rodrigo	140
——	Affairs near Aldea de Ponte	142
1812	Sickness in the First Battalion	145
——	Removed to Lisbon	—
——	Embarked for Gibraltar	147
1812	Success in recruiting the Second Battalion, still in Scotland	—
1813	Major-General the Earl of Dalhousie, K.B., appointed Colonel of the Regiment	148

xiv   CONTENTS OF THE HISTORICAL RECORD.

Year		Page
1814	Disbandment of the Second Battalion	152
1822	The Regiment proceeded from Gibraltar to Ireland	155
1824	Dispersed state of the Regiment	158
1827	Removed to England	163
1828	Embarked for Madras	165
1830	Proceeded to Calcutta	169
1831	Toilsome marches	171
1834	Ordered on Field Service	177
——	Differences with the Rajah of Joudpore arranged	—
1836	Sufferings from Cholera	180
1838	Major-General Sir John Colborne (afterwards Lord Seaton), G.C.B., appointed Colonel of the Regiment	182
1839	Question regarding the PIPERS	184
1840	The Regiment embarked for China	185
——	Names of Officers who proceeded therewith	—
——	Death of Colonel Oglander	186
——	Landing at Chusan	187
——	Dreadful mortality there	—
——	Singular Memorandum, from the Court of Directors, in reference to the health of the Regiment whilst in India	188
1841	Attack upon Cheumpee	189
——	Advance on Whampoa	191
——	Occupation of Howqua's Fort	—
——	Operations against Canton	—
——	Affair near that place	192
——	Complimentary Order by Major-General Sir Hugh Gough	—
——	Attack of Amoy	193
——	——— Koolangsoo	—
1842	Affair near Ningpo	195
——	Attack of Chapoo	—
——	Occupation of Paoushan and Shanghae	196
——	Capture of Chin-Keang-foo	197
——	Landing at Nankin	—
——	Conclusion of Peace	—
——	The Regiment authorised to bear the word "CHINA" with the "DRAGON"	198

CONTENTS OF THE HISTORICAL RECORD. XV

Year		Page
1842	Embarked for Calcutta	199
1843	Complimentary Order on the return home of the Regiment	200
——	Napoleon's Tomb at St. Helena, visited by the Regiment	202
——	Stationed at Edinburgh Castle	203
1844	Presentation of New Colours by Lady Douglas	205
——	Complimentary Order on the Regiment leaving Edinburgh	209
——	Arrived at Newcastle-on-Tyne	211
1845	Recruiting extended to England and Ireland	—
——	The Regiment embarked for Ireland	212
1846	Colonel Mountain appointed aide-de-camp to the QUEEN	213
——	The Regiment marched to Dublin	214
1847	Removed to Buttevant	215
1848	Presentation of the Good Conduct Medal to Colour-Sergeant James Searson	218
1849	Guard of Honour, under Captains Layard and Carey, to receive the QUEEN at Cork	219
1850	The Service Companies embarked for Gibraltar	220
——	The Depôt Companies removed from Ireland to Jersey	221
1851	The Depôt Companies embarked for South Britain	—
1853	The Service Companies proceeded to Canada	222
1854	Major-General Sir Philip Bainbrigge, C.B., appointed Colonel of the Regiment	223
——	The Service Companies removed to Bermuda	—
1855	The Depôt Companies embarked for Ireland	224
——	Returned to England	—
1856	Enfield Rifles supplied to the Regiment	225
——	Yellow Fever at Bermuda	226
1857	Commission appointed to report thereon	227
1858	Plaid Forage Cap of the Regiment authorised to be continued	228
——	The Depôt Companies removed to Ireland	229
1859	The Service Companies arrived at Kingstown in Ireland, from Bermuda	230

xvi CONTENTS OF THE HISTORICAL RECORD.

Year		Page
1860	Interchangeable Rifles issued to the Regiment in lieu of the Enfield	232
1861	The Regiment embarked at Dublin for Edinburgh	233
1862	Presentation of New Colours by Lady Belhaven	—
——	Complimentary Order on quitting Edinburgh	234
——	The Regiment proceeded to Aldershot	235
——	Three PIPERS authorised for the Regiment	—
——	Major-General George Henry Mackinnon, C.B., appointed Colonel of the Regiment	236
1863	The Depôt Companies removed from Ireland to Preston, Lancashire	237
1865	The Service Companies ordered to proceed to Bombay	—
——	District Order prior to Embarkation	—
——	Names of Officers embarked	238
1866	The Regiment stationed at Camp Belgaum	240
1867	CONCLUSION	—

SUCCESSION OF OFFICERS, 1689 to 1867 . . 241

APPENDIX.

I.—Stations and Out-Posts of the 26th Regiment, in Ireland, between October, 1822, and October, 1827 257
II.—Correspondence regarding the PIPERS . . . 258
III.—Questions and Replies relating to the Epidemic Fever at Bermuda in 1856 261
IV.—Correspondence relative to the PLAID FORAGE CAP worn by the Regiment 264

ILLUSTRATIONS.

Illustrations of uniforms after page xvi

1742. GRENADIER. 1750.

THE 26TH CAMERONIAN REGIMENT.

GRENADIER

1768

THE 26TH CAMERONIAN REGIMENT.

1792

THE 26TH CAMERONIAN REGIMENT.

1807.

THE 26TH CAMERONIAN REGIMENT.

THE 26TH CAMERONIAN REGIMENT.

1812

THE 26TH CAMERONIAN REGIMENT.

1826   LIGHT COMPANY.

THE 26TH CAMERONIAN REGIMENT.

THE 26TH CAMERONIAN REGIMENT.

LIGHT AND GRENADIER COMPANIES.
1840

THE 26TH CAMERONIAN REGIMENT

GRENADIER COMPANY

1854

THE 26TH CAMERONIAN REGIMENT.

1854

THE 26TH CAMERONIAN REGIMENT.

1854

THE 26TH CAMERONIAN REGIMENT.

1847.   1854.

THE 26TH CAMERONIAN REGIMENT.

1854.
THE 26TH CAMERONIAN REGIMENT.

1854.   1856.

THE 26TH CAMERONIAN REGIMENT.

1864.

THE 26TH CAMERONIAN REGIMENT.

1864.

THE 26TH CAMERONIAN REGIMENT.

1868.

THE 26TH CAMERONIAN REGIMENT.

1873.

THE 26TH CAMERONIAN REGIMENT.

1879.

THE 26TH CAMERONIAN REGIMENT.

COLOURS OF THE 26TH CAMERONIAN REGIMENT,
PRESENTED BY LADY BELHAVEN,
at Edinburgh, on the 21st April, 1862.

1879.

THE 26TH CAMERONIAN REGIMENT.

1880.

THE 26TH CAMERONIAN REGIMENT.

HISTORICAL RECORD

OF

THE TWENTY-SIXTH,

OR

CAMERONIAN REGIMENT.

THE REGIMENT which forms the subject of this 1688. Record derives its popular designation of CAMERONIANS from the sect (named after one of its first preachers, Richard Cameron) formed at the time when the religious persecutions of the Stuart family enforced against their subjects of the Presbyterian persuasion in Scotland, led to the assembling of bodies of men, who, rendered desperate by ill-usage, occasionally appeared in arms to resist this cruel and ill-judged policy. Looking upon themselves as the remnant who had not bowed the knee to Baal, these devoted men frequently met for worship during the silent hours of night, on many a Scottish hill-side, moor, or in lonely glen—the attempts made for their extirpation tending, as usual, only to increase their numbers. Such an example had its due effect in keeping up the spirit of resistance in the North against arbitrary power; and when the encroachments of James II. on the civil and religious liberties of the nation led to his flight from England, the Camero-

B

1688. nians gave proof of their devotion to the principles of the Revolution of 1688, as several of them, at this era, had volunteered for service in the Cameronian Guard, for the temporary support of the Estates; and, moreover, rendered important service to their country by protecting, together with the militia and some of the Argyle Highlanders, the early sittings of the Convention, wherein the Duke of Hamilton obtained the ascendancy, and thus rendered the new state of things, brought about by the flight of James II. and the arrival in London of the Prince of Orange in November, permanent to the north of the Tweed. The Duke of Gordon, a Roman Catholic, held the Castle at Edinburgh, which had placed the members of the Convention in danger; but apprehension was allayed when Colonel Sir John Lanier appeared with reliefs, and their security was confirmed

1689. towards the middle of March, 1689, by the arrival in Edinburgh of the three Scots Regiments which had been employed for many years in the Dutch service, and had been ordered to Scotland under the command of Major-General Mackay, one of these corps being his own and the other two that of Brigadier Balfour and Colonel Ramsay's.

The Cameronian Guard, consisting principally of inhabitants of Glasgow, being thus relieved, were dismissed with the thanks of the Convention for the timely assistance afforded. A proclamation was issued in April, requiring all men between sixteen and sixty to be ready in arms; and a proposition of the Cameronians, chiefly in and about Douglas, had been canvassed amongst their friends, as to the advisability of supplying a regiment for His Majesty's service. Such was the patriotism of the Cameronians, and their zeal and devotion, that twelve hundred men were raised in one day, on the instant, without beat of drum, and 1689, without levy money; and upon being regimented, they were placed under the command of the young Earl of Angus, not then twenty, only son of the Marquess of Douglas, to whom, as the first colonel, the Estates granted the following commission,* dated 19th of April, 1689:—

"The Estates of the kingdom of Scotland, con-
" sidering that James, Lord Angus has made an offer
" to levie a Regiment of 1200 foot, to be commanded
" by him as Collonell, and to be employed in the service
" of His Majestie, William, by the grace of God, King
" of Great Britain, France and Ireland; and the Estates
" reposeing trust and confidence in the fidelitie couradge
" and good conduct of the said James, Lord Angus,
" have therefore nominated, constituted and appoynted,
" and by these presents doe nominate, constitute, and
" appoynt the said James, Lord Angus to be Collonell
" of the said regiment of foot appoynted by the act
" of the said Estates of the dait of these presents,
" to be levied by him as said is consisting of 20 com-
" panies, and 60 men in each company, with full power
" to the said James, Lord Angus to nominate the
" Lieutenant Collonell and Major of the said regiment,
" and the Captains and inferior Officers of the several
" companies, and to grant Commissions accordingly,
" and to command and exercise the said regiment,
" both officers and souldiers, as Collonell and Captain
" carefully and diligently, and to keep them in good
" order and discipline, and to doe and act all things
" competant and incumbent for any Collonell of foot

---

* Thomson's "Acts of Scottish Parliament."

1689. "to do and performe, requireing and commanding hereby all officers and souldiers of the said regiment to give due obedience to the said James, Lord Angus as their Colloncll and to the respective commanding Officers, and further the estates do hereby command and require the said James, Lord Angus to observe and prosecute such orders and directions as he shall receive from tyme to tyme from them or from Major General Mackay, present Commander in Chiefe of the forces of this kingdome, or any other Commander in Chiefe for the tyme, or any superior Officers, according to the rules and discipline of War, and the estates do declair that such company of both officers and souldiers is to enter in pay after the same is mustered compleat, and the Field Officer after the whole regiment is mustered, and that his Commission shall continue untill the King's most excellent Majestie shall be pleased to grant new Commissions for the said regiment, 'or otherwise dispose' 'thereof signed by warrant,' and in the name of the Estates by the Duke of Hamilton their President."

Alexander Shields was appointed chaplain to the Earl of Angus's Regiment,[*] and his brother, Michael, clerk;

---

[*] Regiments were at first distinguished by the names of their colonels, and were not officially designated by their numerical titles until the Warrant of the 1st of July, 1751, was issued, by which it was required that "the number of the rank of the regiment" should be painted, or embroidered, in gold Roman characters on the colours. Before this period, however, Boards had been assembled to decide on the rank and precedency of regiments; the first was held in the Netherlands on the 10th of June, 1694, by King William III.; the second, in 1713, in Queen Anne's reign; and a third, by King George I., in 1715. The rule followed was, that English regiments raised in England took rank

one of the stipulations being, that the Cameronians should have a minister of their own persuasion, and that each company should be provided with an elder, in order that piety might be promoted, and offenders reproved.

The following officers were appointed to the Regiment:—

Companies.	Captains.	Lieutenants.	Ensigns.
1st	Col. Earl of Angus.	Walsh, *Capt. Lieut.*	Cranston.
2nd	Lieut.-Col. Cleland.	Gilchrist.	Pringle.
3rd	Major Henderson.	Stuart.	Boyd.
4th	Capt. Ker, of Kersland.	Oliphant.	Ferguson.
5th	Monro.	Dalzell.	Campbell.
6th	Roy Campbell.	Hutchinson.	J. Campbell.
7th	Hay.	Forrester.	Nesmyth.
8th	Dhu Campbell.	Cathcart.	
9th	Borthwick.	{ Johnstone. W. Campbell.	} Grenadier Company.
10th	Hume.		Lang.
11th	Craigmoor.	Veitch.	Cleghorn.
12th	Halden.	Tate.	Denniston.
13th	Harris.	Ballantine.	Wilson.
14th	Lindsay.	Blackader.	Kirkland.
15th	Steil.	Calder.	Wilson.
16th	Gilchrist.	Clarke.	Hislop.
17th	Mathison.	Harkness.	M'Cullock.
18th	Caldwell.	Stewart.	Hay.
19th	Stephenson.	Aikeman.	Stephenson.
20th	Gunn.	Fairborn.	Young.

from the dates of their formation, and that English, Scots, and Irish regiments raised for the service of a foreign power, should have precedency from the dates of their being placed on the English establishment. The last Warrant published, which also followed the same ruling as the foregoing, was that of King George III., dated 19th December, 1768. For years the 26th had been popularly known as the Cameronians, on account of the origin of the corps; and this designation was revived, by royal sanction, in 1786, as shown in this Record of its services; but no other numerical title than the present one has ever been authorised.

1689. Lieut.-Colonel Cleland's commission was of the same date and purport, vesting him with power to act and command the Regiment in the absence of the Earl of Angus.

Although the sanction of the Estates had been thus obtained on the 19th of April, yet the organization of the Cameronians was not completed till the 12th of May, when they were embodied at Douglas, and on the 14th were mustered by Mr. Buntine, Muster Master General, on the Holm, a field near that town.

The following terms of agreement were read and explained to the men by their Lieut.-Colonel:—

" 1. That all the officers of the Regiment shall be
" such as in conscience and prudence may, with
" cordial confidence, be submitted unto and fol-
" lowed; such as have not served the enemy in
" destroying, nor engaged by oaths and tests to
" destroy the cause, now to be fought for and
" defended.

" 2. That they shall be well affected, of approved
" fidelity, and of a sober conversation.

" 3. They declare: that the cause they are called to
" appear for is, the service of the King's Majesty,
" in the defence of the nation; recovery and
" preservation of the Protestant religion; and,
" in particular, the work of reformation in Scot-
" land, in opposition to Popery, prelacy, and
" arbitrary power in all its branches and steps,
" until the government of church and state be
" brought back to their lustre and integrity,
" established in the best and purest terms."*

---

* " Memorial of Grievances."—" Faithful Contendings."

Early in June, the Cameronians were at Dumblain, 1689. Stirling, and St. Ninians, where they received an issue of four hundred stand of arms, and shortly after they joined Major-General Mackay, to watch the movements of Viscount Dundee, whose activity, influence, and abilities rendered his operations very dangerous. His success at Killiecrankie, at which battle the Regiment was not present, might have proved prejudicial to the Protestant cause, had it not been more than counterbalanced by the wound and subsequent death of this extraordinary man. Mackay, who had made a skilful retreat with two unbroken regiments, soon regained the ascendancy, having to contend with Brigadier-General Cannon, an adversary every way inferior to his predecessor, Dundee. The Cameronians, whom he had left at Dunkeld the day before the battle, joined the remains of his army on his retreat to Stirling.

In July the Regiment was stationed at Perth as a check on the Highlanders, who had made several irruptions into the lowlands, to plunder and levy contributions. After receiving some reinforcements, Mackay again moved forward to counteract the designs of Cannon, who, however, undertook no enterprise of importance. The Cameronians were then ordered to occupy Dunkeld,* where they arrived on the 17th of August. Cannon, who, from neglect or want of influence, had hitherto not turned to advantage the unexpected result of the battle of Killiecrankie, now brought the whole of his army, consisting of about five thousand men, to bear on the post of Dunkeld. Lieut.-Colonel Cleland, anticipating the danger to which he might be exposed

---

* Blackader.

1689. in an open town—the goodwill of whose inhabitants was doubtful—lost no time in preparing for its defence by availing himself of the localities, which proved of great advantage. The stone walls, which formed the fences of the fields and gardens, were repaired, and the posts of the picquets made tenable against a sudden attack. The Marquess of Athol's house and the church were converted into defensible posts; and every arrangement was made, that the withdrawal of the various picquets might be conducted with regularity. On the 19th, Lord Cardross marched in with five troops of cavalry, and on the morning of the 20th a general reconnaissance of the enemy's position was effected, who, in the course of the operation, were driven into the woods. The troops then retired into the town. The same night the horse marched to Perth, in obedience to a second and peremptory order to that effect. The Cameronians were thus left in a situation of great peril, their escape from which was due to the skill and foresight of Lieut.-Colonel Cleland, and the persevering courage of the officers and men.

The attack of the Highlanders commenced about seven on the morning of the 21st of August. After a brisk action, the immense superiority of the rebels compelled the outposts to retire; an operation which was effected, with scarcely any loss, in strict conformity with Colonel Cleland's previous arrangements. The enemy thus obtained possession of the greater part of the town, an advantage which the official report* made to King James ascribes to the gallantry of Sir Alexander M'Leane and his Highlanders, who alone in it are admitted to have

---

* "Macpherson's Papers," Vol. i. p. 371.

taken part in the engagement; but which was really the 1689. result of Lieut.-Colonel Cleland's plan of defence.

"The Lieut.-Colonel had before possessed some out-
"posts, with small parties, to whom he pointed out
"every step for their retreat. Captain William Hay and
"Ensign Lockhart were posted on a little hill, and the
"ensign was ordered with twenty-eight men to advance
"to a stone dyke at the foot of it. They were attacked
"by the rebels, who were in armour, and the foresaid
"other battalion. And after they had entertained them
"briskly with their fire for a pretty space, the rebels
"forced the dyke, and obliged them to retire, firing from
"one little dyke to another, and at length had to betake
"themselves to the house and yard-dykes; in which
"retreat Captain Hay had his leg broken, and the whole
"party came off without any more hurt.

"Lieutenant Stuart was placed in a barricade at the
"cross with twenty men, who, seeing the other lieutenant
"retire, brought his men from that ground, and was
"killed in the retreat, there being a multitude of the
"rebels upon them.

"Lieutenant Forrester and Ensign Campbell were at
"the west end of the town, within some little dykes,
"with twenty-four men, who fired sharply upon the
"enemies' horse, until great numbers of foot attacked
"their dykes, and forced them to the church, where
"were two lieutenants and about one hundred men."*

The assailants then commenced a vigorous attack both on the castle and church; in the front of the former

---

* "The Exact Narrative of the Conflict at Dunkeld betwixt the Earl of Angus' Regiment and the Rebels."

1689. Colonel Cleland* was killed, whilst encouraging his men, early in the action, and Major Henderson, who received three wounds, died in a few days. This occurred about an hour after the conflict had commenced, when the command of the Regiment devolved on Captain Monro. Undaunted by their loss, the Cameronians kept up a most destructive fire, which, together with the flames of some neighbouring houses, effectually baffled all the persevering and gallant attacks of their opponents, who, despairing of success, relaxed in their efforts about

---

* Colonel Cleland was one of the most accomplished and gallant leaders the Covenanters ever had; but unlike many others of them, little is known of his early history. He was born near Dumfries, and shortly after quitting the University was chosen one of their officers, before he was eighteen. At Drumclog or Louden Hill, where Dundee, then Claverhouse, was nearly taken prisoner, the victory was generally ascribed to a stratagem of Cleland's. At Bothwell Bridge he was a captain. After the defeat at that place he fled to Holland; in 1685 he was again in Scotland, but the Earl of Argyle's expedition having failed, he once more escaped to the Continent. In 1688, he and Dr. Blackader (brother of Colonel Blackader) were sent as agents by the Scottish emigrants in Holland to prepare his countrymen for the expected landing of the Prince of Orange. Captain Cleland was a great favourite with the Earl of Angus, and was appointed Lieut.-Colonel of his regiment. His efforts to withdraw when he was mortally wounded, lest his fall should discourage his soldiers, stamp him as a true hero. Lieut.-Colonel Cleland was a poet of considerable ability, his productions being chiefly humorous and satirical, although he was able to rise to higher and more dignified flights of fancy. This gift was also possessed by his son, William Cleland, Esq., one of the Commissioners of the Customs in Scotland, who was the author of the prefatory letter to Pope's Dunciad, and is believed to have been the original of the famed Will Honeycomb, of the "Spectator."

eleven o'clock, and shortly after withdrew in confusion 1689. to the hills, notwithstanding the earnest attempts of their officers to rally and bring them back to the assault.

Mackay did not approve of the arrangement by which the Cameronians had been sent to garrison Dunkeld. Lord Macaulay, in his History of England, alludes to this fact, and thus describes the foregoing action :—

"It soon appeared that his forebodings were just. "The inhabitants of the country round Dunkeld fur-"nished Cannon with intelligence, and urged him to "make a bold push. The peasantry of Athol, impatient "for spoil, came in great numbers to swell his army. "The Regiment hourly expected to be attacked, and be-"came discontented and turbulent. The men, intrepid, "indeed, both from constitution and from enthusiasm, "but not yet broken to habits of military submission, "expostulated with Cleland, who commanded them. "They had, they imagined, been recklessly, if not "perfidiously, sent to certain destruction. They were "protected by no ramparts, they had a very scanty stock "of ammunition, they were hemmed in by enemies. "An officer might mount and gallop beyond reach of "danger in an hour, but the private soldier must stay "and be butchered. 'Neither I,' said Cleland, 'nor any "' of my officers will, in any extremity, abandon you. "' Bring out my horse, all our horses, they shall be "' shot dead.' These words produced a complete "change of feeling. The men answered that the horses "should not be shot, that they wanted no pledge from "their brave colonel except his word, and that they "would run the last hazard with him. They kept their "promise well. The Puritan blood was now thoroughly "up, and what that blood was when it was up, had been "proved on many fields of battle.

1689. "That night the Regiment passed under arms. On
"the morning of the following day, the 21st of August,
"all the hills round Dunkeld were alive with bonnets
"and plaids. Cannon's army was much larger than
"that which Dundee had commanded. More than a
"thousand horses, laden with baggage, accompanied his
"march. Both the horses and baggage were probably
"part of the booty of Killiecrankie. The whole number
"of Highlanders was estimated by those who saw them
"at from four to five thousand men. They came
"furiously on. The outposts of the Cameronians were
"speedily driven in. The assailants came pouring on
"every side into the streets. The church, however,
"held out obstinately. But the greater part of the
"Regiment made its stand behind a wall which sur-
"rounded a house belonging to the Marquess of Athol.
"This wall, which had two or three days before been
"hastily repaired with timber and loose stones, the
"soldiers defended separately with musket, pike, and
"halberts. Their bullets were soon spent; but some
"of the men were employed in cutting lead from the
"roof of the Marquess's house and shaping it into slugs.
"Meanwhile, all the neighbouring houses were crowded
"from top to bottom with Highlanders, who kept up
"a galling fire from the windows. Cleland, while
"encouraging his men, was shot dead. The command
"devolved on Major Henderson. In another minute
"Henderson fell pierced with three mortal wounds.
"His place was supplied by Captain Monro, and the
"contest went on with undiminished fury. A party of
"the Cameronians sallied forth, set fire to the houses
"from which the fatal shots had come, and turned the
"keys in the doors. In one single dwelling sixteen of
"the enemy were burnt alive. Those who were in the

" fight described it as a terrible initiation for recruits. 1689.
" Half the town was blazing; and with the incessant
" roar of the guns were mingled the piercing shrieks of
" wretches perishing in the flames. The struggle lasted
" four hours. By that time the Cameronians were
" reduced nearly to their last flask of powder, but their
" spirit never flagged. ' The enemy will soon carry the
" ' wall. Be it so. We will retreat into the house;
" ' we will defend it to the last; and, if they force their
" ' way into it, we will burn it over their heads and our
" ' own.' But while they were resolving these desperate
" projects, they observed that the fury of the assault
" slackened. Soon the Highlanders began to fall back:
" disorder visibly spread among them, and whole bands
" began to march off to the hills. It was in vain that
" their general ordered them to return to the attack.
" Perseverance was not one of their military virtues.
" The Cameronians, meanwhile, with shouts of defiance,
" invited Amalek and Moab to come back and to try
" another chance with the chosen people. But these
" exhortations had as little effect as those of Cannon.
" In a short time the whole Gaelic army was in full
" retreat towards Blair. Then the drums struck up;
" the victorious Puritans threw their caps into the air,
" raised, with one voice, a psalm of triumph and thanks-
" giving, and waved their colours—colours which were
" on that day unfurled for the first time in the face of
" an enemy—but which have since been proudly borne
" in every quarter of the world, and which are now
" embellished with the Sphinx and the Dragon, emblems
" of brave actions achieved in Egypt and in China.
" The Cameronians had good reason to be joyful and
" thankful, for they had finished the war."

In this memorable action, the Cameronians had, in

1689. addition to their two field officers killed, five officer wounded, namely, Captains Hay, Borthwick, Steil, Caldwell (died of wounds), and Lieutenant Stuart; Captain Steil after having his wounds dressed, returned to his post. Fifteen men were killed and thirty wounded; the loss of their enemy is stated to have exceeded three hundred men.

No pursuit was attempted, on account of the superiority of Brigadier-General Cannon's army; but resuming their former outposts, with the experience of old soldiers, the Cameronians immediately commenced the repair of their injured defences, and cut down some trees on a little hill, whence the rebels had under cover maintained a galling fire. Their powder was nearly expended, and during the action they had been obliged to employ men to cast slugs, made of the lead taken from the roof of the castle. The "Exact Narrative" (quoted at page 9) quaintly states:—" That a handful of unexperienced men was " wonderfully animated to a steadfast resistance against " a multitude of obstinat furies; but they give the glory " to God, and praised him, and sung psalms, after they " had fitted themselves for a new assault."

The Cameronians remained unmolested at Dunkeld for some days, and afterwards were left in garrison in the north by General Mackay, whose march through Aberdeen and Inverness experienced little, if any, opposition. After leaving garrisons in the castle of Blair and other places, he returned with the body of his army towards Edinburgh. The Highlands, however, continued to be disturbed throughout the following year.

Major-General Mackay, in a letter dated Edinburgh, 22nd October, 1689, thus wrote to Lord Melville, Secretary of State for Scotland, then in London :—

" My Lord— 1689.

" I am of opinion that a battalion of the Earle " of Angus's regiment ought to be entertained so long " as his Majestie may have occasion for such, because " they behaved well against the rebels at Dunkald, as " a testimonie of his Majestie's esteem; but there ought " to be a man of service put upon their head, for at this " time they shall scarcely make up the number of six " hundred men."*

This representation drew forth the following orders for remodelling the Regiment.

" Instructions to our Right Trusty and well-beloved " Cousin and Councellor, our Right Trusty and well- " beloved Councellor, and our Trusty and well-beloved " David, Earle of Leven, Hugh Mackay, Major General " of our Forces, and Sir George Monro.

" 1. You are to remain and modell the six regiments " commanded by the Earle of Angus, the Earle of " Argile, the Earle of Glencairne, the Lord Viscount " of Kenmore, the Lord Strathnaver, and the Laird " of Grant, and you are to forme a regiment to be " commanded by ———— Cunningham; of the said seven " regiments three are to remain in that our ancient " kingdom, and the other four to be employed for our " service in Ireland.

" 2. You are to appoint the above seven regiments " to consist of thirteen companies each, and sixty men " in each company, and one company of each regiment " to be grenadiers.

" 3. For making up the said regiments you are to

---

* Extract from original letter among the papers of the Earle of Leven.

1689. "disband the three regiments of the Earle of Mar,
"Lord Blantire, and the Lord Bargeny.

"4. You are to disband all independant companies,
"and what officers of them are fit for our service, you
"are to employ in situations proper for them as our
"service requires.

"5. You are to appoint fit persons to be Lieutenant
"Colonels, Majors, and other inferior officers to the
"aforesaid seven regiments.

"6. You are to employ what officers you judge fit
"for our service that were in the three regiments,
"which you are to disband, or in the independant
"companies.

"7. You are to turn out of any of the regiments
"what officers you think unfit for our service, and
"put others who are well qualified in their places.

"Lastly. You are to transmit a list of such officers as
"you nominate to George, Lord Melville, our secretary,
"that they may have their commissions accordingly.—
"Given under our royal hand and signet, at our Court
"at Holland House, the 18th day of December, 1689,
"and of our reigne the first year."

1690. In 1690 the Regiment was reduced to thirteen companies, the names of the officers being as follows:—

Companies.	Captains.	Lieutenants.	Ensigns.
1st	Colonel Earl of Angus.	Tate, *Capt. Lieut.*	Cranston.
2nd	Lieut.-Col. Fullarton.	Aikeman.	Pringle.
4th	Major Ker, of Kersland.	Oliphant.	Ferguson.
6th	Captain Roy Campbell.	Green.	J. Campbell.
7th	Hay.	Ferguson.	Nesmyth.
8th	Dhu Campbell.	Johnstone.	Gilchrist.
9th	Borthwick.	{ Stewart. Halden.	} Grenadier Company.
10th	Hume.	Veitch.	Lang.
12th	Halden.	Ballantine.	Denniston.

OR CAMERONIAN REGIMENT.   17

Companies.	Captains.	Lieutenants.	Ensigns.	1690.
13th	Harris.	Blackader.	Wilson.	
14th	Lindsay.	Fairborn.	Kirkland.	
15th	Steil.	Mathewson.	Wilson.	
18th	Caldwell.	Gilchrist.	Hislop.	

In consequence of this arrangement, the third, fifth, eleventh, sixteenth, seventeenth, nineteenth, and twentieth companies were reduced by ballot.

In April, 1690, the Cameronians were stationed in Montrose, where a party of the rebels appeared on the 2nd, but they retired hastily when they saw the dispositions which were made to attack them.

In September following, a plundering party appeared in the neighbourhood of Cardross, and defeated a detachment of thirty men, by which they were opposed. When this news reached Dumbarton, Lieut.-Colonel Fullarton marched the same night with Lord Rollo's troop of horse and one hundred of the Cameronians, with whom he overtook the rebels early the next morning. He immediately attacked and defeated them, with the loss of their commander and forty men killed, and about the same number taken prisoners. The officers and men of the detachment, whom they had taken the day before, were liberated. After this affair, the Regiment was employed under Major-General Mackay in repressing the spirit of opposition which continued to prevail in the Highlands, till they quitted the country for Flanders early in the following year.

The reinforcements for the army in Flanders, of 1691. which Lord Angus's Regiment formed a part, embarked in the Frith of Forth in February, and after some weeks' detention by contrary winds, they landed in Holland. In March, the Cameronians were encamped at Halle, in South Brabant, and were brigaded with the Scots Foot

C

1691. Guards, the first battalion of the Royals, and the regiments of Ramsay, Mackay, and Hodges.* The French besieged Mons, and the confederates being unable to relieve the place, the garrison was forced to surrender on the 31st of March. In May, the Cameronians were encamped near Brussels, and formed part of the brigade under Brigadier-General Ramsay, which consisted of both battalions of the Royals, and the Scots regiments of Mackay, Ramsay, and O'Farrell. In an enumeration of the corps composing the confederate army under King William's command, dated Camp at Gerpynes, 27th July, the Regiment, which is styled the Earl of Angus's, is mentioned, and its facings then are stated to have been *white*.

The summer was passed by the opposing armies in manœuvring, and the campaign, although not signalized by any brilliant or successful operations, nor by any great battle, was most harassing to the soldiers by reason of the frequent marches. It terminated about the beginning of October, when the troops went into winter quarters.

1692. In May, 1692, the active operations of the year commenced, and shortly acquired a high degree of importance by Louis XIV. undertaking in person the siege of Namur, which King William having been unable to raise, the town capitulated on the 20th of June, and on the 1st July the citadel likewise. After this severe loss, no important event resulted from the manœuvres of the two armies till the 3rd of August, when it was resolved to attack the enemy under Marshal the Duke of Luxem-

---

* D'Auvergne's "Campaigns in Flanders."

bourg, at his castle near *Steinkirk*. After a tedious 1692. march, the vanguard, consisting of four battalions of English foot, two of Danes, and a detachment of General Churchill's brigade, fell upon the enemy with such vigour that they were driven from hedge to hedge, so that the Duke of Wirtemberg succeeded in taking post in the wood which fronted the right wing of the French army. Whilst his batteries were playing upon the enemy, King William's forces marched to the head of the defile, where it opened into a little plain, and where they were ordered to halt. The regiments of Cutts (Coldstream Guards), Mackay, Graham, and Angus (Cameronians), being interlined with the horse, were commanded to the right skirts of the wood; while three other regiments of infantry, intermixed with the left wing of the horse, were posted on the other flank of the wood. After this disposition was completed, the main body of the army being still halted, the Duke of Wirtemberg began the attack with the vanguard, and was seconded by the English in the foregoing order of battle. Never was a more terrible, and at the same time a more regular, fire heard; during two hours it seemed to be like continued thunder. The vanguard behaved with such bravery and resolution, that although they received the charge in succession of the enemy's battalions, yet they drove them from a battery of seven pieces of cannon, which, however, they could not send away, as the French had cut the traces and carried off the horses. All the regiments distinguished themselves by their courage and perseverance, driving their opponents from hedge to hedge, often firing muzzle to muzzle through them. The King, being informed of their difficulties, and of the great superiority of the enemy, despatched an aide-de-

1692. camp to Count Solmes* for a re-inforcement, who, from jealousy of the Duke of Wirtemberg, evaded the order,

---

* Sterne, in "Tristram Shandy," has perpetuated the military criticisms of the day upon the conduct of Count Solmes.

"My uncle Toby had just then been giving Yorick an account of the battle of Steinkirk, and of the strange conduct of Count Solmes, in ordering the foot to halt and the horse to march where it could not act; which was directly contrary to the king's command, and proved the loss of the day.

"'Corporal Trim,' replied my uncle Toby (putting on his hat, which lay upon the table), 'if anything can be said to be a fault, when the service absolutely requires it should be done, 'tis I certainly who deserves the blame; you obeyed your orders.'

"'Had Count Solmes, Trim, done the same at the battle of Steinkirk,' said Yorick, drolling a little upon the Corporal, who had been run over by a dragoon in the retreat—'he had saved thee.'

"'Saved!' cried Trim, interrupting Yorick, and finishing the sentence for him after his own fashion—'he had saved five battalions, an' please your reverence, every soul of them.

"'There was Cutts's,' continued the Corporal, clapping the fore-finger of his right hand upon the thumb of his left, and counting round his hand, 'there was Cutts's, Mackay's, Angus's, Graham's, and Leven's, all cut to pieces; and so had the English Life Guards, too, had it not been for some regiments upon the right, who marched up boldly to their relief, and received the enemy's fire in their faces, before any one of their own platoons discharged a musket.'

"'They'll go to heaven for it,' added Trim.

"'Trim is right,' said my uncle Toby, nodding to Yorick; 'he's perfectly right.'

"'What signified his marching the horse,' continued the Corporal, 'where the ground was so straight, that the French had such a nation of hedges, and copses, and ditches, and felled trees laid this way and that, to cover them (as they always

observing, "Let us see what sport these English bull- 1692.
dogs will make." On a second and peremptory order,
the Count advanced with his horse, but, being still unsupported by the infantry, his succour proved insufficient
to maintain the advantages which had been gained; and
the English, overpowered by the repeated charges of
thirty battalions of infantry, and a fresh corps of cavalry
which Marshal Boufflers opportunely brought into action,
were finally compelled to withdraw in confusion. The
retreat was, however, afterwards conducted in tolerable
order, and the loss of the French had been too severe
materially to interrupt it, or to prosecute their advantage.

Thus ended the famous battle of Steinkirk, which
would have been a brilliant success to the allies, but
for the base jealousy of a foreign general. The Earl
of Angus fell at the head of his Regiment, which,
having had its full portion of the glory, must have
equally shared with the other corps in the casualties
of the day, amounting on either side to three thousand killed, and a like number wounded and prisoners.
Besides their youthful Colonel, the Cameronians lost
their two field officers, Lieut.-Colonel Fullarton and Major

" 'have). Count Solmes should have sent us; we would have
" 'fired muzzle to muzzle with them for their lives. There was
" 'nothing to be done for the horse: he had his foot shot off,
" 'however, for his pains,' continued the Corporal, 'the very
" 'next campaign, at Landen."

The corps named by the Corporal have since been disbanded, with the exception of Cutts's, now Coldstream Guards;
Leven's, now 25th Foot—Uncle Toby and Corporal Trim are
represented as belonging to this regiment; and Angus's, now
26th, or Cameronian Regiment.

1692. Ker of Kersland, the first being killed and the latter mortally wounded; the names of the other officers have not been preserved; many privates of Douglas, where they were originally embodied, were killed.

The King bestowed the Colonelcy of the Regiment on Lieut.-Colonel Andrew Monro,* from the Royal Scots, now First Foot. After this battle, no important event occurred, except the relief of Charleroi, which Marshal Boufflers had invested; and about the beginning of November the army was distributed into winter-quarters.

1693. In 1693 the campaign was opened in the month of April, and King William contented himself with defensive operations, by which, however, he was unable to prevent the defeat of a part of the army under the Count de Tilly, and the subsequent loss of the fortress of Huy, on the 23rd of July, by the mutiny of its garrison. After this advantage Marshal the Duke of Luxembourg determined to attack the King, who, though much inferior in numbers, awaited the enemy in a disadvantageous position, with the Geete in his rear, extending from Neer-Winden to Neer-Landen. Brigadier Ramsay with his brigade, of which the Cameronians formed part, was ordered to the right of the whole army, to line some hedges and hollow ways on the further side of the village of Laér, supported by one battalion of Brandenburg on the left. After some preliminary movements, Luxembourg, about eight o'clock

---

* Monro's commission as Colonel is dated 1st of August, 1692, the battle of Steinkirk having been fought on the 24th of July, o.s., England not having then adopted the new style of reckoning.

on the 29th of July, ordered a strong body of troops to attack the villages of Laér and *Neer-Winden*, which they did with various success, but the allies finally maintained their ground. On the side of *Neer-Landen*, however, after being several times repulsed, the enemy, by dint of reinforcements, and with the flower of the French infantry, gained this flank of the position; and they then renewed the attack on Neer-Winden. The King, who had hastened from the left to this position, twice led the English battalions to the charge, where they fought with great bravery; but, having their position turned on both flanks, their ammunition expended, and being assailed by a greater superiority of numbers, and by fresh troops, he at length, seeing no chance of success, ordered them to retire. In this hard-fought, but unfortunate battle, the army lost its artillery, many standards and colours, and two hundred and fourteen officers killed, and two hundred and ninety-six wounded; six thousand and five rank and file killed and prisoners, and three thousand nine hundred and fifty-eight wounded. The casualties of the French were estimated at from eighteen to twenty thousand.

As usual, the English appear to have borne the brunt of the action, having first had very important points of the position at and near Laér and Neer-Winden assigned to their care, and which they defended with success; they were afterwards led to the defence of the entrenchments between Neer-Winden and Neer-Landen, and finally covered the retreat.

The Cameronians, who bore a part both in the glory and loss of this day, which is known as the battle of Landen, or Neer-Winden, were brigaded with O'Farrell's (21st Royal North British Fusiliers), Mackay's, Lauder's (afterwards disbanded), and Leven's (25th),

1693. under Brigadier Ramsay, and had the following officers wounded:—Captain Stewart, and Ensign Hutchinson; Captains Alexander, Campbell, Fullarton, and Munro; the three latter were prisoners of war.* The casualties of the Regiment in non-commissioned officers and men have not been separately recorded.

Luxembourg† did not turn his victory to any immediate account, but remained inactive at Waren for fifteen days. When Marshal Boufflers joined him with some troops from the Rhine, he then formed the siege of Charleroi, which, after a vigorous defence, from the 10th of September to the 11th of October, surrendered on the most honourable conditions. With this event the campaign concluded, and both armies went into winter quarters, the Cameronians being stationed at Ostend.

On the 25th of August, 1693, the colonelcy of the Cameronians was conferred upon Lieut.-Colonel James Ferguson, of the Regiment, in succession to Colonel Monro. After the battle of Landen, the camp at Halle, and also that of the enemy, suffered severely from sickness, occasioned by the excessive heat of the weather, to which Colonel Monro fell a victim.

1694. In 1694, the losses which the British had suffered in the preceding campaigns were repaired by reinforcements

---

* D'Auvergne.

† An excellent anecdote has been handed down in reference to the Duke of Luxembourg's deformed figure. William III., his constant antagonist, is reported to have exclaimed, impatiently, "What! shall I never beat this hump-backed fellow?" This speech coming to the Duke's ears, he is stated to have replied, "How should he know the shape of my back? I am sure he never saw me turn it to him."

from home. The Scots regiments obtained an accession 1694. of seven thousand men; of these three thousand were new levies; and with such expedition were they raised, that although the proclamation for them was not issued till the 14th of March, by the 22nd of April they were not only completed, but all actually embarked in Leith Roads for Flanders.* It does not appear to what extent the Cameronians shared in this reinforcement, but their popularity and services leave it little doubtful that it was to the full extent of their wants.

It was not until the middle of June that the army left its winter quarters, when King William assumed the command. Although his forces were nearly equal in number to the enemy, yet no action whatever took place: Marshal Luxembourg manœuvring on every occasion with great skill, to avoid a battle. In the month of September the King formed the siege of Huy, which surrendered on the 27th, after a defence of ten days. The British troops were not employed in this operation. In October the armies broke up, and went into winter quarters.

In May, 1695, the Regiment, which had been in 1695. winter quarters in the villages near the Nieuport Canal, pitched its tents in the vicinity of Dixmude, where a small force was being assembled under Major-General Ellemberg; the main army, at the same time, took the field under King William. In June, the Duke of Wirtemberg took the command of the troops at Dixmude; reinforcements arrived, and an attack was made on *Fort Kenoque*, situated at the junction of the Loo and Dixmude Canals.

---

* "Blackader's Life and Diary."

1695. On the evening of the 9th of June, the grenadiers of the several regiments employed on this enterprise drove the French from their entrenchments and houses near the Loo Canal. A redoubt was afterwards taken, and a lodgment effected on the works at the bridge, in which service the Cameronians had several men killed and wounded. The total casualties were about four hundred men, of which Ferguson's and Tiffin's regiments (now 26th and 27th) lost the most.* These attacks produced the desired effect, as the enterprise had only been designed as a diversion, to favour the operations of the main army, under King William, before *Namur*, and the Regiment subsequently marched towards the Lys, and joined the covering army under the Prince of Vaudemont, who, on the approach of Marshal Villeroy with an army far superior in numbers, effected his skilful and celebrated retreat from the camp at Arsel to the vicinity of Ghent, leaving his antagonist quite disconcerted by the masterly arrangement of the march.†

While the siege of the *Castle of Namur* was being carried on, Brigadier Fitzpatrick marched, on the 17th of August, to the village of St. Denis, with a body of troops, of which the Cameronians formed part. Two

---

* D'Auvergne.

† Blackader, in an entry in his Diary on the 25th May, 1706, writes :—

"Marching this day to Arsel, a place famous for the retreat of "Prince Vaudemont, made here in 1695, in presence of the "French army, who were thrice as strong as ours. And at this "place I have a monument set up of thankfulness and praise for "merciful deliverance from men who were ready to swallow "us up."

days afterwards, thirty-six grenadiers per company from each of the regiments composing this force were selected to proceed to Namur, the town of which had surrendered on the 25th of July, and every effort was now being made against the Castle. Brigadier Fitzpatrick continued with his force at St. Denis, which, lying upon the skirt of a wood, was strongly fortified by the troops under his orders.

On the 30th of August an assault was made, about mid-day, to storm the breach of the Terra Nova, when the grenadiers rushed forward, under a heavy fire from the Castle, and were followed by the regiments ordered to support the attack; the latter not moving forward in time, the assailants were overpowered by superior numbers, and the survivors received orders to withdraw from the unequal contest. Some partial advantages were gained, but severe loss was sustained. The casualties amongst the grenadiers of the Cameronians have not been separately recorded. Preparations were made for a second assault, which was prevented by the surrender of the Castle. On the 1st of September Marshal Boufflers offered to capitulate, and on the 5th he marched out with his garrison, now reduced from fifteen thousand to five thousand five hundred men. King William III., on the 12th of that month, reviewed the whole of his troops at Lembecque, after which they continued in the field about a fortnight. Towards the end of the month both armies began to separate and take up their winter quarters, Namur being assigned to the Cameronians.

In 1696, the French had taken the field before the allied army could be assembled; but no transaction of consequence distinguished the campaign. The Cameronians, now brigaded with the 23rd and other regiments,

1696. under Brigadier Ingoldsby, were inspected by the King, with eight English and Scots regiments, on the 9th of July, at the camp at Vilvorde. The scheme of Louis was still defensive on the side of the Netherlands, while the active plans of King William were defeated for want of money.

1697. Negotiations for peace were commenced at Ryswick, in the beginning of the year 1697; nevertheless both armies took the field, and the French besieged and took Aeth; King William, however, confined himself to the protection of Brussels, which the enemy vainly endeavoured to attack. During this campaign the Cameronians were brigaded with the 25th and three foreign corps, under Brigadier-General Maitland. The treaty of Ryswick was at length signed, at midnight, on the 10th of September (o.s.).

When the Parliament met, after the peace was proclaimed, owing to the universal ferment in the nation, produced by the terrors of a standing army, the House of Commons voted "that all the forces raised since the year 1680 should be disbanded;" and allotted maintenance for ten thousand men only. The King, though very much mortified by these resolutions, was obliged to comply, and therefore received a part of the British troops into the Dutch pay, of which Ferguson's Regiment was one. It is uncertain whether the corps benefitted by the levy of one thousand men, ordered by the Scottish Parliament, in October, 1696, to be made to recruit the

1700. King's forces in Flanders. In 1700, the Cameronians were taken back into English pay and were sent to Scotland.

1701. When England and Holland armed in 1701, to prepare against any attack to which the latter might be exposed from the French and Spaniards, in consequence of the disputes to which the late King of Spain's will 1701. (Charles II.) had given rise, the Dutch Government claimed from England the stipulated succours. Accordingly thirteen British battalions were embarked for Holland, in June, to assist the Dutch against the advance of the French army towards their frontiers, but the Cameronians did not proceed thither until the year following.

Additional regiments were sent to the Netherlands in 1702. this year, of which the Cameronians formed one; they received orders to join the confederate army on the 1st of February, 1702, and embarked for their destination on the 7th of March. On the day following, the decease of King William III. occurred, but Queen Anne resolved to carry into effect the views of her predecessor. War was proclaimed against France and Spain on the 4th of May, and the Earl of Marlborough was appointed to command the British, Dutch, and auxiliary troops, with the rank of Captain-General. Thus, after a residence of about a year in their native country, during part of which time they had been in garrison at Perth, the Cameronians were recalled to the scene of their former exertions and glory, being destined to bear a conspicuous part in those campaigns, which the skill and conduct of the Duke of Marlborough will ever render celebrated in the page of military history.

In April the allies formed the siege of *Kaiserswaert*, and the Earl of Athlone encamped at Cranenburg during the operation, to cover the siege. The French, under the Duke of Burgundy, vainly attempted to interrupt this siege, and having failed in that object, they afterwards endeavoured to surprise the Earl's camp, in which they nearly succeeded. He was compelled to make a precipitate retreat on *Nimeguen*, in which he had

1702. to sustain the attacks of the enemy's cavalry, which, however, were repulsed, and that place saved from the French. The *London Gazette* stated, "the English "especially, both officers and soldiers, and particularly "the battalion of Her Majesty's Guards, showed a great "deal of valour and gallantry." The Earl's retreat did not lead to the failure of the siege of Kaiserswaert, which surrendered on the 17th of June.

After the embarkation of the Regiment, Captain Blackader was employed for some time about Stirling, Edinburgh, and Leith, in levying the necessary complement of men, in which he was very successful, notwithstanding his disdain of the usual alluring and plausible arts of a recruiting officer.* He thus proved that the good feelings of men are sufficient, when properly addressed, to induce them to enrol themselves in the honourable list of the defenders of their Sovereign and country. On the 13th of July he sailed from Leith with his recruits, and, landing on the 23rd, joined his regiment two days afterwards.

In the beginning of July, the Earl of Marlborough arrived in the Netherlands, assembled his army, and commencing active operations, by his skilful movements, he compelled Marshal Boufflers to retire in every direction before him. Thus, without striking a blow in its defence, the Marshal saw himself obliged to leave Spanish Guelderland to his adversary's discretion. Though thwarted in his designs by the timidity and

---

* "Life and Diary of Colonel Blackader." He, in addition to his recruiting duties, had also to provide a chaplain for the Regiment, in place of Mr. Shields, who had proceeded on the Darien expedition, and died in the West Indies.

jealousy of the Dutch generals and deputies, the Earl undertook, on the 29th of August, the siege of *Venloo*, which capitulated on the 25th of September, after *Fort St. Michael* had been stormed and taken on the 18th by the English troops under Lord Cutts. As volunteers were employed, it is probable that every corps furnished its quota. After this success, *Stevenswaert* and *Ruremonde* were successively reduced, these sieges only lasting a few days, and the Earl having, by a rapid and secret march, anticipated Marshal Boufflers in the occupation of *Liege*, its citadel was carried by storm on the 23rd of October.

At the siege of Liege, the British acted a conspicuous part; for, in a letter to the Earl of Nottingham, dated 23rd October, 1702, forming part of the correspondence discovered in 1842, upon making some improvements at Blenheim, and shortly afterwards published under the superintendence of the late General the Right Hon. Sir George Murray, G.C.B., Marlborough wrote: "The post "not being gone, I could not but open this letter to let "you know that, by the extraordinary bravery of the "officers and soldiers, the citadel has been carried by "storm, and, for the honour of Her Majesty's subjects, "the English were the first that got upon the breach, "and the Governor was taken by a lieutenant of "Stewart's regiment.* The necessary orders are given "for hastening the attack of the Chartreuse."

The *Chartreuse* surrendered on the 29th of October, when the Earl of Marlborough proceeded to Holland, and thence to London, where, on arrival, Queen Anne created him a Duke, as a reward for the successes gained

---

* The present 9th Foot.

1702. during this year. Thus ended a campaign, at the commencement of which the States had trembled for Nimeguen, but they now saw the French driven back into their own territories. The Cameronians, at this period, consisted of forty-four officers, one hundred and four non-commissioned officers, and seven hundred and thirty-six privates.* In November, the British troops quitted the valley of Liege, and marched to Holland for winter quarters.

1703. Upon the Duke of Marlborough's return to Holland, in March, 1703, he made a general inspection of the garrisons and troops, and reviewed the British regiments, in number eight of cavalry and sixteen of infantry, in their respective cantonments, after which he caused them to assemble near Liege. These regiments were the present 1st, 3rd, 5th, 6th, and 7th Dragoon Guards; and the 1st Royal, 2nd Scots Greys, and 5th Royal Irish Dragoons; the Grenadier Guards, the 1st (two battalions), 8th, 9th, 10th, 13th, 15th, 16th, 17th, 18th, 21st, 23rd, 24th, 26th, and 33rd regiments of foot. The Duke again reviewed the whole confederate army (then increased by the 2nd, 3rd, 11th, and 37th foot), near Maestricht, on the 21st and 22nd of May.

In April, 1703, the Cameronians marched towards Maestricht, where the allied army was assembled, and were formed in brigade with the second battalion of the Royals, the 10th, 16th, and 21st regiments, under Brigadier-General the Earl of Derby. The first operation of importance was the siege of *Bonn*, against which the trenches wre opened on the 3rd of May. On the 9th the fort was taken, which loss compelled the Marquess

---

* Harleian MS., No. 7,025, British Museum.

d'Allegre, after a vigorous defence, to capitulate on the 1703. 15th. This success was followed by a series of marches, in which the Duke's objects were frustrated by the jealousy of the Dutch generals, and the summer passed without any important event occurring, except the indecisive battle of Ekeren, in which the Dutch, under D'Obdam, were surprised and defeated, till the siege of *Huy*, which surrendered, after a vigorous defence, on the 25th of August. Being again thwarted by the Dutch in an intended assault on the enemy's lines, between the Mehaigne and Leuwe, Marlborough undertook the siege of *Limburg*, for which service the Cameronians and other regiments were detached from the main army. The place was invested on the 10th of September, and surrendered on the 28th of September, after two days of open trenches. On the 17th of October, *Guelders* capitulated, and with this success terminated a campaign which would probably, but for the intrigues of the Dutch deputies and the jealousy and timidity of their generals, have been marked by more important events.

It was, however, one of great fatigue to the soldiers, as the marches and countermarches were incessant, especially during the months of May and June. The Duke, in a letter to the Dutch General D'Obdam, dated 3rd of July, 1703, of which the following is an extract, has feelingly alluded to the long marches made by the troops, in order to bring the enemy to a battle :—

" Nous avons eu une cruelle marche aujourd'hui pour
" les pauvres soldats, qui ont été la plupart du chemin à
" mi-jambe dans l'eau et la boue, ce qui nous obligera,
" j'ai peur, de faire halte ici demain, mais nous poursui-
" vrons la marche demain pour vous approcher de plus
" près, et attendrons avec impatience vos sentiments,
" avec ceux des généraux, sur les opérations que nous

1703. " aurons à faire pour parvenir au plus-tôt à nos des-
" seins."

Their patience under disappointments, and endurance of suffering, were thus highly proved; and those military qualities exercised, which so greatly contributed to the successes of the next campaign.

The Cameronians were reviewed on the 9th of June.

Shortly after the capture of Limburg, the Regiment marched back to Holland, where it was stationed during the winter.

1704. In the memorable campaign of 1704, in which the Duke of Marlborough's skill and ability as a statesman and a general were so eminently conspicuous, and in which the allied armies achieved victories, alike honourable to the troops engaged, and remarkable for their decisive results, the Cameronians were constantly employed. In that skilfully combined movement, by which the *élite* of the confederate forces were withdrawn from the Netherlands to the Danube, Ferguson's regiment marched from the Basse on the 28th of April (o.s.), and encamped on the 18th of May at Bedburg, where the army was assembled under General Churchill, amounting to fifty-one battalions and ninety-two squadrons, including sixteen thousand English. The Duke, who joined on that day, commenced his march on the 19th, was near Coblentz on the 26th of May, and on the 27th near Brauback; on the 28th at Neustad, and on the 29th he reviewed the British troops at Cassel, in presence of the Elector, who was much pleased with their neat and clean appearance; " they were," as the Duke says in a letter to the Earl of Godolphin, " in the " highest spirits, notwithstanding their long and harass- " ing marches." On the 31st the passage of the Maine was effected by the advanced guard, and on the 3rd of

June that of the Neckar, at a bridge constructed near Ladenburg, but the artillery and most of the infantry were some days' march in the rear.

1704.

His Grace halted two days to refresh his troops, and to afford time for the rear of the army to come up. On the 6th the advance passed through Weslock, and on the 7th encamped at Irpingen. At this time the British had suffered much from the want of shoes, notwithstanding the Duke's care to provide the necessary supplies. On the 9th the Neckar was again passed, at Laufen; and the next day the Duke and Prince Eugene had their first interview. On the 11th, the cavalry were reviewed at Hippah, in presence of the Prince, who expressed his surprise to see the troops in such excellent condition after so long and harassing a march, and he was particularly struck at the appearance and appointments of the English. In this camp there was a halt of three days, to give time for the infantry to approach. On the 20th the army passed through the difficult defile of Geislingen, after which it was reviewed on the 23rd. The following day the advance reached the Danube, and on the 25th the Duke fixed his head-quarters at Langenau.

The Regiment thence continued its march with the grand army, and was present at the attack made, on the 2nd of July, on the enemy's entrenched position at *Donawert.* Count D'Arco, who commanded the French and Bavarians, occupied a position on the heights of Schellenberg, situated on the left bank of the Danube, to cover this important town, between the Brentz and that river: independently of its natural advantages, he had carefully strengthened it with entrenchments. The Duke of Marlborough, who had previously joined the Imperialists under Prince Lewis of Baden, no sooner

1704. heard that the enemy awaited him, than he determined to dispossess them of this important post before they could be reinforced, and, therefore, hastened the march of the army, which only arrived before the enemy's entrenchments late in the day. Not a moment was lost in reconnoitring them with his advanced guard, and, when supported by sufficient troops, of which the English formed a part, he at once began the attack.

About six in the evening the leading division, consisting of detachments from each British regiment,* with the Foot Guards, Royals, and 23rd Fusiliers, commanded by Brigadier-General Ferguson, and a Dutch force under General Goor, advanced under cover of a heavy cannonade, to attack the works. The contest on the hill was severe, lasting until eight in the evening; and, though the enemy made most gallant, and at one time successful, resistance, the impetuosity and perseverance of the allies overcame every obstacle. The entrenchments were carried, the enemy being driven in disorder, and with great loss, into the town, whence they made a hasty retreat. They were pursued across the Danube by the victorious troops, who captured sixteen pieces of artillery, several standards, colours, and tents, with the equipage and plate of the Count d'Arco; he and his generals saved themselves by swimming across the river.

Of the gallantry of the British, the Duke says, in a letter to the Queen,—" I crave leave humbly to add, " that our success is, in a great measure, owing to the " particular blessing of God, and the unparalleled bravery

---

* Colonel Blackader states, "Only four detachments of one hundred and thirty men of the Cameronians were present."

"of your troops." Leopold, Emperor of Germany, also 1704. added his tribute of praise in a letter to His Grace,—
"This will be an eternal trophy to your most serene
"Queen, in Upper Germany, whither the victorious
"arms of the English nation have never penetrated
"since the memory of man."

In this attack the Cameronians had Captain Lawson and Lieutenant Seaton wounded; one sergeant and eighteen men killed; three sergeants and fifty-seven men wounded.

The next day the allies entered Donawert, where they found large magazines of provisions and military stores.

On the 5th of July, the confederate forces crossed the Danube by pontoon bridges, and encamped at Mortingen, where, on the 7th, the Duke ordered a general thanksgiving through the whole army for the late victory. The main body passed the Lech on the 10th, and moved on the 12th to cover the siege of *Rain*, which surrendered on the 17th. On the 18th, the town of *Aicha*, in which the Elector of Bavaria had left a garrison of nine hundred men, was taken by storm, and a position at *Friedburg* was occupied by the army on the 23rd, by which the Elector's communication with his capital was intercepted, and his country left in the power of the allies.

Louis XIV. made every possible exertion to retrieve the fortunes of so faithful an ally, and a fresh army was formed under the orders of Marshal Tallard, who crossed the Danube, and opened a communication with the Elector's forces at Augsburg. During the enemy's march, Prince Eugene had moved in a parallel line on the left of the Danube. The Duke of Marlborough and Prince Louis of Baden quitted their position at Friedburg, and drew off towards that river, and after a

1704. personal interview with Eugene, it was agreed that Prince Louis should remain, and form the siege of *Ingoldstadt*, whilst the Duke and Prince Eugene should march to meet Marshal Tallard, who had then completed his junction with the Elector, having brought to his assistance an army composed of the *élite* of the French troops, and in number equal to renew the contest with a fair prospect of success. In the beginning of August the allies were employed in making the necessary arrangements to enable Prince Louis to form the siege. On the 9th, the Prince left the army with twenty-three battalions and thirty-one squadrons, and the next day Marlborough moved to Exheim; as the enemy's object was apparently to overwhelm the small army on the left of the Danube before the Duke could join it, his utmost exertions were required to anticipate the attack. In this, however, by the activity and decision of his movements, he succeeded and effected a junction with Prince Eugene on the morning of the 11th of August.

This grand object being effected, it now remained to take measures for bringing the enemy to battle, and the two commanders, therefore, proceeded to make a reconnaissance. On approaching Schweningen on the 12th, several hostile squadrons were observed at a distance, but being unable to form an accurate judgment of their force, the allied generals ascended the tower of Dapfheim church, whence were descried the quartermasters of the Gallo-Bavarian army marking out a camp beyond the Nebel, between Blenheim and Lutzingen. This discovery satisfied their expectations, and they determined to attack before the enemy could strengthen themselves in their new position. The rest of the day was spent in repairing the roads, and making other necessary preparations.

At break of day on the memorable 13th of August 1704. the army was in motion, proceeding in nine columns to the attack. The nature of the ground having enabled the Duke to bring the left wing, under his command, into position sooner than the right wing, under Prince Eugene, whose movements were impeded by woods and other difficulties, a delay of some hours took place. The Duke availed himself of this interval to make a solemn appeal to the Giver of Victory, and directed the chaplains to perform the usual service at the head of each regiment. He then rode along the line, and found the soldiers animated by the best spirit, and impatient for the contest.

When all the preparations were completed throughout the line, the Duke gave orders for a general attack, which began on the left about a quarter before one. Major-General Wilks, with five English battalions and four of Hessians, made the first onset, and was supported by eleven battalions, and fifteen squadrons. Brigadier-General Row, who charged with the greatest intrepidity, led on the British troops to the assault of the village of *Blenheim*. They advanced to the very muzzles of the enemy's muskets, but being exposed to a superior fire, and unable to break through the barricades, they were forced to retire, leaving nearly one-third of their men either killed or severely wounded. In this retreat, they were pursued by thirteen squadrons of the French *gens d'armerie*, and would have been entirely cut to pieces, had not the Hessian infantry stopped the charge by a heavy and well-sustained fire. The French, repulsed and forced to fly in their turn, were chased by

---

* Coxe's " Life of Marlborough." Blackader.

1704. five squadrons of English horse, which by this time had passed the rivulet; these being somewhat disordered by their success, whilst regaining their ranks, were vigorously charged by a fresh and greatly superior body of the enemy's horse, and were obliged precipitately to repass the stream. Here the Hessians again performed a notable service, for by their steady and well-sustained fire, they routed the enemy and recovered a pair of colours taken from Row's regiment, the present 21st Royal North British Fusiliers.

Whilst Row's brigade rallied, Ferguson's attacked the village of Blenheim on the left, but without decisive success, and though both returned three or four times to the charge with equal vigour, they were still repulsed with loss, so that it was found impossible to force the enemy on that post, without sacrificing the whole of the infantry. The French horse, which had for a time rendered doubtful the result of the day, having been completely defeated, the confederates remained masters of all the ground between their antagonists' left and the village of Blenheim, the troops in which were thus cut off from the rest of the army. In despair of being able to make their escape, after a resolute attempt to withstand the renewed attacks of the infantry which surrounded the village, they at length capitulated about eight in the evening. They laid down their arms, and delivering their colours and standards, surrendered themselves prisoners of war, on condition that the officers should not be searched. Night coming on, the British troops, to whom this little army had surrendered, rested on their arms all night to guard them. Colonel Blackader mentions that the Cameronians were especially employed on this duty, as a compliment to their courage and conduct during the day. They had the following officers killed and wounded:—

Captain Alexander Campbell; Lieutenants Archibald 1704.
Douglas, George Seaton, and Moncrieffe, and Ensign
James Hay, killed. Lieut.-Colonel Livingstone; Captains Smart, Blackader, Borthwick, and Wilson; Lieutenant Ferguson; Ensigns Barnard, M'Lean, Ogilvy,
Row, Dalrymple, Oliphant, and Marshall, and Quartermaster Stephenson, wounded.*

On the right, victory remained some time doubtful;
but in the end, Prince Eugene overcame every obstacle,
and drove the enemy from the field, though without
obtaining such signal advantages as those which had
been gained on the left. The conquerors lost about
nine thousand men in killed and wounded. The vanquished army was almost entirely destroyed. Of sixty
thousand who had been assembled in Germany,
there escaped not more than twenty thousand; twelve
thousand were left dead on the field of battle; the
greater part of thirty squadrons perished in the Danube;
thirteen thousand were made prisoners; one hundred
pieces of cannon, twenty-four mortars, one hundred
and twenty-nine colours, and one hundred and seventy-one standards, were the trophies of the victory.†

The day after the battle, the Duke and Prince Eugene
made a short march, and encamped between Wittisling
and Steinheim on the Danube, where they halted for
four days to refresh the troops, and make a division
of the prisoners. On the 19th the army again moved
forward, and on the 21st reached Sefelingen, within
a mile of Ulm, the Elector retiring before their
advanced guard. The army again commenced its
movement on the 25th; and on the 28th divided

---

* "Annals of Queen Anne." † Coxe's "Marlborough."

1704. into four columns, marched through Suabia, and formed a junction in the vicinity of Philipsburg.* The English and Danes advanced early in September to Stenfield and Odenheim, to undertake the siege of Landau. On the 5th the allied commanders made a reconnaissance beyond Philipsburg, and the Palatine troops passed the Rhine to occupy the position of the Spirback. On the 7th the English and Danish foot, with the Dutch Lunebergers and Hessians, successively filed over; and on the 8th the whole army was on the left of the Rhine.

During the previous operations of the campaign, the British had suffered so severely, that the Duke about this time stated to Lord Godolphin, that "our battalions are extremely weak, so that if we come to action, I intend to make the fourteen English into seven."

On the 12th of September, *Landau* was invested; and it was agreed that the troops of Prince Louis, which had suffered less than those under the Duke and Prince Eugene, should carry on the operations of the siege, whilst the latter should occupy an entrenched camp at Weissemberg. The post of Lauterburg was also occupied, and as its garrison was British, it is not improbable that the Cameronians formed a part. The prisoners, being found to be a source of embarrassment to the army, were sent to Holland, under an escort of the present 1st Foot (second battalion), and the 4th, 10th, 21st, and 37th regiments, under Brigadier-General Ferguson. As the enemy made no attempt to interrupt the operations of the siege, the covering army remained quietly on the line of the Lauter, and was reviewed on

---

* Kane's "Memoirs."

the 2nd of October, by the King of the Romans, who passed the highest encomiums on the general conduct and appearance of the victors of Blenheim.

Marlborough, finding that it would not be in the enemy's power to interrupt the siege, about the middle of October, caused the rest of the British and the Dutch troops to embark in boats, and descend the Rhine as far as Nimeguen, where the corps separated, and proceeded by land to their respective cantonments. The Cameronians were then commanded by Major Cranston, in the absence of Colonel Borthwick. The cavalry had marched previously.

Landau surrendered on the 24th of November, after a brave defence of eight weeks. Thus ended a campaign signalized by the most brilliant and decisive victories, and conducted through a period of seven months without a single instance of reverse. The British troops had never before acted on so extensive a field of operations, and their character attained a degree of reputation which, although it may have been equalled, yet has never been surpassed.

In 1705, the operations of the army were comparatively unimportant. Captain Blackader, who during the winter had been recruiting in Scotland, embarked in March to join the army, and was present with it on the 22nd of April. The reinforcement, which the exertions of the recruiting officers and men, aided by the popularity of the cause, had succeeded in raising, would appear to have been considerable, as the Duke, in a letter of the 21st of April (o.s.) informed Lord Godolphin of their arrival; of these, the Cameronians, doubtless, obtained their share. On the 14th of May His Grace reviewed the British troops, which, under the command of General Charles Churchill, marched the

1704.

1705.

1705. next day towards the Moselle; and on the 5th of June, Captain Blackader mentions the arrival of the Regiment on the banks of that river, after a march which lasted the whole night. The army now approached the enemy's entrenched position at Sirk; the French commander, although his forces exceeded the Duke's in the proportion of seventy thousand to forty thousand, thought it most prudent to continue on the defensive.

The cabals of the foreign generals, and the unwillingness of Prince Louis to co-operate with the Duke, having frustrated all his plans in this quarter, and he having received pressing demands for assistance from General d'Auverquerque, whose situation near Maestricht had become extremely perilous from the enemy's great superiority, his Grace, leaving some of his German auxiliaries to protect Treves, broke up his camp at Triers, on the 17th of June (o.s.), and marched with such diligence, that he arrived in time to save the citadel of *Liege*, although he lost a great many men and horses by the fatigue incident to so rapid a march in so hot a season. On his approach, the French abandoned Liege; and on the 11th of July, after a few days' siege, he retook *Huy*, making the garrison prisoners of war. On the 18th, the Regiment was present at the attack of the French and Bavarian lines near *Hildesheim*, which were successfully surprised, and forced. The allied cavalry, under the immediate direction of the Duke, had charged the enemy previously to the arrival of the British infantry, whose march had been retarded by some difficulties of ground; and though successful against his cavalry, they had been thrown into confusion by a well-directed fire from the infantry. The opportune arrival of the British infantry, after great exertions, restored the fortune of the day, and the enemy was

compelled to abandon his lines without further con-   1705.
test. In their retreat, ten Bavarian battalions were
repeatedly attacked by the allied cavalry, but being
formed in squares, finally succeeded in effecting their
escape. His Grace, in a letter to the Duchess, thus
speaks of the conduct of his soldiers on this memorable day:—" It is impossible to say too much good of
" the troops that were with me, for never men fought
" better."

In this service, the Cameronians were formed in brigade with the 16th, 28th, and Stringer's (afterwards
disbanded), under their Colonel, Brigadier-General Ferguson, and composed part of the main body of the
army. By a rapid movement, the enemy reached the
camp of Parck, near Brussels; and on the 19th (o.s.)
Major Blackader says—the Cameronians were in sight
of *Louvain*, from the ramparts of which a brisk cannonade was kept up. This place surrendered in a few
days. The army lay encamped within cannon-shot of
the enemy about ten days, which time was employed
in demolishing the enemy's lines, captured on the
18th. On the 21st there was a slight affair of outposts, in which Lieutenant Dalrymple received a wound
in the head. The position of the Cameronians was so
much exposed, that on the 23rd they shifted their camp
to a more secure spot. The following day was appointed by the Duke for a general thanksgiving
throughout the army, for the late successes.

On the 30th of July, an attempt was made to force
the passage of the *Dyle* at Corbeck and Neer Ische,
which was actually successful on the part of the advanced
guard; but at the moment when support only was
wanted to secure the advantage, the Dutch generals
peremptorily refused to continue their advance, and the

1705. Duke was reluctantly compelled to withdraw, which was effected without loss.

Marlborough next made a movement towards the forest of Soignies, with a view to force the enemy's position on the Ische, and the Cameronians were selected as one of the twenty battalions, which, under General Churchill, were to have commenced the attack. The Duke's intention, however, was again overruled by the Dutch generals, who, through timidity or envy, pronounced the enterprise to be too hazardous; and another opportunity, which, in his Grace's opinion, would have led to the complete defeat of the enemy, was thus lost. It is worthy of remark, that the scene of action would have been near to that on which, about a century afterwards, the glorious victory of Waterloo was gained. The enemy then occupied that village as part of his position. On the 20th of August, the Cameronians moved with the rest of the army, which, advancing by various routes, finally occupied a position between Bossut and Meldert, at which latter place the head-quarters were established on the 30th.

After completing the works of Diest and Tongres —which were intended to cover the winter quarters of the army—the Duke, about the middle of September, paid a visit to the Hague, on account of some negotiations which were then carried on with the enemy, but which finally proved abortive. On the 20th of October (o. s.), he fixed his head-quarters at Campthout, with the troops which covered the siege of *Sandvliet* on the Scheldt, the garrison of which had harassed the inhabitants of Zeeland with frequent incursions, but it is uncertain whether the Cameronians were employed in this enterprise, as only a detachment from the grand army, under Count Noyelles, was sent thereon. The place surrendered in three days. On the 22nd of October, 1705. the Duke quitted the army, leaving General d'Auverquerque to complete this operation, and distribute the troops into winter quarters.

Although the campaign passed without any great battle, yet the army, at times, suffered much fatigue and hardship: circumstances which put to a higher and more severe trial the most valuable qualities of the soldier, both of body and mind, than the more appalling, though short-lived dangers, to which he is exposed in action. Deficiency of food, fatigue, and the absence of shelter from cold and wet, assail and wear out the physical strength of the soldier, and his mind, strongly influenced as it is by the sufferings of the body, if not positively depressed by constantly disappointed hopes, is unsupported by the excitements of success; these are trials under which many yield, who have never flinched in the hour of danger. In such circumstances will be experienced the full benefit of those moral feelings which teach men to look beyond the present moment, and to place confidence, under all their difficulties, in that superintending Providence whose timely aid will never forsake them. To cultivate such a reliance, and to fortify and sustain the soldier under these trials, as well as those to which, when in quarters, he is exposed, were objects of constant attention with the Duke of Marlborough. The religious duties of the army were regularly performed by regimental chaplains, and His Grace never failed to set an example, of which his receiving the sacrament in his carriage previous to the battle of Blenheim is a remarkable instance.*

---

* Coxe's "Life of Marlborough."

1705. This year the colonelcy of the Regiment passed from Brigadier-General Ferguson,* who died suddenly on the 13th of September, at the Bush in Brabant, when he was about to be promoted for his services, to Colonel John Borthwick,† whose commission was dated the 24th of October; his promotion raised Major Cranston to the lieut.-colonelcy, and Captain Blackader to the majority, of the Regiment.

When the army went into winter quarters, the Cameronians marched into Holland, and reached the Busse, near Rotterdam, on the 1st of November.

1706. On the 1st of January, 1706, Colonel John Borthwick effected an exchange with Lord John Dalrymple (afterwards Earl of Stair), colonel of a Dutch regiment.‡

---

* " Our Brigadier is dead—Lieut.-Colonel Borthwick is putting " in for the Regiment; Major Cranston to be lieut.-colonel, and " I, as oldest captain, to be major. I know not how it will go, " but I desire to be very easy, go as it may."—" Blackader's Letters."

And in his diary is the following entry:—

" December 15th.—Got my major's commission this day. I " wish it may not be a burden too heavy for my weak shoulders. " I see Providence brings about my affairs, as well as theirs who " have dexterity to manage them."

† " But Mr. Borthwick, lieut.-colonel to Brigadier Ferguson, " was so well recommended to me, that I could not refuse him " the Regiment before I had the honour of your letter."—From letter dated Hague, 26th December, 1705.—" Marlborough Despatches," vol. ii., page 357.

This was in reply to the Duke of Argyle's recommendation of his relative, Lord Archibald Campbell, for the colonelcy of the Regiment.

‡ War-Office Records.

In 1706, the Regiment marched from the Busse on the 30th of April (N.S.), and joined the main army under the Duke of Marlborough, near Tongres, on the 8th of May. It afterwards suffered considerable hardships from the badness of the weather, in the movements which preceded, and, by the Duke's skill, brought on the battle of Ramillies. On the 21st of May (O.S.), Major Blackader remarks, "that he felt pity for the poor " soldiers, who suffered greatly on account of the " badness of the weather and of the roads." On the 22nd the army continued its march, and was joined by the Danes, on whose arrival it consisted of about sixty thousand men, a number nearly equal to the enemy in strength.

On the 23rd, in the morning, on the fog clearing off, the two armies appeared in presence of each other on the open ground between the rivers Gheet and Mehaigne, the enemy having occupied, with twenty battalions, the village of *Ramillies,* and also those of Offuz and Autreglise. In the course of the ensuing action, in which the allies, as usual, were the assailants, the Cameronians were, for some hours, exposed in position to a heavy cannonade, from which they lost several men; and though not employed in any of those brilliant attacks, by which the enemy was driven from all his positions, and put to a complete route, their enduring constancy materially contributed to the final success of the day. Colonel Borthwick, formerly of the Cameronians, and Captain Denon of the Regiment were killed. The pursuit, in which the Cameronians were engaged until interrupted by darkness, was immediate and brisk. The enemy lost about fifteen thousand men, with nearly all their cannon and baggage, while the allies had only one thousand and sixty-six killed, and

1706. two thousand five hundred and sixty-seven wounded and missing. The French and Bavarians, having fled in confusion behind the Dyle, made a show of defending that position; but as the allies prepared immediately to force it, Marshal Villeroy and the Elector evacuated Brussels, and were compelled to abandon the greater part of the Austrian Netherlands. In the course of these movements, the Cameronians were at Louvain on the 25th; at Brussels on the 26th; and on the 30th they underwent a very fatiguing march in pursuit of the flying enemy. On the 1st of June there was a general thanksgiving for the late victory, and on the 5th the Regiment marched to Cambray.

Lieut.-Colonel George Preston was promoted, from the 2nd Dragoons, on the 24th of August, 1706, to be colonel of the Cameronians, in succession to James Earl of Stair, removed to the Scots Greys.

During the siege of *Ostend*, which commenced on the 28th of June, and ended by the town being surrendered on the 8th of July, the Cameronians remained in the neighbourhood of Dendermond, under the command of Brigadier-General Meredith, whose corps (the present 37th) was employed to watch that fortress; they were not actively employed at the siege of Menin, which, being invested on the 25th of July, and the trenches opened on the 4th of August, capitulated on the 25th of the same month. Between the 18th and the 23rd of August, they appear to have been in the vicinity, as on the 19th, they were drawn out at three in the morning to resist an expected attack, which, however, proved to be only a feint. Four pieces of cannon, taken by the French at the battle of Landen or Neer-Winden were found in this fortress, and were immediately sent by the Duke to London.

In the subsequent operations of the campaign, the

Cameronians continued to take an active part, particu- 1706.
larly at the sieges of *Dendermond* and *Aeth*. The former
was invested on the 29th of August, and surrendered on
the 5th of September, in consequence of the capture by
assault of a redoubt which covered it; an enterprise in
which the Regiment shared. This surrender was most
opportune, for, immediately afterwards, heavy rains commenced, which, had they fallen during the siege, would
have materially protracted the capture of the place. At
the investment and siege of *Aeth*, the Cameronians were
constantly employed in the trenches; and, on the 29th
of September, about midnight, the whole Regiment
being on duty, a lodgment was effected in the counterscarp by an ensign and eighteen men, from which the
Regiment had the misfortune to be driven about
two p.m. the next day. This reverse, however, was of
short duration, for at six it had regained the position,
after having suffered considerable loss. The garrison
capitulated on the 3rd of October.

With the capture of Aeth, the campaign terminated,
and the army was distributed into cantonments for the
winter. Before the Cameronians took up their quarters
at Ghent, they were sent to Courtray to assist, under
the command of Colonel the Hon. Robert Murray, in
repairing the fortifications of the town.

In 1707, the hostile armies took the field, but no 1707.
action whatever of importance occurred during the
campaign. The Cameronians joined the grand army
on the 22nd of May, and accompanied it in the marches
which were made previous to the occupation of the
camp at Meldert; where, from the 1st of June, the
troops remained inactive for about two months, owing
to the opposition made by the Dutch to the plans of
the Duke of Marlborough. The French, under the

1707. Duke of Vendôme, occupied a strong position at Gemblours. On the 9th of August, Marlborough made some offensive movements, which obliged them to retire behind Mons. Bad weather, however, interrupted his operations for awhile, but in the beginning of September, he succeeded in driving them behind the Marque, under the protection of the cannon of Lisle. The troops suffered much, at times, from long marches, and from the badness of the weather and of the roads, but had no opportunity of encountering the enemy in the field.

On the 14th of August, after a march which commenced at daybreak, over broken roads, and under a pouring rain, the Cameronians had only one hundred men left with the colours at night; and many men are said to have perished in the sloughs.

The army broke up about the middle of October, and occupied nearly the same winter quarters as the year before. The Cameronians were in Ghent. Colonel Blackader remarks in his diary, that on the occasion of a review of them on the 24th of May, he received a compliment from the General, who thanked him at the head of the Regiment, that "they exercised so well, and were so carefully regulated."

1708. When the French expedition sailed from Dunkirk, early in 1708, to effect a diversion by landing the Pretender in Scotland, ten British regiments embarked, and others, of which Preston's was one, were placed under orders; but the enemy's fleet having been dispersed by a storm in the Firth of Forth, these corps returned to the army, with which the Cameronians had remained.

The operations of the allied forces in 1708, were of the most brilliant character. The Confederates were

OR CAMERONIAN REGIMENT. 53

late in taking the field, having assembled towards the 1708. end of May; and the next month was spent in a variety of marches, during which the enemy, who had numerous friends in Ghent and Bruges, succeeded in surprising those important towns, and in taking the Fort of Plassenberg by storm. The French next attempted the reduction of *Oudenarde*, an object which, by movements skilfully combined and rapidly executed, the Duke of Marlborough completely frustrated. He passed the Scheldt at Oudenarde on the 11th of July, and brought on an immediate battle. The Duke of Burgundy's army was drawn up in a position of great strength, which the French General had occupied in the course of his retreat, his object being to avoid an engagement, if possible.

Marlborough, however, no sooner came within reach of the enemy's columns, than he decided upon and immediately executed his plan of attack. The Cameronians formed part of the first line of the right wing, stationed on the height of Bevere, and they had on this occasion the honour of acting under the immediate command of Prince Eugene, who had some days before joined the Duke, having preceded a reinforcement from the Rhine. His Grace conferred on him the command of this wing, to which the greater part of the British were attached. During the action the Regiment was very much exposed for nearly two hours, and had many killed and wounded; but no record has been handed down of the casualties of each corps. The French are said to have lost upwards of sixteen thousand men. Unhappily the day was so far advanced, that at the time when the victory was secured, and a large part of the enemy's army intercepted,

---

* Coxe's "Life of Marlborough."

1708. night intervened, and protected their retreat. Many corps which had surrendered were thus enabled to escape.

The Duke hastened to improve this victory; and by the 14th, had obtained possession of the lines which the enemy had constructed, with the posts of Warreton, Combres, and Werwick.

After completing the destruction of these works, the confederates entered the French territories, with the view of compelling the Duke of Vendôme to quit his position near Ghent and Bruges; which, however, he pertinaciously maintained. From the 25th of July to the 2nd of August, the Cameronians formed part of a small corps which was detached on an enterprise against Leuwe; but as the enemy withdrew on their approach, no material result was attained, and they rejoined the main army.

The next considerable event was the siege of *Lisle*, the capital of French Flanders, during which the Cameronians were employed with the covering army, except when occasional reinforcements were specially detailed for service in the trenches. This city, which was considered to be the strongest in Flanders, being protected by a series of works constructed under the superintendence of the celebrated engineer Vauban, was amply prepared with every requisite for making a protracted defence, and was garrisoned by twenty-one battalions of the best troops in the French army, under the command of Marshal Boufflers. To increase the difficulties of the enterprise, the enemy intercepted the communications of the allies with their magazines at Antwerp and Sasvanghent, so that they were obliged to bring their convoys from Ostend, along a narrow causeway, exposed to the attacks of an army more numerous than their own. On the 13th of August the city was invested, and on the 22nd the trenches were opened. The enemy now resolved, if possible, to relieve the place; but the Duke, who commanded the covering army, made so skilful a disposition of his forces, that they did not make any decisive attempt. On the 7th of September, the besiegers effected a lodgment in an outwork, in which they lost one thousand men; and on the 12th (23rd N.S.), Major Blackader was employed in an attack, with four hundred grenadiers, of which in his diary he gives the following characteristic account:—

"We marched into the trenches about 12 o'clock; "Prince Alexander of Wirtemberg came in about four, "made the dispositions, and gave us our orders. When "he posted me he bade me speak to the grenadiers, and "tell them that the Duke of Marlborough and Prince "Eugene expected they would do as they had always "done—chase the French; adding, that it was better to "die there than make a false step. I answered, 'I "hoped we should all do our duty,' so he shook hands "with me, and went away. Near seven, the signals "being given by all our cannons and bombs going off "together, I gave the word upon the right, 'Grenadiers, "in the name of God, attack!' Immediately they "sprung over the trenches, and threw their grenades "into the counterscarp; but they fell into some con- "fusion. I then ordered out fifty more to sustain them, "and went out myself, and in a little time I got a shot "in the arm; I felt that the bone was not broken, and "all the rest of the officers being wounded, I thought it "my duty to stay still awhile, and encourage the gren- "adiers to keep their warm post. About a quarter-of- "an-hour afterwards, the fire continuing very hot, I got "another shot in the head. I then thought it was time "to come off. I had a great deal of trouble to get out "of the trenches in three hours' space."

1708. As a great deficiency of ammunition began to be felt, a convoy was prepared at Ostend, and was placed under the command of Major-General Webb, with an escort of six thousand men. On its safe arrival depended the continuance of the siege; and the enemy, therefore, made a great effort to intercept it on its march. On the 27th of September it departed from Ostend; and a corps of one thousand six hundred infantry, composed in part of Preston's or Cameronians, and of the Royals, was detached to Oudenburg, with orders to wait there until the convoy had passed, and afterwards to rejoin the escort at Turout. The Count de la Motte, whose army amounted to twenty-two thousand men, meanwhile attempted to intercept the convoy, and to stop its progress in the wood of *Wynendale;* but General Webb, on the first alarm of the enemy's approach, made a most able disposition of his men, by occupying an advantageous position in the wood, with his main body formed in two lines, between the coppice and wood of Wynendale, the regiments which escorted the convoy, forming a third line as they arrived. Two regiments, and parties of grenadiers, were placed in ambuscade on each side, with orders not to discover themselves till they could take the assailants in flank. Count de la Motte, having formed his army, advanced, in full confidence, to overwhelm a force which did not amount to one-half of his own. The enemy began the attack; but, approaching the allied lines, were received by such a fire from the right ambuscade in the woods, that their left wing fell back on the centre. The fire of the opposite ambuscade was then opened, and soon threw their whole line into confusion. They, however, still advanced, and broke two battalions; but, reinforcements being drawn up from the rear, they were repulsed. A third attempt was made by them, but the fire in front and flanks 1708. again throwing back their wings on the centre, the French retired in the utmost confusion, leaving six thousand men killed and wounded on the field. The loss of the allies was only nine hundred, and that of the Cameronians was only one officer wounded, so that most likely they were in the third line.

The further progress of the convoy experienced no obstacle; and, on the last day of the month, this important supply filed through the camp, and, by its opportune arrival, enabled the allies to continue the siege, which, but for this success, must have been raised the next day.

This gallant exploit excited great admiration, and Major-General Webb received the thanks of Parliament and the approbation of Queen Anne, for his services on this occasion.

Whether the Cameronians, after the action of Wynendale,* returned to the siege of Lisle, has not been ascertained; but it is most probable that they remained with the covering army.

The besiegers continued to advance by the slow movements of the sap, to raise new batteries, to complete the lodgments which had been effected, and to fill up the ditch. Under the direction of Prince Eugene, they carried the tenaillon on the 3rd of October, and the ensuing night established themselves on the salient places of arms, opposite to the great breaches. The slow, but irresistible, progress of the besiegers, induced Vendôme to make fresh efforts; which, after several movements, wherein he was counteracted by corres-

---

* "Blackader's Diary."

1708. ponding ones by the covering army under Marlborough, completely failed of their intended object. By these marches, and especially on the 5th and 6th of October, when the Cameronians had a very harassing one, the Duke succeeded in obtaining fresh supplies from Ostend, notwithstanding that Vendôme had laid the country under water by breaking down the dykes. The operations of the siege were, however, pressed with vigour, and every preparation made on the 21st for a general assault. The next day Marshal Boufflers, with whom Marlborough, in the early part of his military career, had served under the celebrated Marshal Turenne, beat a parley at four o'clock in the afternoon; and the town being surrendered on the 23rd, the remainder of the garrison, now reduced to five thousand men, retired into the citadel on the 25th of October.

Operations against the citadel commenced on the 29th of October; and the French, who boasted that the allies were so cooped up that they must either raise the siege or be famished, made the greatest exertions for its relief. The Elector of Bavaria attacked Brussels with ten thousand troops, but was repulsed by the garrison with a loss of two thousand men; and this important town was freed from further danger by the approach of the allied commanders; who, on hearing of the enterprise, marched with the covering army, and passed the Scheldt on pontoons, notwithstanding the strength of the enemy's entrenchments. This difficult enterprise had been so skilfully arranged, and every movement ordered with such secrecy, that when the different columns arrived at their assigned points during the night and early on the morning of the 26th of November, expecting—as an eye-witness observed—" to engage in " the bloodiest day they had ever yet experienced," they found the enemy totally unprepared, and unconscious of danger. The bridges were laid at Gavre and Kirkhoff before the dawn, and the whole army successively passed without opposition. The enemy retired to Tournay, and the allied columns moved to attack his main body on the heights of Oudenarde.

1708.

Instead, however, of aiding the general disposition by a sudden sally, as was directed, the Governor retained his troops quietly within the works, alleging, in excuse, a counter order from the Dutch deputies. The enemy were thus enabled to withdraw to Grammont, with a loss of only about twelve hundred men. The allies, on their arrival at Oudenarde, heard of the Elector's retreat, whereon the Prince returned to Lisle, and the Duke proceeded to Brussels. His Grace afterwards took post at Oudenarde, in order to maintain his communication with the Prince.

During these operations the Cameronians seem, at one time, to have been with the army, but shortly after to have returned into Lisle, where they were stationed previous to the surrender of the citadel. Colonel Blackader, who rejoined them on the 24th of November, having then recovered from his wounds, which he received at the assault and lodgment effected on the 23rd of September, found them in Lisle. They received orders to be in readiness to march on the 25th of November, but did not leave the town; where they remained, doubtless taking their share in the siege, till the fall of the citadel.

The works being now very far advanced, a summons was sent to offer an honourable capitulation, provided the garrison surrendered before the batteries opened; and Marshal Boufflers accepted the offer. On the 9th of December, the garrison marched out with the honours

1708. of war. After its surrender, the Cameronians remained for some days quartered in the town of Lisle.*

Not content with this conquest, Marlborough was determined to strike another blow before the troops marched into winter quarters; to which he was encouraged by the incautiousness of the enemy, whose army had already taken up its cantonments. *Ghent* was invested on the 18th of December; and on the 30th, the batteries being ready to open, the Count de la Motte agreed to capitulate.

1709. On the 3rd of January, 1709, thirty battalions and sixteen squadrons marched out, and were conducted to Tournay; the town and citadel were then taken possession of by six British regiments, under the Duke of Argyle. The French, in consequence of this loss, abandoned Bruges, Plassendahl, and Laffengen.

Thus ended this protracted campaign, in which the Cameronians bore a very distinguished part, having been actively engaged in the four principal events, viz.: the battle of Oudenarde, the siege of Lisle, the action at Wynendale, and the siege of Ghent. The Cameronians continued to be stationed throughout the winter, at Ghent, where Colonel Blackader rejoined them in March 1709, from leave of absence.

The campaign of this year did not open till the end of June, when the allied army, numbering one hundred and ten thousand men, was assembled in the plain of Lisle. The Cameronians had quitted Ghent on the 17th of that month, on their way to join; and arrived on the 21st, after a long and fatiguing march from five in the morning to five in the afternoon over very bad roads.

---

* " Blackader's Diary."

The French army, under Marshal Villars, occupied an entrenched camp at Lens. As the Duke did not deem it prudent to attack him in that position, the allied commanders, after a series of well-combined marches, by which Ypres was made to appear as the intended object of their attack, suddenly undertook the siege of *Tournay;* the garrison of which, in order to strengthen his army, Marshal Villars had imprudently weakened. The investment took place on the 27th of June; and though the garrison did not exceed twelve weak battalions and four squadrons, the works were so strong, both by art and nature, and De Surville, the governor, displayed so much skill and bravery, that the siege was protracted much beyond the expectation of the allies, and was attended with great loss. On the 29th of July, the besiegers having affected a practicable breach, the town capitulated, and the garrison retired into the citadel.

After an abortive treaty for its surrender, hostilities recommenced on the 8th of August. As the besiegers now proceeded by the method of sap, their miners frequently met with those of the enemy under ground, and fought with bayonet and pistol. The volunteers on both sides presented themselves for these subterraneous combats, in the midst of mines and countermines, ready primed for explosion. Sometimes they were kindled by accident, and sometimes sprung by design; so that great numbers of these brave men were stifled below, and others blown into the air, or buried in the rubbish. It was not till the 3rd of September, when all the provisions were consumed, and preparations were complete for a general assault of the trenches, that De Surville surrendered at discretion.

During the continuance of this siege, the Cameronians

1709.

1709. were employed with the covering army, and remained in the same camp about two months.

The reduction of *Mons* became the next object of the confederates, who passed the Scheldt on the 3rd of September, and detached the Prince of Hesse, to endeavour, by a rapid march, to occupy the lines which the enemy had formed on the Trouille. Having traversed a distance of forty-nine English miles in fifty-six hours, the Prince passed the Haine at two in the morning of the 6th, and entered the lines at Trouille, without opposition. The main body of the army was held in readiness to support, and, on the news of his success, its march was accelerated, after a few hours' repose in rain and mud; so that in the course of that and the next day, the passage of the Haine was completed, and Mons invested on the side of France. On the 9th of September, the two armies were so near that a heavy cannonade ensued, and the Cameronians were posted, with two other regiments, in so exposed a part of the line, that they suffered a considerable loss, and had Captain Lawson, and Lieutenant Simson wounded.*
The enemy, who occupied a position between the woods of La Merte and Taniers, fortified it with triple entrenchments. Their camp was so covered with lines, hedges, entrenchments, cannon, and trees laid across, that it seemed quite inaccessible. On the 11th, early in the morning, the allies, favoured by a thick fog, erected batteries on each wing, and in the centre, and, about eight o'clock, the weather clearing up, the battle of *Malplaquet* began. Eighty-six battalions on the left, with a support of twenty battalions, attacked the right

---

* "Blackader's Letters."

of the enemy with such vigour, that notwithstanding all 1709. the natural and artificial advantages of their position, in less than an hour they were driven into the woods. The Prince of Orange, with thirty-six Dutch battalions, advanced against the right of the French centre, posted in the wood of La Merte, and covered with three entrenchments; here the battle was maintained with the most desperate carnage on both sides. The Dutch carried the first, but were repulsed in their attack on the second entrenchment, with great slaughter, whereupon the Prince renewed his efforts; and though the French defended themselves with an obstinacy of courage bordering on despair, they at length made an orderly retreat under Marshal Boufflers, when they saw their lines forced, and their left and centre giving way.

Thus the field of battle was abandoned to the confederates, with about forty colours and standards, sixteen pieces of artillery, and a large number of prisoners. The victory was, however, dearly purchased by the loss of five thousand five hundred and forty-four killed, and twelve thousand seven hundred and six wounded, including two hundred and sixty-two officers killed, and seven hundred and sixty-two wounded, making a total of eighteen thousand two hundred and fifty of their best troops, whereas the enemy did not lose above half that number. In consequence of the severe casualties which the allies had sustained, they halted near the field of battle on the plain beyond Malplaquet, whilst the French were enabled to make an orderly retreat across the Renelle, reassembling their troops in a camp between Quesnoy and Valenciennes.

The share which the Cameronians had in this desperately fought battle was, first, in occupying a situation in which they were exposed to a cannonade

1709. the most severe they had ever suffered, and by which they experienced a considerable loss. "But the soldiers "(states Blackader), however, endured it without "shrinking, very patiently, and with great courage."

They were next entrusted with a duty on which their discipline and resolution underwent another severe trial, and, with some other regiments, rendered good service, for it was by the success of Lieut.-General the Earl of Orkney's attack on the enemy's centre that the victory was secured to the allies. They were ordered to occupy a retrenchment, which the French had left, where they had to sustain the cavalry which were repulsed by the enemy; but, being thus supported, the allied horse were able to maintain their ground, and the ruinous consequences which must have attended their defeat were avoided. On this occasion the *gens d'armerie* of France were checked in their successful charge on the allied cavalry under the Prince d'Auvergne, and finally driven back. This affair took place under the immediate observation of Marshal Boufflers, who, in his despatch, attributed his loss of the battle to the conduct of the allied infantry, of which the Cameronians formed a part. Speaking of the battle, and of the general demeanour of the troops, Major Blackader adds, " It was the most deliberate, solemn, and well-ordered " battle that ever I saw. It was a noble and fine dis- "position, and as nobly executed. Every man was at " his post, and I never saw troops engage with more " cheerfulness, boldness, and resolution. In all the " soldiers' faces appeared a brisk and lively gaiety, " which presaged victory." In the marches previous to this battle the troops had suffered greatly from exposure to the weather, which was very bad, and also the want of provisions. Major Blackader says, on the 9th,

"Our men have wanted bread these five days, and are 1709. "faint." Yet, two days after was that great battle, in which they forgot all their hardships, and fought with so much bravery.

The Cameronians suffered severely, for the cannon-balls came thick among them, and swept away whole files of men; they lost their commanding officer, Lieut.-Colonel Cranston, who was killed by a shot, which passed through his body as he was riding at the head of the Regiment. Captain Shaw, and Ensign Inglis were killed; Lieutenant Cockburn, Ensign Burnet, and Sergeant Wilson were wounded.*

After this victory, the allies remained undisputed masters in the field, and prosecuted the siege of *Mons*, which surrendered on the 23rd of October. The Cameronians returned to the neighbourhood of Mons the evening after the battle, where they remained in camp, with a full expectation of being employed in the siege, till they were relieved by some regiments from the garrisons, on whose arrival they marched to join the covering army. During this operation the troops suffered greatly from the inclemency of the weather; but before the end of the month they went into winter-quarters, and the Cameronians proceeded to Ghent,† where they arrived

---

* Major Blackader, in a letter to his wife, after the sanguinary battle of Malplaquet, thus consoles her: "When you grow anxious "and thoughtful, take my riddled hat and hang it up before "you, and trust in God, who hath delivered and doth daily "deliver."

† After the Cameronians had taken the field this campaign, during which they so much distinguished themselves, the arrival of a body of recruits, who joined from Scotland on the 19th of July, completely filled up the vacancies in their ranks, occasioned

1709. on the 31st of October; here they remained during the whole winter.

1710. The confederates took the field in 1710 unusually early. Prince Eugene and the Duke set out for Tournay on the 15th of March, to assemble the troops which were quartered on the Meuse and in Flanders; but the Cameronians did not leave Ghent until the 14th of April. On the 20th the army suddenly advanced to *Pont à Vendin*, to attack the lines, which the enemy had made during the winter, with the hope of being able to cover Douay and other frontier towns. The troops left for their defence at once retired. It was on the 21st that the Cameronians came in sight of the lines, just after their evacuation. Lieut.-Colonel Blackader writes, that when "he saw the pass and " bridge which they were to have attacked, he could " not but admire the goodness of God; for it was so " strong a morass, that they could hardly have made " a-head to attack it." The Duke of Marlborough remarked, "It was a happy beginning of the campaign;" for had the enemy remained at Pont à Vendin, the result would have been doubtful. On the 22nd a similar

---

by their active services the year before; for when reviewed on the 21st of August, by the Duke and Prince Eugene, Major Blackader says, that "all went on very well, and our Regiment appeared in good order and full." Thus their character at home seems to have remained unimpaired, and that military ardour and zeal for their country's cause, which were so conspicuous at their formation, operated among their countrymen to induce them to repair the casualties of war. Major Blackader obtained his promotion to the lieut.-colonelcy on the 28th of October (o.s.), two days after the Regiment commenced its march for Ghent.

success attended the operations of the allied army; for 1710. on the front of it appearing, the French quitted the line of the Scarpe, and left Douay uncovered.

Having laid bridges over the Scarpe, the Duke passed with his division, and encamped at Vitry. Prince Eugene invested Douay on the 23rd of April, but the trenches were not opened until the 5th of May.

One thousand infantry, chiefly grenadiers, and two hundred dragoons of the garrison, under Brigadier the Duke of Montemar, made a sortie about ten at night on the 7th of May, when Sutton's regiment (since disbanded), which covered the workmen, was nearly cut to pieces, and a Swiss corps also suffered greatly. The assailants were, however, in the end repulsed with loss. This circumstance caused the Cameronians, who had till then been with the covering army, to be ordered into the trenches to replace Sutton's regiment. Their first turn in them was on the 12th of May, but they were relieved the next morning without the loss of a man. They were in the trenches when a second sortie was made by the enemy on the 17th of May (as Lieut.-Colonel Blackader states in his Diary), "a little before " break of day. They came on silently, expecting to " surprise us; but by the goodness of Providence, we " were ready. .Our sentinels gave us warning, and we " put ourselves in a posture, and received them so " warmly that they immediately retired in confusion, " without firing a shot."* Thus, the vigilance of the sentries saved their comrades who were at work, from

---

* Lediard, in his Life of the Duke of Marlborough, thus describes this sortie : "On the 17th of May, in the morning, the " besieged in Douay made another sally, with nine companies of " grenadiers, towards the left of the left attack ; but Colonel

1710. the severe loss with which a successful sortie is so often attended, and which was unhappily experienced on other occasions during this siege, but from such negligence the Cameronians appear to have been altogether free.

The Regiment joined the main army on the 30th, when it was threatened with an attack by Marshal Villars, who, having viewed the position of the confederates, marched back, and fixed his camp at St. Laurens. The Cameronians returned the next day to the trenches, in which they continued to take their share of duty, but without any severe casualties, excepting on the 3rd of June, when, by an unfortunate explosion of some powder and grenades, Lieutenant Graham, Sergeant Davidson, and sixteen rank and file, were burnt and wounded, two of whom died; and on the 20th, when, out of a detachment of thirty-nine men employed in making a lodgment in a raveline, thirty-two became *hors-de-combat*. On many other occasions, when it came to their turn to be in the trenches, they appear to have been much favoured, as no other considerable loss is recorded, though altogether it was large. Lieut.-Colonel Blackader states that, in riding on the afternoon of the 17th of June, he went to their hospital, "where was a melancholy sight of wounded men." It is elsewhere recorded that, previous to the 30th of May, they had lost between forty and fifty killed and wounded; but they were in daily expectation of the arrival of eighty-five recruits, who were much wanted to fill up their ranks. The total loss sustained by the Regiment was one

---

" Preston, who commanded there, gave them so warm a reception, " that, upon the first firing of his men, the enemy retired in great " confusion, and left above one hundred men prisoners." Vol. III., p. 42.

captain, three sergeants, and forty-seven soldiers killed; 1710. one captain, five subalterns, eleven sergeants, and one hundred and seventy-five soldiers wounded—in all, two hundred and forty-three casualties.*

The aim of the French Marshal was, by continued alarms, to interrupt and protract the siege of Douay, and thus aid the defence, which was vigorously conducted by the numerous garrison under General Albergotti, until the besieged, being reduced to the last extremity, were obliged to capitulate on the 27th of June.

On the 7th of July the Cameronians were on the march, and on the 14th they were reviewed. During these movements in the field, the Duke, finding it impracticable to force the enemy's position near Arras, resolved to besiege *Bethune*, which was invested on the 15th of July, and surrendered on the 29th of August. The Cameronians then formed part of the covering army.

After this success, the allies undertook at once the sieges of Aire and St. Venant, but the Cameronians were not present at either. The former surrendered on the 9th of November, and the latter on the 30th of September. After their reduction, the army broke up, and went into winter quarters, the Regiment occupying its old quarters at Ghent.

In 1711, there is reason to believe that the Came- 1711. ronians were actively employed before any other part of the army. They left Ghent on the 21st of March, and advanced into the enemy's territory, where, on the 24th, they took possession of a post, which they fortified and retained till the forces assembled, about the middle

---

* "Annals of Queen Anne," p. 63.

1711. of April,* at Orchies, the French troops being then concentrated between Cambray and Arras. On the 23rd of May, the Duke, whose army was encamped between Douay and Bouchain, was joined by Prince Eugene. He, however, soon after quitted the Low Countries, with the Imperial and Palatine troops, to protect Germany. The Duke, repassing the Scarpe, encamped on the plains of Lens, from whence he advanced towards Aire, as if he had intended to attack the French lines in that quarter. These lines, beginning at Bouchain on the Scheldt, were continued along the Sanset and the Scarpe to Arras, and thence by the Upper Scarpe to Canche. They were defended, by redoubts and other works, in such a manner that Villars deemed them impenetrable, and named them the *ne plus ultra* of Marlborough. Having prepared a great quantity of fascines, and made every arrangement for an immediate attack, and caused a report to be circulated, which was soon carried to the enemy, that it would take place on the 4th of August, the French commander was induced to collect his whole army in the full expectation of a battle. Calculating that the passage of the Sanset by *Arleux* would be left unguarded, Marlborough had ordered Lieut.-Generals Cadogan and Count Hompesch to

---

* In the course of this spring, also, a draft of recruits joined the Regiment from Scotland. In the beginning of July, Lieut.-Colonel Blackader speaks of being busied with them in preparing for a review by the Earl of Orkney. It would seem probable that every year, from the frequent mention made of them, the Regiment had received reinforcements from home, which must have been very necessary to maintain it in that effective state in which it appears constantly to have been kept, notwithstanding the severe losses that attended its arduous services.

assemble twenty battalions and seventeen squadrons from 1711. the neighbouring garrisons, and march to that place. Brigadier-General Sutton was despatched with the artillery and pontoons, to lay bridges over the canal near Coulezon, and over the Scarpe near Vitry; while the Duke, with the whole army, began his march for the same place about nine in the evening of the 4th, moving with such expedition, that by five in the morning of the 5th of August he had passed the river at Vitry. There His Grace received intelligence that Count Hompesch had taken possession of the passes on the Sanset and Scheldt without opposition, the enemy having withdrawn their detachments from that side, just as had been anticipated.

With his vanguard of fifty squadrons, Marlborough directed his march towards Arleux, and before eight arrived at Bacca Bacheul, where, in two hours, he was joined by the heads of the columns into which he had divided his infantry. Villars being certified of this intention, about two in the morning decamped with his whole force; and placing himself at the head of the household troops, marched all night with such expedition that, at about eleven in the forenoon, he was in sight of the Duke, who had by this time joined Count Hompesch. Villars immediately fell back on the main body of his army, which had advanced to the high road between Arras and Cambray; while the allies encamped on the Scheldt, between Oisy and Estrun, after a march of ten leagues without halting, which is scarcely to be paralleled in history. By this plan, so happily executed, Marlborough fairly out-manœuvred Villars, and without the loss of one man, entered the lines which had been so confidently pronounced to be impenetrable.

The Duke was thus enabled to pursue the object, with

1711. a view to which he had engaged in these arduous movements; and passing, almost within cannon-shot, in front of Cambray, he threw bridges over the Scheldt; and, on the 6th of August, crossed that river, in presence of the enemy. So well were his measures taken, that Villars remained in his camp, and suffered the allies, without molestation, to proceed to the investment of *Bouchain*. This enterprise was deemed impracticable, as it was situated in a morass, and was strongly fortified, and defended by a numerous garrison, in the neighbourhood of an army superior in numbers to that of the allies. The place, however, was invested on the 10th of August; and, whilst the Duke exerted his utmost skill to ensure its capture, Marshal Villars had spared no pains for its safety. He had reinforced the garrison to six thousand chosen men, commanded by officers of known ability; some efforts were made by him to raise the siege, which were rendered ineffectual by Marlborough's consummate prudence and activity: and he was equally unsuccessful in an attempt to surprise Douay. The trenches were rapidly advanced, and the Cameronians, towards the conclusion of the siege, were one of the corps employed in them.*

In the execution of this plan, the English General was obliged to form lines, erect regular forts, raise batteries, throw bridges over a river, make a causeway through a deep morass, and provide for the security of convoys against a numerous enemy on the one side, and the garrisons of Condé and Valenciennes on the other. This was, therefore, considered as one of the boldest enterprises of the war. It displayed all the fortitude, skill,

---

* "Blackader's Diary."—Smollett's Hist.

and resolution of the General, and all the valour and intrepidity of the troops, who had scarcely ever exhibited such amazing proofs of courage on any other occasion. In twenty days after the trenches were opened, the garrison, on the 13th of September, were obliged to surrender themselves as prisoners of war. This was the last military exploit which the Duke performed; for, when the breaches were repaired, the army went into winter-quarters; and their illustrious Chief, who returned home, was deprived of his command by the counsels of the new ministry.*

1711.

---

* Colonel Blackader, who had been twenty-two years in the Regiment, and had shared in all its dangers and honours, now quitted the service, being permitted to sell his commissions. He left the army at Bouchain on the 12th of October, after a melancholy parting with some of his kind friends, and the corps with which he had so long served. His diary, to which this Record is much indebted, must rank as a singular and interesting work. The original manuscripts having been overlooked for many years, were sold with other papers to a tobacconist at Stirling, by whom they were rescued from destruction. He was born at Glencairn on the 14th of September, 1664, and was the son of the Reverend John Blackader, minister of Troqueer, expelled at the Restoration for non-compliance with episcopacy. This may account for his remarks regarding the "Ebenezers" he set up through Germany, and for his practice of visiting the field of battle after the stern conflict was over, in order to get "a preaching from the dead." He seems to have enjoyed a high reputation, and to have been particularly favoured by the Duke of Marlborough; for, on taking leave of him, he says he was quite ashamed to hear of the kind and obliging things which His Grace spoke about him to the generals present at the interview. He then proceeded to Holland, and after narrowly escaping a party of the enemy near Sas, he reached Rotterdam, and thence proceeded to England. Thus, nearly at the same time that the

1711. During the course of this campaign the army suffered considerably from the weather; which the Duke noticed,

---

army was deprived of its great General, under whom it had been led through an uninterrupted course of victory, and who, by his bitterest enemy, Lord Bolingbroke, was acknowledged to be "the greatest General and the greatest Minister that our or any other country had produced," the Cameronians lost a commander in Colonel Blackader, who had shared their fortunes in all the numerous situations of difficulty and trial in which they had been placed from the time of their levy. Zealous in all his duties, he must earnestly have co-operated in that excellent system of discipline, which, by raising the moral character of the soldier, increases the efficiency of an army in the field, by withholding him from those excesses which are alike injurious to health and character; and, by protecting the persons and property, and by conciliating the feelings of the people, whose country may be the scene of operation, tends materially to diminish the effects of their hostility, as carried out in later times in the Peninsula and France by the Duke of Wellington. The chief principles on which this discipline was grounded are thus described by Lediard, who himself served under the Duke of Marlborough's command, and could speak as an eye-witness of its salutary effects. "The "Duke discountenanced the slightest degree of intemperance or "licentiousness; and laboured to impress his officers and troops "with the same sense of religion which he himself entertained. "Divine service was regularly performed in all his fixed camps, "both morning and evening; and, on Sundays, sermons were "preached, both in field and in garrison. Previous to battle, "prayers were offered up at the head of each regiment, and the "first act, after a victory, was a solemn thanksgiving. By these "means, aided by his own example, his camp resembled a quiet, "well-governed city. Cursing and swearing were seldom heard "among the officers, a sot and a drunkard was the object of "scorn, and the poor soldiers, many of them the refuse and dregs "of the nation, became, at the close of one or two campaigns, "tractable, civil, sensible, and clean, and had an air and spirit "above the vulgar."

on one occasion, with his usual humanity, for which he was so much beloved. "We have had miserable wet weather ever since we came into the field; and I pity the poor men so much, that it makes me uneasy to the last degree; for it can't be otherwise but great numbers must be sick." At other times the heat was excessive. Colonel Blackader writes of the 15th of June, that this " was one of the severest he ever saw. Several men, " marching in the ranks, fell down, and died upon the " very spot. The whole fields were like a field of battle, " men lying panting and fainting. Most of the regiments " did not bring above sixty or seventy men to the camp " with their colours." The length and frequency of the marches, also, added to the fatigue of the troops; who, however, bore every hardship with cheerfulness, being full of confidence in the skill of their illustrious leader.

During the course of their services under the Duke of Marlborough, Colonel Blackader states, that his Grace bestowed on the Cameronians his special thanks no less than seven different times, for their distinguished gallantry and conduct.

The army broke up from its camp near Bouchain on the 27th of October, but it does not appear in what Flemish town the Regiment was quartered during the winter.

In 1712, the army, under the command of the Duke of Ormond, who had succeeded Marlborough, took the field early; and, in the beginning of March, the Earl of Albemarle was sent, with a considerable force, to bombard *Arras*, which he reduced to a heap of ruins. In May, the Duke of Ormond joined Prince Eugene at Tournay, and the allies passed the Scheldt, encamping at Haspre and Solenmes; but when the Prince proposed to attack Marshal Villars, his new coadjutor declined, being restrained by his orders from fighting a battle.

1712. The Prince then undertook the siege of *Quesnoy* with his own army, the Duke of Ormond consenting to cover it with his troops, a service which led to its surrender on the 4th of July. The Prince then invested Landreçy; but, as the terms of peace were now arranged between France and England, the Duke of Ormond withdrew the British troops, consisting of eighteen thousand men, and proclaimed a suspension of arms for two months. The allies, being highly exasperated at this separation of the British, refused them leave to enter Douay, Lisle, Tournay, and many other towns; but the Duke continued his march, and seized Ghent and Bruges. He then reinforced the garrison of Dunkirk, which the French had surrendered to a force sent from England to occupy it, as a security on the part of France for the due execution of the terms of peace.

On the 5th of August, the following corps of infantry, which were encamped near Ghent, commenced their march for Dunkirk, viz.:—two battalions of the Royals, the 15th, 16th, 19th, 21st, and the Cameronians, together with Newton's, Evans's, and Leigh's regiments—the three latter were disbanded in the year following. All arrived at Dunkirk on the 10th, and the remains of the French garrison then quitted the place.

When the campaign between the French and the remainder of the allies, which (after the separation of the British) had been attended with uniform misfortune to the latter, was terminated by the armies going into winter-quarters, the Duke of Ormond proceeded to London, leaving the English in garrison.

1713. After the occupation of Dunkirk, several movements of the British troops in the vicinity took place, with a view to the demolition of the fortifications and port. The treaty of Utrecht, which terminated the wars of Queen Anne, was signed on the 11th of April. On the

3rd of May, 1713, three regiments, viz.:—the 3rd, 24th, 1713. and 26th, occupied Nieuport, of which fortress Brigadier Preston, the colonel of the Cameronians, was, on the 19th of that month, appointed governor. On the 13th, three other regiments, viz.:—8th, 21st, and Wynne's, formed part of that garrison. The Cameronians remained there till the 16th of August, when they marched with the 34th, and 7th Dragoon Guards, to Dunkirk, and encamped on the esplanade, permission to enter the town being refused. The two youngest companies of each infantry regiment were then reduced. The 24th, 26th, and 34th, embarked on the 20th for Ireland, whilst the 4th Dragoons and Pocock's regiment sailed for Dover, where the latter was disbanded. Wynne's regiment had previously been disbanded in June. On the 17th of August, five cavalry regiments proceeded from Dunkirk for Ireland, and a short time afterwards the Marquess of Harwich's (7th Dragoon Guards), and Ross's Dragoons (5th Lancers) embarked for England. Thus, by the end of August, all the British troops had quitted the Low Countries.

The Cameronians continued in Ireland from September, 1715. 1713, until the autumn of 1715, when, from the implicit confidence placed by the Government in their tried fidelity, they were brought over on the breaking out of the rebellion in the Highlands of Scotland, and in the North of England, in favour of the Pretender. In the former, the Earl of Mar had collected a body of fourteen thousand men, and commanded all the country as far as the Frith of Forth. He had even succeeded in transporting a body of twenty-five thousand men across, under Brigadier Macintosh, which, after threatening Edinburgh, marched to the borders, and finally entered England under the command of Mr. Foster, who was

1715. commissioned as General by the Earl of Mar. Here they were joined by the Earl of Derwentwater, and then advanced to Penrith, where the *posse comitatus* of Cumberland, which, to the number of ten thousand men, had been collected by the Earl of.Lonsdale, dispersed precipitately at their approach. Foster then proceeded triumphantly, by Kendal and Lancaster, to *Preston*, whence Stanhope's Dragoons (since disbanded), and a regiment of militia, immediately withdrew.

Their success, however, now terminated. Major-General Wills, with six regiments of horse and the Cameronians, reached the bridge of Ribble before Foster received intelligence of their approach; but when apprised of his danger, the latter forthwith began to raise barricades, and to put the place in a posture of defence; in which he was interrupted on the 12th of November by the King's troops. Though so weak in infantry, Major-General Wills determined at once to attack the town in three different places.

The main attack was formed by the Cameronians under Lieut.-Colonel Lord Forrester, supported by fifty dismounted men of each of the six dragoon regiments, and directed against the barriers, by which the several entrances into the town were defended. After making their way through the lanes and narrow approaches, they were received with a very heavy fire from the entrenchments and houses; and being without artillery, after some unavailing attempts to force their way against superior numbers, they were compelled to fall back. During the heat of the.action, it was however discovered that the entrance into the town by the Wigan road was less strongly fortified, and that part of the Highlanders there stationed had been withdrawn. Lord Forrester immediately availed himself of this opening; and, though exposed to a heavy and destructive fire from a concealed enemy, he succeeded, at the head of his gallant men, in occupying two houses, the superior elevation of which gave them considerable advantage over the rebels: who, in this quarter, in their turn, sustained a severe loss both of officers and men. The Pretender's adherents maintained themselves at the other two points of attack, no impression having been made on their position, except by Lord Forrester.

1715.

In this attack, his Lordship's coolness and judgment were particularly noticed. He placed his men in a narrow passage, where they were out of fire, and then entered the street alone to reconnoitre the rebels' entrenchment; from which, and from the houses, he was exposed to a heavy fire. Having accomplished his object, his Lordship returned, and leading out his men, drew up one division across the street, to keep under by its fire that of the enemy; whilst, with the remainder, the houses were secured; by which a tenable lodgment was effected in the rebels' line of defence. It was in the course of these operations that he received several wounds.* An eye-witness of the action states that the men "upon all occasions behaved with a great deal of bravery and order."

Major-General Carpenter having joined on the following day (13th of November) with three regiments of dragoons, the place was surrounded, and the rebels, fearful of the result of another attack, sent to propose a capitulation. Major-General Wills refused to grant them any terms, and they were under the necessity of unconditionally laying down their arms. Thus the

---

* "Patten's History."

1715. Cameronians, the only infantry regiment present during these operations, contributed, by their great exertions, to suppress this dangerous rebellion. They suffered, however, a considerable loss—of the one hundred and forty-two casualties, ninety-two were from their ranks, and amongst the wounded were their lieut.-colonel, Lord Forrester, Major Lawson, and Captain Preston; the latter died of his wounds.*

The following anecdote shows the spirit of loyalty which animated the Cameronians:—It is related that a soldier of the Regiment, who was lying with two other wounded men, prisoners with himself, when Mr. Patten, a clergyman of the rebel army, offered to pray with them, immediately replied, " If you be a Protestant we " desire your prayers, but name not the Pretender as " King."†

Great encouragement had been given to the disaffected by the indecisive battle of Dumblain or Sheriffmuir, which was fought on the very day of the surrender of the rebels at Preston (13th November), and which was increased by the subsequent arrival of the Pretender; but as the Government was now able to direct an undi-

---

* *List of Killed and Wounded of the King's Forces in the attack on Preston, in Lancashire, on the 12th of November,* 1715.

Two captains, one ensign, and fifty-three men, including sergeants, killed; one lieutenant-colonel, one major, two lieutenants, one cornet, four ensigns, and seventy-seven rank and file wounded; making a total of one hundred and forty-two, of which number ninety-two belonged to the Cameronians. Lieut.-Colonel Lord Forrester and Major Lawson were wounded, and Captain Preston died of his wounds.—*Vide* "Rae's History," "Patten's History," and "Colonel Blackader's Life."

† "Patten's History."

vided attention to Scotland, by the end of January, 1716. 1716, so formidable a force was collected that the Chevalier relinquished the enterprise in despair. After his departure, the royal army in vain attempted to overtake his adherents, who, being deserted by their chiefs, dispersed, and rejoined their respective clans.*

The whole of the Duke of Argyll's army, which consisted of fourteen battalions and ten squadrons, including the six regiments of Dutch auxiliaries, were quartered in the Highlands during the winter, the better to secure the tranquillity of that part of Scotland. The Cameronians subsequently proceeded to Ireland.

On the 3rd of May, 1720, Lieut.-Colonel Philip 1727. Anstruther was promoted Colonel of the Regiment, in succession to Brigadier-General Preston, who retired by the sale of the colonelcy, under the regulations of the 27th of February of that year.

The Cameronians remained in Ireland from 1716 to 1726, when they were put on board the fleet. In the following year, in consequence of the attempt made by the Spaniards to recover Gibraltar, fresh

---

* During this Rebellion, Colonel Blackader held a temporary commission as Colonel of the Glasgow Volunteers, a corps raised in that city to support the Government. As an additional reward for his services he was appointed, on the 27th of March, 1717, to be Deputy-Governor of Stirling Castle. He was also returned a member to the General Assembly: this afforded him opportunities of showing his talents as a public speaker, and there is a degree of pride about him to become an orator, as from his own account he was slow of speech and a stammering tongue. He discontinued his Diary at the end of the year 1728, and did not live many months after. His death occurred on Sunday morning, the 31st of August, 1729, within a few days of completing his sixty-fifth year. A plain marble tablet was erected to his memory in the West Church of Stirling.

1727. troops were sent out to strengthen that garrison. They sailed under convoy of Admiral Sir Charles Wager's fleet, and reached the bay on the 12th of February, in fifteen days from their embarkation at Portsmouth. The Cameronians formed one of the regiments composing this reinforcement, and had a post of danger immediately assigned to them. On the 6th of February their alarm-post was the covertway at Southport. About the 22nd of that month, the batteries of the Spaniards opened against the place, and, according to their own gazettes, they fired at the rate of seven hundred shot an hour, the cannonade lasting from daybreak till noon, and from one till sunset. This bombardment lasted twelve days, and then ceased, owing to the running of nearly all their guns. They still, however, persevered in carrying on the siege, and maintained a slow firing till the 11th of June.

On the 1st of April, 1727, the alarm post of the Cameronians was on the road to Wills's, beyond the hospital; and on the 3rd of May, the Regiment marched out of the town, and encamped on the red sands, having the line wall between the town and the new mole as their alarm-post. They were relieved by a battalion of the Guards and Colonel Clayton's regiment (14th Foot), which had just arrived. On the 25th of May, their alarm-post was Southport glacis, where they continued till the 29th of July, when the Regiment was again quartered in the town.

During this siege no brilliant action on either side is recorded; and, on the part of the garrison, their duties were chiefly confined to a patient endurance of danger and fatigue, circumstances very trying both to the health and temper of the soldiers, and affording little excitement or hope of distinction. The Cameronians had six rank

and file killed; three died of wounds, and six of sick- 1738.
ness;—twenty-nine were wounded. They formed a
portion of the garrison till the 13th of June, 1738, when
they embarked for Minorca,* and remained in that island
until their removal to Ireland in 1748.   1748.

In the Royal Warrant of the 1st of July, 1751, for 1751.
ensuring uniformity in the clothing, standards, and
colours of the army, and regulating the number† and
rank of regiments, the facings of the 26th Regiment
were directed to be *pale yellow*. The first, or King's
colour, was the great Union; the second, or Regimental
colour, was of pale yellow silk, with the Union in the upper
canton; in the centre of the colour was the number of the
rank of the Regiment, in gold Roman characters, within
a wreath of roses and thistles on the same stalk.

In 1754, the Regiment returned to its native country, 1754.
after an absence of about thirty-two years. In the
spring of 1757 the Cameronians again proceeded to 1757.
Ireland, and remained there for ten years.

Colonel Edward Sandford was removed from the
colonelcy of the 52nd to that of the 26th, on the 27th 1760.
of November, 1760, *vice* Lieut.-General Anstruther,
deceased; and Colonel John Scott was appointed to the
colonelcy, on the 14th of January, 1763, in succession 1763.
to Major-General Sandford, removed to the 10th Foot.

In May, 1767, the Regiment embarked from Ireland 1767.
for North America, and was stationed there in the discharge of the ordinary duties of the country, till the
American Revolution broke out in 1775, when the 1775.

---

* Lieut.-General Anstruther of the 26th was Governor during
part of this time; being replaced, on his election as a Member of
Parliament in 1747, by Lieut.-General Blakeney.

† *Vide* Note, page 4.

1775. Cameronians were found in the posts of greatest danger, and to them, of misfortune. The British ministry, which had provoked the colonists to resistance by the impolicy and violence of their measures, had made little or no preparation in any part to support by force those orders, the voluntary and peaceable execution of which, in the existing temper of men's minds, could not reasonably be expected. When they, at length, roused themselves from their apathy, and determined to put forth the strength of the kingdom, to crush a rebellion which was now openly declared, their attention was diverted from Canada to those states where the danger appeared most imminent, and the whole of Lower Canada was therefore left to the protection of two regiments, the 7th and 26th, at a weak peace establishment of three hundred and forty men each, the 8th Foot being stationed in Upper Canada. They were, moreover, separated in several remote garrisons; so they were not disposable to occupy a point of *appui*, where the provincial militia might assemble, and be instructed in discipline. Though the military did their duty, yet they were able scarcely at all to contribute to the safety of the province, which was due to the skilful defence of Quebec by Lieut.-General (afterwards Sir Guy) Carleton.

The Americans, whose attention was unwearied, did not fail to remark, and to take advantage, of the defenceless state of the Canadas. Brigadier-General Montgomery (a native of Ireland, who had quitted the British service a short time before, and settled at New York), and Colonel Arnold, collected a considerable force, with which they advanced against Montreal and Quebec. The first blow, however, was struck by a volunteer, named Ethan Allan, who, on the 3rd of May, 1775, assembled, of his own accord, about fifty men, and proceeded towards *Fort Ticonderoga*; which was garrisoned 1775. by sixty men, under Captain Delaplace, of the 26th Regiment. Allan, who had often been at Ticonderoga, had remarked a great want of discipline in the garrison, and the negligence of its commander was such, that the gates were never shut; disposing his small force in the woods, he went to Captain Delaplace, with whom he was well acquainted, and prevailed on him to lend him twenty men, for the pretended purpose of assisting to transport some goods across the lake. Having contrived to make these men drunk, at night-fall, drawing his own people from their ambuscade, he advanced to the fort, of which he immediately became master. As there was not one person awake, though there was a sentry at the gate, they were all taken prisoners[*] owing to the shameful negligence of the officer, and the drunkenness of the men. *Crown Point* also shared the same fate.

Notwithstanding these advantages, the Americans had not sufficiently completed their preparations to enable them immediately to attack St. John's, to which the remainder of the 7th and 26th Regiments had withdrawn from Montreal, and where they had been employed in constructing two redoubts. In some incursions, previous to their engaging in this operation, they were repulsed with loss. Allan (now Colonel), with a party of one hundred and fifty men, marched to the St. Lawrence, and, crossing the river, about three miles below Montreal, attempted to surprise that place; but, on the 25th of September, he was encountered by eighty men, thirty-six being Cameronians, under Major Campbell, and was defeated, with the loss of sixteen killed, and thirty prisoners, of whom the Colonel was one. On the 18th

---

[*] Stedman's "History of the American War."

1775. of the same month, a party of two hundred men, which had approached St. John's, was attacked by a detachment of the garrison of one-half its strength, and defeated.

General Montgomery having now completed his preparations, turned the siege into a blockade, and invested Fort Chambly, where Major the Honourable Joseph Stopford, of the 7th Royal Fusiliers, and about eighty men, were in garrison. This post kept up the communication between St. John's and Montreal, but the place could not be held against the very superior numbers of the enemy, and the garrison surrendered on the 20th of October. The General then resumed the siege of *St. John's*, which had been strengthened by some new works. The garrison, consisting of five hundred and fifty men of the 7th and 26th, and a few Canadian volunteers, were commanded by Major Charles Preston, of the Cameronians, and had but a small supply of ammunition and provision, while the works were only in an imperfect state.

Nevertheless, its defence was gallant and protracted; the soldiers were often knee-deep in mire, and were reduced to half-allowance of provisions; ammunition at length ran short, and seeing no chance of relief, the garrison was obliged to surrender on the 13th of November as prisoners of war.

After this success General Montgomery rapidly advanced towards Montreal, which was evacuated on his approach, and Colonel Easton, whom he detached in pursuit, having overtaken the bateaux, in which Major-General Prescott, his staff, and about one hundred and fifty men, chiefly Cameronians, had embarked to descend the St. Lawrence to Quebec, succeeded in taking prisoners the whole party. On this occasion the Regiment lost its colours, which, when the detachment found themselves closely pursued, had been stripped from the staves 1775. and carried by an officer round his body; but finding escape impossible, they were then wrapped round a cannon-ball and sunk in the river.

Thus, before the end of November, the whole of the small regular force, to which the defence of the provinces had been entrusted, was captured; and no further obstacle remained to impede the further progress of the enemy. Lieut.-General Carleton narrowly escaped being taken, when obliged to leave Montreal by night, with a few attendants, he passed through the American flotilla unobserved, in a boat with muffled oars, landing without being discovered, at Quebec, just as General Arnold arrived at Point Levi, opposite the town.

The British General, to whose timely arrival the safety of this important town is to be ascribed, immediately took the most active measures for its defence. The inhabitants were armed and disciplined; and the sailors, belonging to the transports and merchant ships in the harbour, were landed, and appointed to serve the artillery. In the beginning of December, Generals Montgomery and Arnold commenced the siege; which, lasting till the breaking up of the frost, in the spring, allowed the approach of reinforcements from England. As few, if any, of the 26th Regiment could have participated in this siege, any details are here unnecessary. It was remarkable for the skill and resources of the Governor; and for the patience and endurance of the most harassing duties and privations on the part of the garrison. The enemy also displayed the greatest perseverance; and many of their assaults, though unsuccessful, were marked by enterprise and courage, in one of which Montgomery was killed and Arnold wounded.

On the decease of Major-General Scott, Major-General

1775. Lord Adam Gordon, from the 66th Regiment, succeeded him as Colonel of the 26th, by commission dated 27th December, 1775.

1776. On the 6th of May, 1776, three King's ships entered the basin; and, as soon as the detachment of the 29th Regiment and Marines were landed, Lieut.-General Carleton marched out, at the head of the garrison, to attack the enemy; who made a hasty retreat, leaving their guns and military stores in their works.* As a detachment of recruits for the 26th composed part of the force which landed on this occasion, under the command of Captain the Earl of Harrington, of the 3rd Foot Guards, the Regiment may assume the honour of having participated in the brilliant termination of this glorious defence.†

To a gallant and successful attack, made by Captain Forster, of the 8th Foot, on a body of five hundred of the provincials, at the Cedars, in which a large body of prisoners was taken, an agreement for the release of an equal number of the 7th and 26th Regiments was due.‡ This agreement, though confirmed by Congress, was for some time evaded, as is shown by the correspondence between Generals the Honourable Sir William Howe and Washington, in April. Subsequent letters, in July, intimated that the cartel was then in course of execution. It is, therefore, highly probable, that the 26th was reformed in the course of this year, though the degree of efficiency to which the Regiment had been brought cannot be exactly ascertained.

In the autumn, the 7th and 26th Regiments, which

---

* Short's "Journal and Siege of Quebec."
† "Military Library," vol. i.
‡ "Gentleman's Magazine," August, 1776.

had been companions in misfortune in Canada, were transferred to the grand scene of contest in New York and New England,* the detachment of the latter, which had arrived in May, having now joined the head-quarters. During the winter they were stationed at Amboy, in Middlesex county. At this period a British force under Lieut.-General Burgoyne, was advancing from Canada upon Albany; at the same time another British army, under General Sir William Howe, was proceeding against Philadelphia; and Lieut.-General Sir Henry Clinton, who commanded at New York, resolved to penetrate into Jersey as a diversion in favour of both armies. The 7th Royal Fusiliers, with several other corps, were accordingly embarked for this service, and on the 12th of September effected a landing at four different places, without meeting with serious opposition. The 7th, 26th, and 52nd Regiments, with a body of German grenadiers and three hundred provincials, under Brigadier General Campbell, landed at *Elizabeth-Town-Point*, at about four in the morning, and advanced up the country: the enemy opposed the march, and a sharp fire was kept up throughout the day. The King's forces, however, had the advantage; they took Newark, and were advancing on Aquakinack, when they received orders to halt and wait the advance of the troops which had effected a landing at the other points. The enemy afterwards appeared in force, when several skirmishes occurred, and the British succeeded in capturing four hundred head of cattle, a like number of sheep, and a few

---

* In a letter from Sir William Howe to Sir Henry Clinton, the former says, "I have directed the 7th and 26th Regiments of "Foot, and the Regiment of Anspach, to remain here under your "orders."—*Howe's Narrative.*

1777. horses.* On the 16th of September the force marched to Bergen Point, where it re-embarked and returned to Staten Island.

Towards the end of September, Lieut.-General Sir Henry Clinton having been joined by some recruits from Europe, determined to attack *Forts Montgomery* and *Clinton*, on the Hudson River. After some preliminary feints, the troops, in number two thousand one hundred, were landed, on the 6th of October, at Stony Point; and after a difficult march of twelve miles, they reached the forts about an hour before sunset. The attacks were commenced on that very day, and Fort Montgomery was carried with ease. The attack of Fort Clinton was a more serious enterprise, as it was built on a rocky elevation, the only approach to which was by a species of pass about four hundred yards wide, between a lake and a precipice which overhung the River Hudson. This spot was covered with felled trees, so that the approach of the assailants could not be conducted with rapidity, nor with much regularity. Ten pieces of artillery bore on this narrow pass, whilst there was not a single cannon to cover the assault of the British, whose only chance was to press forward with as much rapidity as the ground would permit; but they were strictly ordered on no account to fire. The flank companies of the 7th and 26th, with a company of Anspach grenadiers, led the attack upon one point, whilst the 63rd Regiment endeavoured to penetrate on another.

In no instance during the war was greater resolution evinced than on this occasion. The British and

---

* " Records of 7th Royal Fusiliers," Official Despatches, &c.

Foreign troops pressed forward silently, under a dreadful 1777. fire; and, arriving at the foot of the work, actually pushed one another up into the embrasures. The garrison, consisting of four hundred men, for a short time longer contested the rampart; and some of the King's troops were killed in the very embrasures, while several were wounded with bayonets in the struggle; a proof of the determined courage with which it was defended. At length, however, the rampart was cleared; and the Americans, retiring to the other side of the esplanade, after discharging a volley, threw down their arms. Notwithstanding this great provocation, no retaliation was made, and none fell except in the actual struggle on the rampart.

In this expedition the 26th had Brevet-Major Francis Stewart and one man killed; Lieutenant Lawrence Dulhuntry and one private wounded.

This enterprise, which was so highly honourable to the troops employed, was not productive of any lasting advantage; and with it ended the campaign on the part of Sir Henry Clinton's corps, while the capture of Philadelphia terminated the progress of General Sir William Howe. Though some barren laurels were gained by the British troops, yet, the permanent results of the campaign were decidedly favourable to the Americans. Franklin observed, on this capture, that "Sir William Howe had not taken Philadelphia, but "that Philadelphia had taken Sir William Howe."

The 26th Regiment continued with the portion of the 1778. army under Sir Henry Clinton, until the whole became united, in consequence of the evacuation of Philadelphia, which was effected in June, 1778. This operation was deemed necessary, in consequence of the declaration of war by France, and the expectation of the provincials

1778. that powerful military and naval reinforcements would be sent out by the king of that country, who had agreed to aid them. It was successfully accomplished, before the Count D'Estaing reached Rariton bay, on the 11th of July; and Sir Henry Clinton, who had succeeded to the command on the resignation of Sir William Howe, was able to baffle all the attempts which the French and Americans made to dispossess him of such districts as were still retained by the British forces. It does not however appear what particular share the 26th took in the desultory operations of this campaign, during part of which the Regiment was at Staten Island.

In the northern provinces the British army had been 1779. weakened in 1779 by the expedition which was sent to Georgia under Major-General Prevost and Lieut.-Colonel Campbell, whose activity and skill secured the reduction of the province, and General Sir Henry Clinton, therefore, confined himself this year to the same system which had been so fruitlessly pursued by his predecessor. The efforts and achievements of his troops bore fresh testimony to British valour, but produced no important results. He even withdrew them from Rhode Island; and thus no progress was made towards the attainment of the objects of the war.

No particular mention is recorded of the 26th during this campaign, but they continued to form a part of Sir Henry's army till the autumn, when they were drafted into other corps, and the staff, under Captain Myers,* embarked in December at New York for England. On 1780. their arrival, in February, 1780, they were ordered to

---

* Afterwards Lieut.-General Sir William Myers, Bart., who died on the 29th of July, 1805.

Tamworth, in Staffordshire, to recruit. On the 1st of 1780. October the Regiment mustered only one hundred and seventy-two rank and file, which by the end of the year was increased to two hundred and four.

In April, 1781, the 26th marched to Shrewsbury, and 1781. remained there until December, when the Regiment, which then numbered three hundred and thirty-six rank and file, proceeded to Tynemouth Barracks, where it arrived in January, 1782, and it continued at that place 1782. until March, 1783.

Major-General Sir William Erskine, Bart., was removed from the Colonelcy of the 80th Royal Edinburgh Volunteers (since disbanded), to that of the 26th Regiment, on the 16th of May, 1782, in succession to Major-General Lord Adam Gordon, appointed to the 1st Royals.

The Regiment in March, 1783, proceeded to Scotland, 1783. and was stationed at Musselburgh until October following, when it embarked for Ireland, where it remained for upwards of three years.

In 1786, the title of "Cameronian" was revived by a 1786. Royal Warrant. How or when this original and appropriate name fell into disuse does not appear; but Sir William Erskine, then Colonel of the Regiment, having remarked the omission, applied to the King for its restoration, a favour which was officially granted in February of that year, as shown in the following notification:—

"*Adjutant General's Office, Dublin,*
"16*th February*, 1786.

" His Grace, the Lord Lieutenant, has received
" a letter from Sir George Yonge, Secretary at War,
" acquainting his Grace that his Majesty has been most
" graciously pleased, at the request of Major-General

1786. "Sir William Erskine, to grant his Royal permission "that the 26th Regiment may in future assume the title "of the 26th, or Cameronian Regiment of Foot.

(Signed)   "H. PIGOT,
"Adjutant-General."

1787. On the 24th of May, 1787, the Regiment, consisting of twenty-one officers, sixteen sergeants, ten drummers, and three hundred and forty rank and file, embarked at Monkstown, Cork, in the transports "Lord Shelburne" and "General Eliott," but the ships did not sail for some days. The head-quarters under the command of Major William Duffe, arrived at Quebec in July, and the remainder in August following. They were cantoned at Beauport, Charlebourg, and other villages on the north shore of the St. Lawrence, in the vicinity of Quebec. The monthly return of the Cameronians for October shows them to have been only four rank and file below their establishment of three hundred and fifty-four rank and file. The number of deaths which had occurred from the date of disembarkation is therein stated to have been three; and thirteen transfers were received during the interval, from the 29th, 31st, and 34th Regiments; these were returning to Europe, and the men, to a certain extent, were, by authority from the Secretary at War, permitted to enlist into such corps remaining in Canada, as were not complete to their establishments.

In October the Regiment was removed to Quebec, and remained there till the month of August, when it proceeded to the frontier posts of the Montreal district, and the head-quarters were fixed at St. John's, four companies occupying the Isle-aux-Noix, and one being stationed at Chambly.

The Regiment in July, 1789, was stationed at Montreal, where, in the month of October, Lieut.-Colonel Andrew Gordon joined, and assumed the command. 1789.

In August, 1790, the 26th proceeded to the Niagara frontier, and occupied the stations between Lakes Erie and Ontario. In this month the increase in the establishment of infantry regiments was notified to the troops in Canada. By the return of the Regiment there appeared as present, twenty sergeants, fourteen drummers, and three hundred and fifty rank and file; the numbers wanting to complete, being ten sergeants, eight drummers, and two hundred and thirty-one rank and file; while that of the preceding month showed only a deficiency of thirty-six rank and file. 1790.

In June, 1792, the Regiment returned to Lower Canada, and occupied its former quarters at St. John's, &c., in which it remained during that year. 1792.

The 26th, in 1793, still occupied the posts of St. John's and Isle-aux-Noix; and was inspected by his Royal Highness the Duke of Kent, father of Her Majesty, then Prince Edward, and Colonel commanding the 7th Royal Fusiliers. His Royal Highness expressed himself satisfied with the appearance of the Regiment, and the excellent system of interior economy which existed in it. In October the command devolved upon Major Duke. 1793.

In August, 1794, the Regiment proceeded to Montreal: before quitting the frontier it was inspected by Lieut.-Colonel Beckwith (afterwards General Sir George Beckwith), Adjutant-General to the forces in Canada; and he seems to have been equally well pleased as his Royal Highness with its discipline and appearance. 1794.

Major-General the Honourable Sir Charles Stuart, K.B., was removed from the Colonelcy of the 68th, to

1794. that of the 26th, on the 25th of March, 1795, in succession to Lieut.-General Sir William Erskine, Bart., deceased.

1795. The Regiment, in July, 1795, was ordered to the Quebec district, and cantoned in the villages north of that city. In September it was ordered into the garrison of Quebec. From August till November, it was in cantonments at Chateau Richer, about fifteen miles below Quebec, and in the last-mentioned month the Cameronians proceeded to Montreal.

1797. In May, 1797, the 26th returned to Quebec. The review return of this year notices a draft of three hundred and fifty men, received from the 4th or King's Own. The greater part of these men were transferred without their consent; for, as soldiers were then enlisted for general service and not for special regiments, they were not allowed to return home with their corps, when those remaining in a settlement were incomplete. The improved principle of enlisting for particular regiments took place in the following year. In October, Major William Blakeney Borough was in the command of the 26th, which were still in garrison at Quebec, with two companies at Three Rivers.

1799. In May, 1799, the Regiment was removed to the Montreal district; the head-quarters, with three companies, being at St. John's, and the remainder in Montreal and Chambly. In September following Lieut.-Colonel Lord Elphinstone having arrived from Europe, assumed the command of the 26th, then on an establishment of ten companies. In November the monthly return of the Regiment was dated on board the "Asia" transport, having embarked that day. A malignant fever having broken out in the 41st foot, which had just arrived in the "Asia," the 26th disembarked on the 15th

of November and went into cantonments in the neigh- 1799.
bourhood of Quebec, at Charlebourg, Beauport, &c., and
on the 16th of May, 1800, they again embarked, and 1800.
proceeded in the above vessel for Nova Scotia.

On arrival at Halifax, the Cameronians landed, and
performed the duties of that garrison until the 26th
of September, when the Regiment again embarked for
England. Two of the transports reached Portsmouth
in safety, and the men landed on the 5th of November;
but that in which Captain Campbell's company had
been embarked was captured in the chops of the Channel, by the "Grande Decidée," French privateer. A convention was entered into, by which the troops were
bound not to serve till exchanged; and Lieutenant
Edward Shearman and Ensign Adam G. Campbell
were taken on board the privateer as hostages; after
which the transport was allowed to pursue her voyage.
The agreement was confirmed by Government. These
two officers were afterwards sent from Corunna, where
they were landed from the privateer, to Portugal, whence
they returned by Oporto to England.

Lieut.-General Andrew Gordon was appointed 1801.
Colonel of the 26th Regiment on the 28th of March,
1801, in succession to Lieut.-General the Honourable
Charles Stuart, K.B., deceased.

After a few months' duty in the garrison of Portsmouth and its neighbourhood, the 26th were called
on to reinforce the army in Egypt, which had successfully landed in that country, and gained two victories in March, near Alexandria, but had suffered the
loss of their veteran commander, Sir Ralph Abercromby.
The Regiment, consisting of twenty-four officers, thirty-one sergeants, fourteen drummers, and four hundred
and sixty-two rank and file, accordingly embarked at

H

1801. Portsmouth, under the command of Lieut.-Colonel Lord Elphinstone,* on the 28th of May, 1801, in the ship "Madras," and after an unusually favourable voyage, it landed at Aboukir, on the 18th of July following. Lieut.-General the Honourable Sir John Hely Hutchinson, K.B. (afterwards Lord Hutchinson), who had succeeded to the command of the army, advanced to Grand Cairo, which capitulated on the 27th of June. General Menou refusing to accept this capitulation, was closely besieged in Alexandria. The reinforcements which joined Major-General Eyre Coote's corps near *Alexandria*, consisted of the late 22nd Dragoons, a detachment of the Guards, 20th (second battalion), 24th, 25th, and 26th Regiments. After their landing, the first movement of importance in which the Cameronians were concerned, took place on the 16th of August, when, together with the second battalion of the 54th, under the command of Major-General Finch, they embarked on Lake Mareotis. It was intended to disembark between Marabout and Alexandria, but Major-General Coote, perceiving some of the enemy's troops on that part of the isthmus, left Finch's brigade opposite to them to make a feint : and pursuing his course with the remainder of his .corps, about three miles further, effected a landing without opposition.†

This success was shortly followed up by the engagement of the 22nd, which is thus described in Major-General Coote's official despatch of the following day:—
" The necessary arrangements having been made on the
" morning of the 22nd, the troops advanced against the

---

* Official Records.
† Sir Robert Wilson's "Narrative of the Campaign."

"enemy, who was strongly posted upon a ridge of high 1801.
"hills, having his right flank secured by two heavy
"guns, and his left by two batteries containing three
"more, with many field pieces placed in the intervals of
"the line. The army moved through the sand hills in
"three columns, the Guards forming two upon the right
"near the lake, and Major-General Ludlow's brigade
"the third upon the left, having the 1st battalion of the
"27th Regiment in advance. Major-General Finch's
"brigade composed a reserve, and was destined to give
"its support wherever it might be required. In this
"manner, having our field artillery with the advance
"guards, the troops continued to move forward with the
"greatest coolness and regularity, under a very heavy
"fire of cannon and small arms, forcing the enemy to
"retreat constantly before them, and driving them to
"their present position within the walls of Alexandria."

In this action the 26th were in reserve, and did not fire a shot, although exposed to a very heavy fire, particularly of grape, the fatal effects of which were prevented by the inequalities of the ground, so that their loss was only four men wounded. They shared in the remaining operations of the siege, which were, however, soon terminated by the surrender of Alexandria on the 2nd of September.*

It is on record that after the terms of capitulation were concluded, an invitation to dinner was given to Brigadier-General Hope, by General Menou, the repast being remarkable for consisting entirely of horse-flesh.

During the progress, and after the conclusion of these operations, the efficiency of the Regiment was greatly

---

* Walsh's "Narrative of the Campaign."

1801. impaired by the prevalence of ophthalmia, which not only attacked the men, but extended to the officers. The effective strength was so reduced that there were scarcely sufficient men for the ordinary camp duties. The sick might often be seen in long files, led by the soldier whose eyes were least affected. From this afflicting state they began to be relieved, after their embarkation on the 23rd of October, on which day the Cameronians, mustering twenty-one officers, thirty-two sergeants, fourteen drummers, and four hundred and forty-two rank and file, embarked at Alexandria, under the command of Lieut.-Colonel Lord Elphinstone, in the ships "Chatham," "Doncaster," and "Flora;"* but though many recovered on the passage, the disease continued to show itself long after their return home.

Thus terminated the campaign in Egypt; the achievements of the British army in that country being a prelude to future victories. Both Houses of Parliament voted their thanks to the troops, and all the regiments received the Royal authority to bear on their colours the word "EGYPT," with the SPHINX,† to perpetuate the fame of

---

* Official Records.

† The Royal authority was signified in the following circular letter to the Colonels of Regiments which had served in Egypt:—

"*Horse Guards, 6th July,* 1802.

"SIR,—I have the honour to inform you, that HIS MAJESTY
" has been graciously pleased to grant permission to the several
" regiments of His army which served during the late campaign
" in Egypt to assume and wear on their colours a badge, as a
" distinguished mark of His Majesty's royal approbation, and as
" a lasting memorial of the glory acquired to His Majesty's arms
" by the zeal, discipline, and intrepidity of His troops in that
" arduous and important campaign.

the expulsion therefrom of the self-styled "invincible" 1801. legions of Bonaparte, who, by this expedition, expected to have been able to extend his conquests throughout Asia.

The Grand Seignior established the Order of Knighthood of the Crescent, of which the general officers were made members; he also presented large gold medals to the field officers, and smaller ones of the same pattern to the captains and subalterns of the several regiments, which their Sovereign permitted them to receive and wear. As a further proof of the estimation in which the Sultan held these services, he ordered a palace to be built at Constantinople for the future residence of the British ambassador.

The following officers of the 26th received the above medal:—

Lieut.-Colonels.

Hildebrand Oakes (*Colonel*).*
John Lord Elphinstone (*Colonel*).

" His Royal Highness the Commander-in-Chief has directed
" me to make this communication to you, in order that the regi-
" ment under your command may avail itself of the honour
" hereby conferred by His Majesty; and I am commanded at the
" same time to apprize you, that a pattern of the badge approved
" by His Majesty is lodged at the office of the Comptrollers of
" Army Accounts, there to be had recourse to as circumstances
" may require.
" I have, &c.,
" HARRY CALVERT, *A.-G.*"

* Colonel Hildebrand Oakes, the senior Lieut.-Colonel of the Regiment, had joined the army under General Sir Ralph Abercromby in the Mediterranean in August, 1800, and served as a brigadier in the campaign in Egypt, and was wounded at the battle of Alexandria, on the 21st of March, 1801.

1801.

Majors.
William Blakeney Borough (*Lieut-Colonel*).
Erskine Hope (*Lieut.-Colonel*).

Captains.

William G. Dacres (*Major*).	William Garstin.
Hugh Henry Mitchell.	Fountain Hogg.
Christopher Davidson.	William Hoggins.
William Gifford (*Major*).	Samuel Nicoll.

Lieutenants.

Frederick Jones.	Thomas Conolly.
Jephson George Forth.	Charles Stuart Campbell.
Anthony W. Wainhouse.	Adam G. Campbell.
James Conolly.	William Walker.

Ensign.—James Hunt.
Paymaster.—Duncan Campbell.
Adjutant.—Frederick Jones.
Quartermaster.—John Robertson.
Assistant-Surgeon.—Duncan Campbell.

1802. The convoy put into Falmouth on the 10th of February, 1802, and then proceeded to Plymouth, where the Regiment landed on the 14th. The peace of Amiens was signed on the 27th of March, but was not destined to be of long duration, and only heralded the general European war which afterwards ensued.

Major-General Richard England inspected the Regiment after its landing, when a considerable number of non-commissioned officers and men were invalided for length of service and for medical incapacity. The recruiting company had previously arrived at Plymouth, to which had been attached some old soldiers and the undrilled recruits, who had been left behind on the embarkation for Egypt, together with some others intermediately enlisted. During the stay of the 26th in Plymouth about eighty men were received, who volunteered in Jersey from the Royal Irish Fencibles, but no recruits were obtained in the West of England. A few parties were sent to Scotland, which furnished about twenty men.

The 26th embarked for Leith, in two frigates, on the 1st of November. They disembarked on the 13th, and proceeded on the 15th to Linlithgow, and on the following day reached Stirling, where they remained till the 1st of February, 1803, when they commenced their march in three divisions for Fort George, and arrived there on the 29th, having passed through Perth, Dundee, Aberdeen, Keith, and Elgin.

At this period the recruiting in Scotland was very unproductive; and some parties were therefore sent to Ireland, but their joint exertions did not obtain more than forty, of whom eleven were from a fencible regiment disbanded at Kilkenny.

Hostilities were renewed with France in May, 1803; and preparations were made to repel the threatened invasion by Napoleon Bonaparte. The "Army of Reserve Act" was passed in June for raising men for home service by ballot; and numerous volunteer and yeomanry corps were formed in every part of the United Kingdom.

About the 31st of July the 26th embarked in two transports, and, after being a couple of days at sea, disembarked at Leith, whence they marched to Stirling, leaving two companies at Falkirk.

When the "Army of Reserve Act" came into operation, all recruiting for the regular army ceased, owing to the enormous bounties given to procure substitutes for those on whom the ballot had fallen, and who did not wish to serve personally. These fluctuated in amount from £20 even to £70; and one man, a bookbinder, received from a tradesman at Falkirk a bounty of £100.

1803.
2nd Batt.

Upwards of one thousand men, raised under this act in Scotland, joined the Regiment at Stirling and Linlithgow in August; and the second battalion, for which letters of service had been previously received, was then formed. Half of the old soldiers of the first battalion were drafted into it, to the number of about two hundred and fifty; and a similar division of the army of reserve men was made between the two battalions. Upon this arrangement being completed, the second proceeded to Linlithgow and Borrowstownness, where part of the army of reserve men afterwards joined it—the total number received into the Regiment being about one thousand three hundred. They were remarkably fine men, and nearly all natives of Scotland.

The two battalions were at this period respectively commanded by Brevet-Colonel Lord Elphinstone and Lieut.-Colonel Borough.

When permission was given for the men to volunteer for general service, at a bounty of £7. 12s. 6d., it applied at first to the army in general; but on a representation of the inconvenience arising from the interference of other regiments, it was restricted to their own corps, and it was not again rendered general till 1806. In order to induce the men to make this extension of their services, a recruiting system was established in the Regiment, and weekly accessions were thus gained to the permanent strength of the corps, without any alteration of its apparent numbers; as advantage was taken of this influx of prime soldiers, to remove those whose length of service or other incapacity rendered them less eligible.

1st Batt.

Early in December, the first battalion quitted Stirling on its route for Port-Patrick, where it arrived on the 13th, passing through Glasgow, Kilmarnock, Ayr, and

Maybole. At this last place a strong instance of 1803.
national feeling was manifested towards the Corps, by 1st Batt.
the mayor and corporation giving each man refreshments, for which the battalion was halted there, as requested, a mark of good will arising out of recollections connected with the earliest periods of its history. It embarked on the 14th, and reached Donaghadee on the 15th, and the next day Belfast, whence, after two days' halt, the Cameronians proceeded to Armagh, where they arrived on the 19th. Thus, after a stay of little more than one year in its native country, in which, with the exception of the year 1783, the Regiment had not been quartered since 1757, it quitted its shores, and did not again revisit them, as a corps, until 1843.

The second battalion followed the first so closely, that it was mustered on the 24th of December, at Belfast, where it remained. The two battalions continued in these towns, Athlone and Belfast, till they commenced their march, about the 4th of June, 1804, with a view 1804. to their forming part of the corps assembled under the command of Lieut.-General Lord Cathcart, on the Curragh of Kildare, the first remaining six weeks at Ballinasloe, and the second about the same period at Athlone. On the 2nd of August they quitted these places, and on the 5th they reached the Curragh, which, by a well combined movement, the different corps of infantry, cavalry, and artillery, to the amount of twenty-one thousand men, entered from different points nearly at the same time. The ground having been previously appointed, and the tents apportioned, the camp was formed simultaneously through the line. The light companies of the several regiments were formed into a brigade. The two battalions of the 26th Regiment were in the right brigade, under the command of Major-

1804. General Francis Grose. On this fine ground the troops continued in active practice of the grand manœuvres of an army till the 30th of September, when the troops marched and encamped on Maryborough Heath; and, on the next morning (1st of October), the different corps proceeded on their route to their respective winter cantonments. The first battalion reached Ballinasloe on the 3rd, and on the 2nd marched to Athlone, at which places they continued the remainder of the year, the two light companies proceeding to Dublin with their brigade.

During the course of this year, the attached men of the "Army of Reserve" were still allowed to extend their services in their own corps; but this permission, supported as it was by so large a bounty, did not produce the effect which might have been expected. When, in the month of December, the first battalion was prepared for foreign service by passing over to the second battalion all the army of reserve men, to the number of four hundred and twenty-seven, it received in exchange, the unlimited service men of the second battalion, to the number of only two hundred and fifty-one; it would appear that, besides the four hundred and twenty-seven thus transferred, the second battalion must then have had about five hundred and thirty-eight of the same class, making a total of nine hundred and sixty-five, who rejected every inducement for the extension of their services. In these numbers of four hundred and twenty-seven and five hundred and thirty-eight, there may indeed have been men, who for unfitness or other causes, were left with the second battalion, for whom an abatement of one hundred may be made, leaving eight hundred and sixty-five for those who, out of the gross number of about one thousand three hundred, 1804. received from the army of reserve, adhered to their original terms of service. The actual gain of disposable men would thus seem to have been nearly four hundred and fifty, which, considering all the advantages possessed by the two battalions to induce these men to volunteer, was certainly small. During the course of the same month, above two hundred more men from the army of reserve were attached to the second battalion from the contingent of Scotland. The result of these arrangements was, to leave the first battalion with only six hundred rank and file, whilst the second was increased to one thousand one hundred and sixty-six.

The first battalion was stationed at Ballinasloe, and the second at Athlone, till the 16th of June, 1805, when the latter changed its quarters for Dublin, and the first was removed to Athlone, where it remained till the 13th of August, when it commenced its march, in three divisions, for Cork, passing through Cloghan, Birr, Nenagh, Limerick, Bruff, Charleville, and Mallow. The first battalion continued at Cork from the 23rd of August to the 19th of November, when it embarked at Monkstown, in three transports, namely—the " Aurora," " Pelican," and " Maria." The total numbers embarked were thirty-two officers, fifty-four sergeants, twenty-two drummers, and eight hundred and eighty-two rank and file, ninety-seven women, and forty-one children, under the command of Lieut.-Colonel Hope. These ships sailed on the 22nd, anchoring at Spithead on the 2nd of December, where they continued till the 6th; they then weighed for the Downs, and remained at that anchorage from the 8th to the 10th. The battalion, which had been crowded in three transports, was transhipped into two other

1805.
1st Batt.

1805.
1st
Batt.
small vessels, so that it was now broken into five divisions of unequal strength. These sailed with the rest of the fleet destined for Germany, but after encountering most tempestuous weather, had to put back on the 16th, excepting the "Maria" transport, which was wrecked on the night of the 14th, on the Haak Sands, off the Texel.

In this catastrophe there perished five officers, and nearly all the men of two companies and-a-half. Captain Frederick Jones, and Assistant-Surgeon Armstrong, with a few men who volunteered to go in a small boat to obtain assistance from the shore, were saved. This enterprise, which at the moment was deemed almost hopeless proved their safety, as they were taken by the Dutch, who, however, were unable to render any assistance to the "Maria," which soon went to pieces, or was swallowed up in the sands. Captain Jones and his companions were kindly treated, and afterwards exchanged.

The misfortunes of the Regiment, however, did not end here, for the "Aurora" transport, in which were the head-quarters of the battalion, under Major Christopher Davidson, in endeavouring to make the Downs, was wrecked on the Goodwin Sands, and every one on board was drowned; the violence of the tempest being such, that even the known skill and resolution of the Deal boatmen, ever ready as they are, at the peril of their lives, to render aid to vessels in danger, were of no avail. By this double visitation, the 26th, which had been completed in May to an establishment of one thousand rank and file, by four hundred volunteers from the Irish Militia, lost half its effective strength, its grenadier company forming a part. There perished in these ships fourteen officers, and four hundred and seventy-four non-commissioned officers and men,* leaving about five hundred, who were embarked in the other three transports. These sailed once more with the expedition on the 22nd of December; but one was again driven back, and the men were landed at Deal, whilst the other two reached the coast of Germany, one landing at Cuxhaven, on the 27th, the other at a place on the Weser, whence the men marched to Penningbuttel, in which, and subsequently in some other villages, they were quartered during their stay on the Continent.

1805.
1st Batt.

Thus four companies only reached their destination, and joined the expedition, which was intended to have effected a diversion in favour of the allies. The great victory of the French over the Russians and Austrians, at Austerlitz, was followed by a treaty concluded at Vienna, wherein it was stipulated that Hanover should be occupied by the Prussians; this led to the British troops being withdrawn, in February, 1806, after occupying the country between the Elbe and the Weser for about six weeks.

---

* Drowned, on the 14th December, 1805, in the "Maria" Transport—Captain William Garstin, Lieutenants John Campbell and C. B. Marshman, Ensigns William Cunningham and George Matheson, and ten sergeants, eleven corporals, two hundred and three privates, twenty-two women and children. Saved—Captain Jones, Assistant-Surgeon Armstrong, one sergeant, and fifteen privates.

Drowned, on the 16th of December, in the "Aurora" Transport —Major Christopher Davidson, Captains William Hoggins and Archibald Cameron, Lieutenants William Browne and Hopkins, (Adjutant) Ensign George Dalzell, Quarter-Master Robertson, Paymaster Duncan Campbell, and Surgeon Robert Dewar, two hundred and fifty non-commissioned officers and privates, and thirty women and children.

1805.
2nd Batt. During the remainder of the year, after its departure from Athlone in June, the second battalion continued in garrison in Dublin.

1806.
1st Batt. Upon the return of the remains of the first battalion from Germany, after a boisterous passage, they landed on the 21st of February, 1806, at Ramsgate, and, on the 24th marched through Canterbury to Ospringe and Feversham, where they were quartered till the 18th of March, when they moved to Ashford. On the 3rd of July, two companies were detached to Canterbury, and on the 26th of October the battalion marched for Dover, and went into barracks on the heights. On the 19th of December it proceeded to Deal. In April Lieut.-Colonel Maxwell assumed the command of the battalion, in succession to Lieut.-Colonel Hope, who retired from the service by the sale of his commission.

Major-General Lord Elphinstone was appointed Colonel of the Regiment on the 24th of April, 1806; in succession to Lieut.-General Andrew Gordon, deceased.

2nd Batt. The second battalion remained during the year 1806 in garrison in Dublin, where its light infantry company rejoined in August, after an absence of two years, during which it had formed part of the light brigade, and had been at the camps on the Curragh in 1804 and 1805. The effective strength of the battalion was above one thousand rank and file; but as the greater portion of the men belonged to the Army of Reserve, who, perhaps, for reasons connected with the discipline of the Regiment, were unwilling to extend their services in it, the permission to volunteer for general service was extended to other corps, of which about four hundred men availed themselves between April and October. The chief part went into the First or Royal Regiment, induced by the persuasions of those who were themselves influenced, and who contrived to influence others by **1806.** various unredeemed pledges of promotion and individual **2nd Batt.** advantage. When it became evident that the rest of the Army of Reserve men were not to be induced by any considerations to extend their services, Government determined to form them into garrison battalions, and four hundred and sixty-two men of the second battalion of the 26th were transferred in December to the fifth garrison battalion, which was at the same time completed by a similar draft from the 42nd Regiment. After this arrangement, the second battalion, now reduced below two hundred and fifty rank and file, changed its quarters from the Royal to the Old Custom House Barracks.

This irreparable loss was not in any degree compensated by success in any other quarter, as the number of men raised by recruits, or from the militia, was inconsiderable in either battalion. It was the more to be regretted, both on account of the urgency of the demand to supply the wants of the first battalion, and also on account of the superior character of the men, and their military discipline, which rendered them an object of imitation to other corps in the garrison. The formation of the garrison battalion having taken away all hope of aid from the reserve, the only resource was in the regular recruiting, on which service, about Christmas, numerous parties were despatched.

The first battalion continued in quarters at Deal till **1st** the 5th of May, 1807, when it marched to Ramsgate **Batt.** and embarked in three transports for Ireland. These sailed immediately, and after anchoring during the 12th, at St. Helen's, finished their voyage on the 20th, on which day they arrived in the Cove of Cork. Landing there on the 23rd, the battalion marched on the 25th

1807.
1st Batt.
for Mallow, and continuing its route on the following days, reached Limerick on the 28th of May, where it remained in garrison till the 26th of June.

Another change in the station of the battalion was produced by the frequent alterations which were at this period made in the stations of regiments, sometimes owing to the demand for troops for foreign service; and at other times in the course of the ordinary removals which were occasionally ordered. On the 26th of June it commenced its march, one wing to Charleville, and the other to Doneraile, whence on the 27th of September it was again recalled to Limerick. The remainder of the year was passed in garrison in that city, sending, however, a few small detachments to some of the neighbouring villages.

2nd Batt.
The second battalion terminated its protracted residence in Dublin in the month of January, and, embarking at Donaghadee, landed at Port-Patrick and proceeded to Ayr, where it continued from the 28th of January till July, in which month it was removed to Glasgow, where it passed the rest of the year.

In consequence of the second battalion being nearly a skeleton, and the first reduced to little more than five hundred men, the recruiting became a service of the utmost importance, but it was not productive. The demand for men at this period of the war was such as could only be met by the volunteering from the militia—a measure which afforded a large supply of men not only of the best description, but often completely trained. The influence of the second battalion was exerted with considerable effect, and its efforts were highly instrumental in rendering the first battalion effective for service in the course of the next year. The drafts were obtained from several regiments of militia; but the

Dumfries furnished the largest, in number about eighty men. Whilst the second battalion was thus maintaining the credit of the Cameronian name in Scotland, the first battalion was wholly unsuccessful in England and Ireland, as its strength was less by thirty men at the end, than it had been at the beginning of the year. This decrease was owing to a mistaken policy which had caused the offers that were made by the men of several Regiments of Irish militia to be rejected, and particularly by those of the Galway, who would have volunteered into the 26th; and thus the services of some hundreds were lost to the corps. Its nationality was indeed a principle of great value, and well worthy of every reasonable effort to maintain the same; but wholly to sacrifice the efficiency of the Regiment to any abstract principle, was an extreme which cannot be justified. Had there been a choice, so that the deficiency on the establishment could have been filled up from Scotland without draining the second battalion, and thereby depriving it of the opportunity of seeing foreign service, by rendering it again a skeleton, such a preference would have been laudable; but in so great an exigency, assistance from any quarter should have been gladly received. The men who were thus unadvisedly rejected entered into other regiments, and the first battalion, on the 24th of December, mustered only five hundred and fourteen bayonets.

1807.
2nd Batt.

1st Batt.

In January, 1808, the first battalion quitted Limerick and proceeded to Rathkeale, Newcastle, and Listowel, at each of which places three companies were quartered, with its remaining company at Tarbert. In April it received a route for Castlebar and Westport, commencing the march on the 18th and ending it the 26th; proceeding through Limerick, Ennis, Gort, Galway,

1808.

I

1808.
1st
Batt.
Tuam, and Ballinrobe. A wing of the battalion was stationed in the towns of Castlebar and Westport. On the 8th of June it began to march for the Curragh, where it arrived on the 16th, by way of Ballinrobe, Tuam, Ballinamore, Athlone, Moate, Kilbeggan, Philipstown, and Edenderry. When it afterwards left the camp on the 22nd of July, it proceeded by Athy, Carlow, Kilkenny, Callan, Clonmel and Clogheen to Fermoy, and arrived there on the 31st of July.

During the encampment on the Curragh a detachment of two hundred and sixty-five men arrived in June from the second battalion in Scotland; and on the 4th of August a second draft of two hundred and twelve men reached that place. By the exertions and popularity of the second, the causes which operated against the first battalion so unfortunately in December 1805 were removed; and its establishment was again raised to that of one thousand rank and file, with the additional Lieutenants.

These timely reinforcements gave the first battalion a place in the expedition fitted out for the south of Spain, under Lieut.-General Sir David Baird. It marched to Cork on the 9th of September, and embarked the next day at Monkstown. The battalion mustered forty-nine officers, fifty-three sergeants, twenty-two drummers, and eight hundred and sixty-six rank and file;* sixty-two women and seventeen children also proceeded with it. The names of the officers were:—*Lieut.-Colonel,* Wil-

---

* By the monthly return of the battalion, dated Salamanca, 1st December, 1808, its strength in rank and file was then seven hundred and forty-five fit for duty, one hundred and twelve in hospital, and nine absent on command; total, eight hundred and sixty-six, as embarked.

liam Maxwell; *Majors*, Fountain Hogg, Patrick Nugent
Savage ; *Captains*, William Fotheringham, Jephson
George Forth, Edward Shearman, James Conolly,
Charles Stuart Campbell, William Walker, Percival
Pym, Edward Whitty, Adam G. Campbell, James Hunt;
Lieutenants, Charles Grant, Robert Haggerstone, William Chartres, John Brooks, Joseph Smith, Andrew
Lett, Francis Shearman, James Stedman, Joseph Nunn,
Thomas Thomson, Robert Smith, Philip Espy, George
Platt, Lawrence Chevers, John Westlake, James Dunn,
Thomas Murray, John Law, George Pipon, Hugh Law,
Hugh McLatchie, Frederick Campbell Heatley ; *Ensigns*, John Maxwell, Colin Campbell, William Keary,
William Laurie, William Johnstone, J. F. Ross, P.
James Robertson, John Kirk ; *Paymaster*, Thomas
Boyes; *Adjutant*, James Nash; *Quarter-Master*, John
Connell; *Surgeon*, Henry Messiter, and *Assistant-Surgeons*, John Coldstream and Archibald Armstrong. The
fleet sailed on the 23rd, and anchored at Falmouth on
the 28th. On the 8th of October the fleet again sailed,
and on the 13th entered the Bay of Corunna; one
transport, which met with some damage on the voyage,
arriving eight days after the rest. The battalion disembarked on the 30th, and on the following day marched
for Betanzos.

After the "Convention of Cintra," which followed
the first two victories of Roliça and Vimiera, gained in
the Peninsula by the army under Lieut.-General the
Honourable Sir Arthur Wellesley, Portugal was freed
from the French. Lieut.-General Sir John Moore,
who had assumed the command, made dispositions for
entering Spain, and the first battalion of the 26th, with
the third battalion of the Royals and the 81st Regiment,
accordingly formed a brigade under Major-General

1808.
1st
Batt.

1808.
1st Batt.
Manningham in the *corps d'armée*, destined to march through Gallicia, and effect a junction with Sir John's army from Portugal in the very centre of Spain. This operation, it was at first supposed, would be conducted wholly through a friendly country, to whose aid the British troops were hastening, and in rear of the Spanish armies. Nor was this expectation disappointed, as far as friendly feeling was concerned; as nothing could exceed the enthusiasm of the Gallician patriots; but though there were no limits to their zeal, yet it was a blind impulse, little guided by judgment. The absence of well directed measures, such as an administration conducted by enlightened and experienced men would have ensured, not only rendered the force of this extensive and populous province inefficient, but deprived their allies of many essentials to their speedy progress through it, and prevented their timely arrival on the banks of the Ebro. As Sir John Moore's army experienced similar difficulties in its march—and in both cases the arrival of authentic intelligence respecting the enemy's movements was tardy and uncertain—those of the British column from Corunna were marked by hesitation and doubt; so that after its head had reached Astorga it retrograded to Lugo.

The French, on the contrary, whose movements were directed by Napoleon in person, after retiring from Castille and Leon behind the Ebro, immediately on his arrival, resumed the offensive; and with that promptitude of action which ever marked his command, the Emperor beat in detail the Spanish armies opposed to him, and after the victory of Tudela he pushed on to Madrid, and entered it by capitulation; a fact which was long concealed from the British general, to whom the Spanish authorities held out the flattering expectation of a protracted resistance, like that by which the inhabitants of Zaragoza had so greatly signalized themselves. All hope of co-operation with the numerous Spanish armies, which had not long before traversed their country from the south to the north in an almost uninterrupted course of triumph, was now at an end. The enthusiasm excited by the defeat of Dupont and his capitulation at Baylen, the defeat of Marshal Moncey at Valencia, the liberation of Portugal by the battle of Vimiera, and the expulsion of the intruder from Madrid, with the glorious and successful defence of Zaragoza; all these advantages were lost in a few short weeks, and the military forces of Spain, which, responsive to the call of their country, had sprung up in every quarter with a spontaneous growth, now seemed to be trampled to the ground. When the capital which might have offered a glorious defence, had the zeal of its inhabitants been supported by an efficient leader, was treacherously delivered up, without resistance, to the conqueror, his work appeared complete. There remained, however, in the north and upon the flank of his line of operations, an enemy undaunted by the terror of his arms; whose power to injure him none more fully appreciated than Napoleon. Though the roads to Lisbon, Cadiz, and Valencia were open to him—points of such paramount importance, and the value of which, his former efforts to possess them, though baffled, had shown that he duly estimated; yet these he at once and without hesitation relinquished, in order that he might pounce with undivided force upon the prey of which he now thought himself secure. Sir John Moore, though he had once hesitated, now resolved to throw himself into the gap; and by a desperate struggle, if still possible, preserve from the invader's grasp the southern and western provinces of the Peninsula.

1808.
1st Batt.

1808.
1st Batt.
In the advance of the army through Gallicia, the conduct of the inhabitants was very friendly, and the instances of hospitality, as far as the manners of the people led them so to manifest their feelings, were frequent; but a change was observable, when those retrogade movements occurred which preceded the junction of the two corps beyond the Esla. They could little appreciate the military or political causes which produced them; and as their direct consequences seemed to be, that their allies, whose aid was daily becoming of more importance, were about to desert the defence of the country in the hour of its increasing danger, the people became naturally disgusted. The degree of attention shown to the army varied according to circumstances; when a larger body of troops was assembled at one time in the same place, the power of the inhabitants was necessarily diminished in proportion; and the advanced guard thus experienced greater civility than the troops which followed in the rear. In the large towns the men were usually placed in convents, the extensive corridors of which afforded ample space even for whole regiments; the officers were in billets, except those on duty with the men, who were accommodated in the cells of the monks. In the villages the officers and men were alike quartered in private houses; and in these cases their numbers rendered them very troublesome to the natives. Good discipline was however maintained, and kindly feelings were preserved, notwithstanding the privations which, even in this stage of the campaign, the soldiers underwent from the defective organization of the commissariat.

After the supply of ship provisions, which the soldiers took with them from Corunna, was exhausted, no regular attempt was made by the commissaries to provide for their wants, who, with an unbounded command of money and in a district of ample resources for the temporary supply of a moderate corps, whose progress through the country was slow and measured, left them almost wholly destitute. Frequently it happened, that after their arrival the parties sent out to collect sheep or oxen were taken from the baggage carts; wood had to be fetched from a distance, and wine brought from stores, instead of these articles being conveyed to the convents by hired labourers. The soldiers' meal was thus deferred till midnight, and when obtained, was indifferent in quality. These defects in arrangements, so necessary to the well being of any army, were owing in part to the remissness and want of energy of the Spanish authorities; but much more to the inexperience of the officers in the commissariat. This branch of the service was one which had almost to be created; and if its short-comings were striking on the advance of the troops, they became fatal on the retreat; the department was but little hurried in its execution of demands, till the enemy left Lugo, when the privation of food, and the want of shoes, which the soldiers suffered, were wholly unwarranted by circumstances. Large depôts of stores had been formed at Astorga, Villa-Franca, and Lugo, which, with proper arrangement, might have been issued to the soldiers: these were destroyed in great quantities, when the men were exhausted from hunger, and at a time when the enemy did not press so as to prevent the issue. Hungry and barefoot they had to undergo the fatigue of a march along ruined roads, at a most inclement season.

 A junction was effected with the force, under Sir David Baird, at Majorga, on the 20th of December. Every arrangement was now made to attack the corps of Marshal Soult, posted on the line of the Carion. At night fall, on the 23rd of December, the troops we e

1808.
1st Batt.

1808.
1st
Batt.

under arms, and had begun their march, animated with a spirit which may be said almost to command victory. A frosty evening, which ensured good roads, and a sufficiency of light, seemed to favour their progress, when about midnight the columns were ordered to return. Disappointment then pervaded every heart; and the retreat, which commenced on the following morning, excited universal discontent, the feeling of the British soldier being ever adverse to such a movement. The cavalry had already met with that of the enemy, and the infantry were within two hours' march of him, when an intercepted letter informed the British Commander that the French Emperor was near at hand, with a superior army, as regards numbers.

The weather, which was fine and frosty till the night of the 23rd and 24th of December, broke up on the 24th, when the retreat commenced; but the Regiment remained at Sahagun until Christmas-day, when it quitted that place, and on the 26th passed the Esla at Valencia de Don Juan, which had nearly proved an insurmountable barrier to further progress. The river had there no bridge, and the ferry-boat being in a wretched state, was quite useless; but the fortunate discovery of a ford, as it was said, by the accidental enterprise of an individual officer, relieved the division from a situation of difficulty, if not of danger. The rains had so swollen the river, that the men could with difficulty support the weight of the current, and pass with their arms and accoutrements carried over their heads. Being uninterrupted in the passage, it was effected without loss of life, but not without that of some of the luggage. Thence the brigade marched to Santa Maria, and reached Astorga on the 30th of December.

Here Sir John Moore had at one time contemplated

the possibility of making head against the enemy, but the concentration of the whole disposable French army, in order to overwhelm him by an irresistible superiority, and the little efficient aid which the Marquis de Romana's force could afford, decided him to continue the retreat. Even in the five days' march between Sahagun and Astorga the discipline of his army had become much impaired, partly owing to the impatience and inexperience of the troops, to the extreme severity of the weather, and to the failure in supplying the men with provisions, the want of which must always lead to irregularities and excesses. His order of the 27th of December animadverted in strong terms on them, and forcibly described the qualities, which are most valuable in a military body. "These," he says, "are not bravery "alone, but patience and hardship, obedience to com- "mand, sobriety, firmness and resolution in every dif- "ferent situation in which they may be placed. It is "by the display of such qualities alone, that the army "can expect to deserve the name of soldiers; that they "can be able to withstand the forces opposed to them, "or to fulfil the expectations of their country." From any participation in the excesses which were committed, the 26th or Cameronian Regiment appear to have been singularly free, as one man only was punished; and he, though taken in company with others, was supposed, from being somewhat idiotic, to have been a spectator rather than a sharer in the plunder.

On the 31st of December, the Regiment quitted Astorga on its march to Lugo. At this time, Sir John Moore's despatch showed that the hope of disputing the passes of the mountains, which afforded positions of great strength, as expressed in his correspondence with Romana, was finally relinquished; for, besides the de-

1808.
1st Batt.

struction of the ammunition and stores collected there, the sick were abandoned, and he stated, "we must all "make forced marches to the coast from the scarcity of "provisions, and to be before the enemy, who by roads "upon our flanks may otherwise intercept us." He added, "I hope to find upon the coast transports for the "embarkation of the troops." Under these discouraging circumstances, the retreat was continued to Lugo.

Shortly after the British evacuated Astorga, Napoleon arrived, and was joined by Marshal Soult. The whole French army that was assembled there amounted to nearly seventy thousand men, besides other corps which were countermanded from their former destination, though not yet come up. The British army, when assembled to attack Marshal Soult, on the Carion, mustered only about twenty-five thousand four hundred men. What greater compliment could be paid to them, than that the French Emperor should thus check his armies in their career of victory, to concentrate so overwhelming a force for their destruction, and what greater disappointment to him, than to find that by the masterly arrangements of his adversary it was impossible to intercept them. Unable, therefore, to secure a triumph, suited to his own renown, he halted to watch the event, and despatched two of his Marshals, with as many divisions, with orders to follow the British closely, and to destroy them either before, or during their embarkation.

In the fatigues and sufferings from hunger and bad weather, the 26th, which formed part of the reserve, had their share, but in the actions which occurred were not engaged. Ready to support, their assistance in aid of the light troops and cavalry was never required.

1809.

On the 4th of January, 1809, Sir John Moore determined on retreating to Corunna instead of Vigo, as was originally intended; and orders were sent for the transports to proceed immediately to the former place. The reserve reached Lugo on the 5th. The irregularities attendant on this march were very serious, and produced a severe order of the day on the 5th. The army occupied its position in front of Lugo on the 7th, and in the evening the 26th were obliged to exchange their quarters in the town for the field, but they were not brought into action. The stragglers from the Regiment, who were not numerous, had nearly all rejoined on the 6th, and the corps was quite efficient when it took its place in the line. It was not, however, the enemy's policy to fight the British army on such strong ground, but to delay and harass its march. After offering battle all day, the troops began to draw off at night fall; and then was renewed, even in marching to Lugo, the disorder which had before prevailed, but which was now aggravated ten-fold. Neither had the commissariat made much effort to alleviate the suffering of the soldiers during the halt; for though they then received some provisions, they were insufficient for the march which followed. Hunger, sickness, want of necessary clothing, bad roads and inclement weather, were all combined to complete their misery; and in the eleven leagues which they had to travel to Betanzos, no supply could be obtained but wine, which proved only a source of evil. The French, who were not apprised of the retreat till the morning, did not overtake the rear guard before the evening of the 9th; and, but for the protection which was afforded to the loiterers, the enemy would have caused scarcely any trouble. To save these men, Lieut.-General Lord Paget remained some miles from Betanzos, whilst the army generally was quartered at that place on the 10th.

1809.
1st Batt.

1809.
1st Batt.

The 26th arrived there close upon eleven in the morning, with about fifty men, fourteen officers and the colours. Twenty-three of the men belonged to the light company. The greater part, however, came in during the day. Other corps were even more reduced. Here provisions were plenty; but shoes, the want of which had occasioned the loss of so many men, were not to be procured. Between Lugo and Betanzos the troops, during the short halts which were unavoidable, were without shelter, as it was preferable that they should endure the cold and rain even of a severe night, rather than encounter the risk of intoxication.

On the 11th of January, the army left Betanzos on its last day's march to *Corunna*, which was conducted with more regularity than on former occasions. The 26th were quartered in the town.

Though all the baggage had been at different times lost, mostly before arriving at Astorga, and the men's clothing, who remained with their colours, had become miserably tattered; yet, in spite of all their sufferings, the spirits of the soldiers continued unbroken, and their arms and accoutrements were all complete and in a fairly serviceable state. As the transports had not arrived, the sick only embarked in the few ships then in the bay.

The result of the march was, that the army arrived entire and unbroken; and in a military point of view the operation was successful. Nearly seventy thousand Frenchmen, led by their favourite Emperor, with a great superiority of cavalry, had endeavoured in vain to surround or to defeat twenty-six thousand British; two hundred and fifty miles of country had been traversed; and mountains, defiles, and rivers had been crossed in daily contact with the enemy. Though frequently engaged, even their rear guard was never beaten or thrown into confusion; but was successful in every encounter. However great the sacrifice of baggage and of stores from want of adequate means of conveyance, and the state of the roads, "neither Napoleon "nor the Duke of Dalmatia won by force a piece of "artillery, a standard, or a single military trophy from "the British army."*

1809.
1st Batt.

As the position was found to be bad, and the transports not arrived, some recommended Sir John Moore to treat with the enemy, which advice he properly rejected. On the 12th the French appeared in force on the right bank of the Mero, and on the 13th Lieut.-General Sir David Baird marched out of Corunna with his division, to occupy the position on the rising grounds in front, and to remain out all night. The 26th were in this division. On the 14th Marshal Soult made some demonstrations, accompanied by a cannonade, which was soon returned with effect, when he drew off his guns, and on the 15th his whole army made a forward movement, and took up a strong position in front of the British; in the evening the transports from Vigo hove in sight, and an attempt was made to seize two of his guns, which failed by the death of Lieut.-Colonel John Mackenzie of the 5th Regiment, who led the attack.

On the morning of the 16th the enemy remained apparently quiet, and the preparations for embarking the army during the night were completed. Sir John Moore had passed the morning in transacting business, and having made his arrangements for the ensuing night, if the French should not move, he set off at one o'clock

---

* "Narrative of the Campaign," by James Carrick Moore.

1809.
1st
Batt.

to visit the outposts, when he was met on the road by a messenger from Lieut.-General the Honourable John Hope, (afterwards Earl of Hopetoun), to report that " the enemy's line was getting under arms." Sir John expressed the highest satisfaction at this intelligence with a feeling truly British, and only regretted that there would not be day-light enough to profit sufficiently from the advantages which he anticipated as certain. The battle soon after began on the right, which was the weak part of the position, against which the enemy made the most vigorous efforts, but they were constantly repulsed. In the course of the conflict, first Sir David Baird, and afterwards Sir John Moore were carried off the field wounded. The soldiers, however, continued the contest with success, although they had witnessed the fall of their two leaders, and Marshal Soult was compelled to draw back his left wing.

Finding that he was not likely to succeed in his first attempt, his efforts became more forcibly directed towards the British centre, where the French were successfully resisted by Major-General Manningham's brigade, forming the left of Sir David Baird's division, and by a part of that under Major-General Leith, composing the right of Lieut.-General Hope's division. Before five o'clock in the evening, not only was every attack successfully repulsed which was made on the position, but ground was gained at almost all points, and a more forward line was occupied than at the commencement of the action. Lieut.-General the Honourable John Hope observed in his despatch, that " the brunt of the action fell upon " the 4th, 42nd, 50th and 81st Regiments, with parts of " the brigade of Guards and the 26th Regiment ;" and in his general orders, of the 18th of January, thus expressed his appreciation of their conduct :—" Major-

"General Manningham, with his brigade, consisting of 1809.
"the Royals, the 26th and 81st Regiments, and Major- 1st Batt.
"General Warde, with the brigade of Guards, will also
"be pleased to accept his best thanks for their steady
"and gallant conduct during the action."

The victory was complete, and gained under many disadvantages. The British had been reduced by sick and stragglers, and by the detachment of Brigadier-General Craufurd's brigade sent to Vigo, to barely fifteen thousand men, whilst the French army, though also diminished from the same causes, still mustered full twenty thousand. Their position was more favourable, and their cannon of much heavier calibre; yet by the daring courage of the troops, by the skilful disposition of the army, and by the manœuvres during the action, Soult was completely discomfited. The British loss was between seven and eight hundred men in killed and wounded, whilst that of the French was about two thousand. This was owing to the quick firing and steady aim of the former, the enemy's veteran officers afterwards declaring that they had never before been in so hot a fire. In commemoration of this victory the 26th subsequently received the royal authority to bear the word "CORUNNA" on the regimental colours and appointments.* The army also received the thanks of

---

* The following is the authority for bearing the word "CORUNNA," by which justice was at length rendered to the services of the 26th on that memorable occasion:—

"*Horse Guards*, 22*nd April*, 1823.

"MY LORD,—I have the honour to acquaint your Lordship,
"by direction of His Royal Highness the Commander-in-Chief,
"that HIS MAJESTY has been pleased to approve of the 26th (or
"Cameronian) Regiment bearing on its colours and appointments,

1809.
1st Batt.
both Houses of Parliament, "for its distinguished discipline, firmness, and valour in the battle of Corunna."

Lieut.-General Hope, under the circumstances in which the British army was placed, and knowing that reinforcements would soon reach the French, considered it would be impossible to maintain his position for any length of time. He therefore judged that the only prudent step that could be taken was to embark the army. At ten o'clock the troops, by brigades, moved from the field and marched to Corunna. Strong pickets were left to guard the ground, and Major General William Carr Beresford commanded the rear guard of two thousand men. He occupied the lines in front of the town, and Major-General Rowland Hill was stationed with a reserve behind the town. The boats were all in readiness, and the previous measures had been so well concerted, that nearly the whole force was embarked during the night.

When the army quitted its position on the night of the 16th, the regiments marched off, left in front, and the 26th, who were on the left of Lieut.-General Sir David Baird's division, led the way; as it was from that flank the movement was made. Pickets were left

---

"in addition to any other badges or devices which may have
"heretofore been granted to the Regiment, the word "CORUNNA,"
"in commemoration of the distinguished services of the Regiment
"in the action fought near Corunna on the 16th of January, 1809.

"I have, &c.,
"J. MACDONALD,
"D.-A.-G.

' Lieut.-General the
 "Earl of Dalhousie, G.C.B.,
   "Colonel of the 26th (or Cameronian)
   "Regiment of Foot."

by each corps, of one captain, two subalterns, and fifty men; the 26th furnishing one of the same strength for the 81st, in consequence of that corps having suffered so great a loss in the action. The embarkation of the Cameronians was made from Santa Lucia, a suburb on the land side, and the boats being ready, the men were quickly taken on board; as it came on to blow hard, and it was difficult, owing to the darkness of the night and the roughness of the sea, to find the right ships, the men were put into those nearest, by which a great mixture of corps ensued. The greater part of the Regiment was embarked in transports, but twenty-nine men and five officers proceeded in the "Implacable."

1809. 1st Batt.

At two o'clock, on the 17th, Major-General Hill's brigade embarked under the citadel, notwithstanding that the enemy had erected some batteries on the heights and had so alarmed the masters of some of the transports, that they cut their cables, and four ran aground. These were burnt, and the troops removed to other ships. During that night, and the morning of the 18th, Major-General Beresford sent off all the sick and wounded, whose condition admitted of their being removed; and lastly, the rear guard embarked without the slightest opposition being made by the enemy.

Most of the women, who had been allowed to follow their husbands in the proportion of six to each hundred men, succeeded in effecting their escape, and many had accompanied them through the whole campaign, having suffered almost incredible hardships. The condition of all ranks, when on board, was wretched, as the officers were without baggage, and the men's kits were reduced nearly to nothing; their health became impaired from want of cleanliness, which, without the necessary change of clothes, and in the crowded state of the vessels, could

K

1809.
1st Batt.

not be attained. Disease broke out amongst them on the passage, and in their subsequent removal from Plymouth and Portsmouth to other parts higher up the channel. Numbers were landed, and sent into the hospital, of whom many never recovered; whilst the remainder were gradually collected at the quarters assigned for the several corps.

The 26th disembarked chiefly at Portsmouth, but others were landed at Plymouth, Liverpool, and Ramsgate, and as soon as circumstances permitted, the Regiment was assembled at Horsham, to which place the disposable part marched direct from Portsmouth, and arrived there on the 1st of February, where it remained till the 27th of June.

It is difficult to ascertain the loss which the Regiment experienced during this campaign, owing to the peculiarities of the service, which impaired the accuracy of the returns, both during its continuance and after the arrival of the army in England. It appears to have lost by death to January, 1809, inclusive, thirty-five men; and two sergeants, three drummers, and one hundred and eighty-seven men were left in Spain. Of these, forty-three afterwards returned, having escaped through Portugal, where, with those of other corps, they were, for a short time, formed into a provisional battalion. The actual strength at Horsham on the 25th of February was four hundred and three men fit for duty, which increased as the sick rejoined. The casualties among the officers at the battle of Corunna were Lieutenants Lawrence Chevers and Joseph Nunn, killed; Lieutenant-Colonel Maxwell, who lost his arm; Lieutenants Francis Shearman, and Thomas Thompson, and Surgeon Henry Messiter, wounded.

The second battalion, which had proceeded to Glasgow in July, 1807, remained in that city till the 26th of May, 1809, when it was removed to Haddington, where it was quartered the remainder of the year. It was occupied, during this period, in endeavouring to replace, by recruiting and by volunteers from the militia, the losses which the first battalion had sustained. [margin: 1809. 2nd Batt.]

On the 7th of May, the first battalion was inspected by Major-General the Earl of Dalhousie, when it was about six hundred strong, and on the 16th of June it received a draft of two hundred men from the second battalion; which, being the only aid obtained from that quarter, shows that the second battalion, itself too weak for service, had not been very successful in recruiting. Its influence was, however, so great at this time, when men could hardly be procured, that between thirty and forty men volunteered from the Lanark militia, a corps which had always shown a decided disinclination to enter the line. By this reinforcement the nominal strength of the first battalion was raised to one thousand and twenty rank and file, though its effectives, when it marched in two divisions from Horsham on the 27th of June, were only about eight hundred. A depôt, composed of the actual non-effective men then with the corps, who were transferred to the second battalion, was left there in charge of the heavy luggage, and the absentees in Spain were still retained on the strength of the first battalion. [margin: 1st Batt.]

The first battalion of the 26th was subsequently encamped near Portsmouth, and was brigaded with the first battalion of the 5th, the second battalion of the 23rd, and the 32nd Regiment, under the command of Brigadier-General Gore Browne.

Immense preparations had been made by the British

1809.
1st
Batt.

Government to fit out the most formidable armament that had for a long time proceeded from England. The troops amounted to forty thousand men, commanded by Lieut.-General the Earl of Chatham; the naval portion consisted of thirty-nine ships of the line, thirty-six frigates, and numerous gun-boats and bomb-vessels, together with other small craft, under Admiral Sir Richard Strachan. The object of the expedition was to obtain possession of the islands at the mouth of the Scheldt, and to destroy the French ships in that river, with the docks and arsenals at Antwerp. The first battalion of the 26th, or Cameronian Regiment, embarked at Stoke's Bay for Walcheren, on the 16th of July, on board of the "Marlborough" and "Hero," 74 guns. The strength of the battalion was forty-one officers, forty-seven sergeants, sixteen drummers, and six hundred and sixty-three rank and file. The names of the officers were:—*Lieut.-Colonel*, William Maxwell; *Majors*, Fountain Hogg, Honourable Henry Murray (2nd battalion); *Captains*, Frederick Jones, William Fotheringham (Deputy-Assistant Adjutant-General), James Conolly, Charles Stuart Campbell, William Walker, Percival Pym, Edward Whitty, Adam G. Campbell; *Lieutenants*, Robert Haggerstone, John Brooks, Joseph Smith, Andrew Lett, Francis Shearman, James Stedman, Thomas Thomson, Robert Smith, George Platt, John Westlake, James Dunn, Thomas Murray, Hamilton Maxwell, George Pipon, Hugh Law, Hugh McLatchie, Frederick Campbell Heatley, Henry Maxwell, Standish Lowcay; *Ensigns*, Patrick James Robertson, George Bray, John Grimshaw, George W. Charleton, Edward James White, Francis R. Masters (2nd battalion); *Paymaster*, William Laforest; *Adjutant*, James Nash; *Quarter Master*, John

Connell; *Surgeon*, John Cairroll; *Assistant-Surgeon*, John 1809. Coldstream. Captain Hope, of the 26th, was on the 1st Batt. staff, as aide-de-camp to Lieut.-General the Honourable Sir John Hope. The ships sailed on the 25th, and anchored in the Downs on the 27th; and weighing on the 29th, they again anchored in the evening off Walcheren. The troops landed during the evening of the 30th, and took up a position about half a mile from the shore. The next day they marched five miles, and encamped near the village of Domberg. On the 1st of August, the troops advanced towards Flushing. The Cameronians marched by West Capelle, and leaving Middleberg to the left, they halted at West Soberg. On the 2nd, the right wing was ordered to the support of the 5th Foot, and afterwards the left, the enemy having attacked that corps. After this affair had ended, two companies remained on picket.

In reference to the operations which followed the landing of the army, the Earl of Chatham stated, on the 2nd, that the " loss will not appear to have been " great, when the serious impediments it was in the " power of the enemy to oppose to our progress are " considered, as well as the formidable state of the " batteries of Flushing, to which our troops were ex-" posed." Having succeeded in the investment, active measures were taken for the reduction of the fortress by a regular siege, and his Lordship wrote on the 7th, that " we have been unremittingly employed in bringing up " the artillery of siege, the ammunition and stores to " the vicinity of Flushing; and the troops have been " occupied in the construction of the batteries, and in " carrying on the several works before the place, but " which have been necessarily interrupted by the heavy " rains which have fallen here. The enemy is active

1809.
1st
Batt.

"and enterprising, and the garrison has certainly received considerable reinforcements from the opposite coast, nor has it been in the power of the flotilla hitherto to prevent it."

The 26th were actively engaged in these operations, and on the 3rd and 5th they suffered some loss. On the latter day Lieutenant Henry Maxwell was dangerously wounded, and died in September following. On the 7th they changed their post in consequence of an attack on the British right. From the 8th to the 11th they were employed alternately in working in the trenches, and in protecting the working parties. On the 13th, the batteries having commenced to fire, the Cameronians were ordered to protect them. The fire proved so destructive, and the Congreve rockets and other missiles had done such damage, that on the 15th a flag of truce was sent out. On the 16th and 17th the arrangements for the surrender were complete, and on the 18th, the 26th had the honour of taking post at the East gate, whilst the garrison defiled as prisoners of war before them. After remaining two days in camp, they marched on the 21st to Armuyden, where they again came under the command of Brigadier-General Browne, who had been wounded during the siege; his brigade then consisted of the first battalion of the 26th, and the second battalions of the 23rd, 81st, and 84th Regiments.

During the three weeks of these operations the Cameronians were not only exposed to danger from the enemy's fire, and in skirmishes which occurred with the outposts, but from exposure to the weather, which there, and in St. Joostland, laid the seeds of the disease that afterwards proved so fatal. The actual casualties from the 30th of July to the surrender of Flushing were five rank and file killed, and two sergeants and nineteen rank and file wounded. Many deaths from sickness afterwards occurred. The total loss from sickness during the year amounted to seven sergeants, one drummer, and ninety-two rank and file. On the 7th of September the battalion was removed into farmhouses nearer the Scheldt. During this month the sickness increased fearfully—from ten to fifteen men were daily sent into hospital—whence they afterwards proceeded to England; and on the 25th of September only two hundred and eighty-seven men were fit for duty. Captain Fotheringham, Lieutenant Law, Ensign Charleton, and Surgeon Carroll, died of fever.

1809.
1st Batt.

All hope of success for the ultimate object of the expedition against Antwerp having been relinquished, and the French having recovered from their first alarm, the greater part of the armament and its commander returned to England; but a considerable garrison was left for the security of Flushing; these troops had little to contend with but the pestilential climate of this marshy island, which was more certain in its effects than any efforts of the enemy could have been for their defeat and expulsion.

After struggling in vain against this most destructive climate, which reduced every corps to a mere skeleton, insufficient for the ordinary duties of the places in which they were quartered, the tardy and reluctant consent of the ministry to the abandonment of this dearly purchased conquest was extorted. The works of the fortress and the arsenal were mined and destroyed, and the troops re-embarked for England.

The Cameronians landed at Portsmouth on the 30th of December, and marched back into Horsham barracks on New Year's Day, 1810, with ninety men. Thus

1810.

1810. ceased this ill-fated enterprise; and though the troops,
1st Batt. "when in presence of the enemy showed the greatest "intrepidity," "and sustained with pleasure and cheerful- "ness the laborious duties they had to perform;" yet, as they were not afterwards brought into a fair field of action, they lost their spirits, and became the ready victims of a contagion, the progress of which no medical skill could arrest.

This short campaign proved even more fatal to the Regiment than that in Spain, with all its protracted toil and hardships. The total casualties of the 26th on these two occasions appears to have been about two hundred and twenty-four, who died or were killed; one hundred and twenty of the absentees on the Corunna retreat were never afterwards heard of, and twenty men were discharged, and fifty-six transferred to the second battalion. Not including the last (though many of them were unfit for the service), the gross number at the time lost to the corps amounted in these two years to three hundred and sixty-four. It would be difficult to give a correct statement of the casualties attributable to the one or the other of these campaigns, as the sick were spread through so many hospitals, and the returns were so irregular and uncertain as to prevent any accurate distribution of them. Besides this positive loss, the constitution of very many, both officers and men, received a shock from which they never recovered, and death, or premature discharge with pension, followed.

2nd Batt. During the whole of 1810, the second battalion remained at Haddington, and its strength was not sufficient to provide a draft for the first, which much needed a reinforcement. The recruiting continued, but without any remarkable success.

OR CAMERONIAN REGIMENT. 137

On the 6th of April, 1810, in consequence of the riots which ensued when Sir Francis Burdett was sent to the Tower, the first battalion proceeded to the neighbourhood of London by a sudden route received at midnight. The officers and men were quartered for some days at Dorking, Epsom, Mitcham, and Wimbledon, where they remained without being brought into the metropolis, as the riots gradually subsided. The battalion was therefore shortly after ordered back to Horsham, where it continued till the 4th of June, when it marched to Portsmouth. On its arrival on the 7th it embarked in transports; and on the 11th, they sailed from Spithead. Having reached Jersey on the 14th of June, the battalion landed, and marched the same day to Grouville, where it continued the rest of the year. Whilst quartered in England, it was not successful in its recruiting.

1810.
1st Batt.

The first battalion remained in Jersey till June, 1811, when it was ordered to join the army in Portugal. It left Grouville on the 23rd, and on the same day embarked in three transports. During the periods of its being stationed in this island, it obtained scarcely any accession to its strength, a score of recruits and volunteers who joined having about balanced the various causes of decrease. On embarkation there were on board thirty-three officers, thirty-four sergeants, twenty-one drummers and six hundred and eighteen rank and file, including eighteen volunteers from the Stirlingshire militia, leaving seventy non-commissioned officers and men behind. The following officers embarked for the Peninsula:—*Lieut.-Colonel*, William Maxwell; *Major*, Edward Shearman; *Captains*, James Conolly, Charles Stuart Campbell, William Walker, Edward Whitty, Adam G. Campbell, Robert Child; *Lieutenants*, Andrew

1811.

1811.
1st Batt.

Lett, Francis Shearman, James Stedman, Thomas Thomson, Robert Smith, John Westlake, James Dunn, Thomas Murray, George Pipon, Hugh McLatchie, Hugh Pollock, Standish Lowcay, Edmund Jordan (second battalion), Thomas Hay (second battalion); *Ensigns,* Francis R. Masters, Robert Robson, Alexander Arnott, George Anderson, John Wilkinson, Thomas Taylor; *Paymaster,* William Laforest; *Adjutant,* James Nash; *Quarter Master,* John Connell ; *Surgeon,* John Butt Taylor; *Assistant Surgeon,* William Mayben. Captain James Archibald Hope and Lieutenant William Chartres, of the 26th, were already in the Peninsula; the former as *aide-de-camp* to Lieut.-General Sir Thomas Graham, and the latter doing duty with the Portuguese army.

After a fine run of ten days, the transports entered the Tagus on the 4th of July, and on the 5th, the battalion disembarked at Lisbon, and was quartered in the convent of St. Paulisto. The 32nd and 77th Regiments, which had sailed under the same convoy, arrived and landed with it. They proceeded on the 18th, up the Tagus in boats to Velada, where they disembarked, and marched the following day to Santarem, and thence by Golegao and Punhete to Abrantes, where they arrived on the 22nd, and were quartered in Pega, a small village on the left bank of the Tagus. They remained there till the 27th, when they continued their route on the 29th to Alpalhao, and there joined the first division under Lieut.-General Sir Brent Spencer, K.C.B., on the 31st, upon its arrival that day, and were brigaded with the 24th, 42nd, 60th, fifth battalion (first company) and 79th regiments, under Lieut.-Colonel Lord Blantyre.*

---

* The strength of the brigade in rank and file was as follows:—

The main body of the army about this time quitted the Alemtejo, where Lieut.-General Viscount Wellington had continued since June, when Marshals Marmont and Soult united on the Guadiana to relieve Badajoz, which, with an army of sixty-two thousand infantry and eight thousand cavalry, they were enabled to effect, as Wellington could only oppose to them a body of fifty thousand men, including four thousand cavalry. It might have been expected that with so decided a superiority of numbers, the enemy would have sought a general action, for which the British General was prepared, and had his army so concentrated near and on the Caya, as to be ready, in a few hours, to occupy a defensive position wherein he had determined to give him battle. The French Marshals, after their reconnaissance, on the 22nd of June, from which they retired without gaining any information regarding the numbers and position of the allied army, as it was skilfully concealed in the woods and behind the hills, were content to remain quiet for above a month, during which the reduction of Ciudad Rodrigo was planned, and the preparations for the attack commenced.*

1811. 1st Batt.

It was at this period that the 26th arrived; and as it joined that part of the army which moved to the north, it avoided all exposure to the climate of the Alemtejo,

---

24th (second battalion)	289
26th (first battalion)	590
42nd (second battalion)	346
79th (first battalion)	595
60th (fifth battalion, one company)	26
Total	1,846

* "Jones's Campaigns."

140   HISTORICAL RECORD OF THE TWENTY-SIXTH,

1811. which, in the summer, becomes very unhealthy. Between
1st   the 1st and 10th of August, the Regiment had marched
Batt. from Alpalhao to St. Estivao, where it remained till the
28th, on which day it moved by Sabugal and Alfayates,
to Mealhada de Sorda, where the Cameronians were
stationed from the 1st to the 23rd of September. This
was an easy march, and although not conducted through
a country affording good accommodation to the troops,
yet it tended to the preservation of their health.
Change of scene and climate, even when the men are
obliged to be out, are at the fine season always con-
ductive to the well being of soldiers, whose minds and
bodies alike need to be kept in active employment.

The Portuguese villages were wretched, both in the
construction of the houses and in their cleanliness, and
offered a striking contrast to those within the Spanish
boundaries, which were, in every respect, but especially
in neatness, very superior. Mealhada de Sorda was an
ordinary village, which, however, was made to contain
the whole corps. The frontier villages were, in a great
measure, deserted by the inhabitants, which enabled
the troops more easily to find accommodation.

After its removal from the Alemtejo, the British army
was collected, with a view to the blockade of Ciudad
Rodrigo, which being situated in a country decidedly
hostile to the French, was obliged to be provisioned by
convoys escorted from a distance, and with the allied
troops encamped in its neighbourhood, it could only be
relieved by a force equal to contend successfully with the
British. As the enemy's garrison began to be straitened
for supplies, Viscount Wellington had placed some corps
of his army in advance of Fuente Guinaldo, so as completely to command the country about Rodrigo, and
ascertain the strength with which the French might

advance to protect their convoy. On the 23rd of September, its head appeared in the plain in front of Rodrigo, and on the following day, a string of loaded cars, mules, and wagons, several miles in length, entered the fortress. On the morning of the 25th, thirty squadrons of cavalry, and a body of infantry, with artillery, crossed the Agueda, as a reconnaissance. The French troops, on the advance of the British at El Bodon, were hard pressed, and the better to avoid a conflict with superior numbers, their commander judiciously crossed to the right of the Agueda, and re-passed at a ford higher up. On the left, the only force to oppose the enemy's formidable cavalry were two British and one Portuguese battalion, with three squadrons of dragoons and four guns. They maintained their ground for some time, and when ordered to fall back, the infantry being formed in two squares, retired in admirable order, only halting occasionally to repel the attacks of the French cavalry. Thus a brilliant retreat was successfully effected, the British cavalry completing, by well-timed charges, the disorder which was occasioned by the fire of the squares.

1811.
1st Batt.

Thus alternately covering each other, this small corps fell back on the supports, which, though distant, were ordered up in sufficient time to preserve it from being overwhelmed by the vast superiority of the enemy. Lieut.-Generals Thomas Picton and the Honourable George Lowry Cole's divisions were then placed in the position of Guinaldo, and the enemy halted in front of it. On the 26th, Major-General Robert Craufurd's division took ground on the same alignment. As the English left flank fell abruptly into a spacious plain, it was necessary to post a strong body of troops on it to prevent the French from manœuvring in rear of the

1811. position. The Cameronians, on the alarm of the enemy's
1st approach, had moved up with the first division towards
Batt. Fuentes d'Onor, whence they afterwards retired to join
with, and protect, the left of the position. In the course
of the day, Marshal Marmont had collected thirty-five
thousand infantry, and a numerous cavalry, within a few
hundred yards of the heights forming Wellington's position; and at dusk, the head of another very large column
appeared in sight; which, when united, would have increased the enemy's force to sixty thousand infantry, and
five thousand cavalry. After dark, the British army was
therefore withdrawn, being followed, on the 27th, by
two columns of the French, when some smart affairs took
place between them and Sir Lowry Cole's division, near
Aldea de Ponte. At night, the whole army again fell
back, according to a preconcerted plan, to a position
selected on a chord of the arc, formed by the Coa, near
Sabugal, and on the 28th battle was offered to the enemy,
when the latter, having effected his object of re-victualling
Rodrigo, declined the challenge, and returned to Salamanca. The British troops were replaced in cantonments,
but more retired than before, as it was no longer an
object to watch the fortress so closely.

The 26th proceeded to Maçal de Chao, where they
remained from the 30th of September to the 24th of
November, and then, after being ordered up to Fuentes
d'Onor with the brigade, owing to some unfounded
reports of the enemy's movements, they marched to
Villa Torpin and Vermioza, and the adjacent villages, in
which they were quartered, from the 30th of November
to the end of the year.

While thus stationed, working parties were furnished
from the Regiment, under officers, to assist in repairing
the fortifications of Almeida, which the French had

blown up on the 10th of May, when General Brennier, 1811. the governor, by skill and promptitude of movement, 1st Batt. effected his escape, penetrating the British line of investment. Other parties were at the same time engaged in preparing fascines and gabions, with a view to the intended attack on Ciudad Rodrigo.

It was after the *alerte*, which had been occasioned by the operations attending upon the relief of Ciudad Rodrigo, that the Cameronians began to suffer materially from sickness. Then fever and ague made great havoc in their ranks, which were fearfully thinned. Several causes may have concurred to render them more susceptible to the variations of climate than the regiments which were more used to it. A large number had before suffered from the Walcheren fever, to which the disease prevalent in some of the valleys of Beira had an affinity. On leaving Lisbon, they did not get any blankets, neither were they issued afterwards, and the want of them was greatly felt. The men were, indeed, generally housed, but a roof might literally be said to constitute the whole accommodation afforded by these wretched villages. The pay of the army being in arrear, the 26th were not enabeld to obtain any advance of money, and they were thus deprived of many comforts, especially salt, which even the soldiers could have obtained either from the country people or the settlers, had they been able to make payment. These, and perhaps some other casual disadvantages of management, placed both officers and men under circumstances of great difficulty, which afterwards unhappily increased, and ultimately led to their quitting the Peninsula.

Whilst engaged in the defensive movements between the 23rd and 29th of September, the detachment under Major Hogg reached the battalion near Fuentes d'Onor.

1811.
1st Batt.

This reinforcement, which consisted of the following eleven officers, viz., *Major*, Fountain Hogg; *Captain*, Charles Addison; *Lieutenants*, Hamilton Maxwell, Frederick Campbell Heatley, John Wright, Henry Roberts, Jesse Collins, John Marshall, and George Bray; and *Ensigns*, Thomas William Boyes and Charles Frederick Sweeney; ten sergeants, one drummer, and one hundred and eighty-seven rank and file, proceeded by sea from Leith to Gravesend, and thence by land to Portsmouth, where they embarked on the 3rd of July in the "Mercury" frigate. After being at sea about seven weeks, of which three were passed at Spithead, and one at Falmouth, they arrived at Lisbon on the 22nd of August, and were quartered, on arrival, in the convent of St. Carmo. Six days afterwards they re-embarked, and sailed for Figueira, where they landed, and proceeded to join the army by the route of Coimbra, Vizeu, and Celorico. In the course of the march, they were obliged to leave behind sick about four sergeants, and twenty-five rank and file, a loss which was partly attributable to eating fruit in excess, and that unripe. In countries where fruits are abundant, no pains should be spared in impressing strongly on the men's minds, the absolute necessity of great moderation in the use of them, and of especial care that such as are not ripe may be avoided. To men accustomed to live in countries where fruits are scarce, few objects are more tempting to the appetite, or more gratifying to persons overcome by fatigue; yet, excepting strong liquors, none are more fatal. The natives, even, who are used to them, partake of them in great moderation, and select, with the utmost care, only such as are ripe. The soldiers, however, would devour them as though they could never be satiated, and in consequence, bowel complaints ensued. In other respects,

the detachment was in very good order, and might fairly
have ensured, at least, in point of numbers, to the
Regiment its place in the army for the ensuing campaign.   1811. 1st Batt.

The second battalion passed the year 1811 between
Haddington and Glasgow, having removed to the latter
on the 20th of June, after a march of four days. Its
popularity whilst at Glasgow gained it a considerable
number of recruits, and the Lanark and Argyll regiments of Militia had turned out some volunteers when
the corps was at Haddington. Though unable to augment its strength sufficiently to be fit for active service,
it ever maintained the efficiency of the first battalion,
under a combination of most untoward events.   2nd Batt.

In consequence of the lamentable sickness which continued to prevail among the Cameronians, as well as in
some other corps, they were deprived of their expected
share at the siege of Ciudad Rodrigo, which commenced
on the 8th of January, 1812, and terminated by the
capture of the place by assault, on the night of the
19th of that month. The 26th had quitted Vermioza
on the 31st of December, and continued their march
direct to Vizeu, where they arrived on the 5th of
January, and remained in that town with the 79th Regiment, which had also been sent there from sickness, till
the 25th of February.   1812. 1st Batt.

Lieutenant-General Sir Thomas Graham (afterwards
Lord Lynedoch) was ordered to inspect the battalion,
with a view to ascertain its efficiency for the field, but
unhappily the sickness still prevailed to such an extent
that he recommended its removal to Lisbon.

Leaving Vizeu on the 25th of February, the Cameronians reached Coimbra on the 28th, where they halted
till the 2nd of March. They were then quartered at
Montemor o Velho, whence on the 8th of April they

L.

1812. proceeded down the Mondego in boats to Figueiras, and
1st Batt. embarked on the 9th in three transports for Lisbon. They entered the Tagus on the 10th, and disembarking the next day, were first quartered in the Castle, and in about three weeks were removed to the barracks at the Campo d'Orique, as it was considered a more healthy station. On the 23rd of April they were joined by a draft of three sergeants and ninety-eight rank and file, under Captain Thomas Best and Lieutenant John Brooks, who had left the second battalion at Glasgow on the 26th of February. Although this reinforcement raised the effectives to upwards of eight hundred non-commissioned officers and men, yet Major-General Warren M. Peacocke, who commanded at Lisbon, at his inspection did not deem the 26th fit to return to the army, and they were therefore ordered to Gibraltar to replace the first battalion of the 82nd, which proceeded to the Peninsula.

This unfortunate result shows the importance of anticipating, by every effort of foresight and care, the causes which are likely to produce an unfavourable influence on the health of the soldiery, so as altogether to counteract, or else to lessen by every practicable means, their effect. Disease is an enemy, which in war is commonly more destructive than the sword; and it is moreover one, to which an undue power is often given by the neglect of precautions, which, if they fail to prevent, would, when adopted in time, at least mitigate the evil. The zeal and valour of both officers and men become paralysed at the moment when their exertions are most needful for their country's cause; because objects which might tend to the preservation of health, have been deemed to be trifling and unworthy of notice.

On the 26th of May the battalion, under the command

of Major Edward Shearman (Lieutenant-Colonel Maxwell being on sick leave in England), consisting of thirty-seven officers, fifty-one sergeants, twenty-one drummers, and seven hundred and forty-one rank and file, embarked in three transports, which sailed from the Tagus on the 2nd of June. On the 4th they anchored at Gibraltar, and on the 8th the battalion landed, and occupied the barracks at Windmill Hill.

1812. 1st Batt.

At this time a large number of men continued to be unfit for duty, and a separate building was assigned for the accommodation of convalescents, who at first amounted to upwards of one hundred. Sixty men had also been left sick in Portugal, most of whom afterwards rejoined. Though they came to Gibraltar at a season considered very unfavourable to the health of young soldiers, of whom there was a very large proportion in the battalion, owing to the heavy and repeated losses which they had experienced, yet the change had a favourable influence on them; and towards the end of the year their efficiency was completely restored. The opportunity, however, of employment with the army was quite lost, and they were obliged to become a permanent part of the regular garrison of the fortress, being brigaded with the 11th Regiment and the Fourth Veteran Battalion, under Major-General D. L. T. Widdrington.

The second battalion had much success in recruiting at Glasgow, and obtained some volunteers from the Lanark and Argyll regiments of militia. On the 25th of May it was removed from Glasgow, and arrived at Dumfries on the 28th, where it continued the remainder of the year. In this town also the battalion was successful in recruiting, and received twenty volunteers from the Lanark and thirty from the Dumfries militia.

2nd Batt.

1813. Major-General the Earl of Dalhousie, K.B., was removed from the colonelcy of the Sixth Garrison Battalion to that of the 26th Regiment, on the 21st of May, 1813, in succession to Lieut.-General Lord Elphinstone, deceased.

1st Batt. In 1813 the first battalion was engaged in the ordinary duties of the garrison of Gibraltar, which did not admit of any occurrence worthy of remark, till the bilious remittent fever broke out, and towards the end of the summer acquired a virulence equal to the plague. All the ordinary business of civil life was interrupted, trade ceased, the intercourse of friendship was suspended, the streets were deserted, except by those compelled by duty to frequent them, and by the dead cart, and a general system of quarantine was established between house and house, as by mutual consent. The Lieut.-Governor, Lieut.-General Colin Campbell,* on the 9th of September placed the garrison under quarantine, and adopted additional sanitary measures of the greatest strictness, which, however, the emergency of the case fully justified. The lower classes of the inhabitants, who had not sufficient house-room to secure them from being overcrowded, were obliged to remove to the neutral ground to the number of three or four thousand, where they were furnished with tents to encamp, and provided with rations at the public expense, when they had no other means of support; all the sick were instantly removed to the Lazaretto, between the north end of the rock and the inundation, where they were placed under proper medical superintendence.

There were also about three thousand of the inhabi-

---

* Died at Gibraltar on 2nd of April, 1814.

tants, who quitted the garrison, and these, with the exception of a few rich individuals, who fled from the danger, were persons without any claim to reside in it. In the town all access to houses in which there were sick, was placed under restrictions by palisades across the streets, and by sentries, the necessary communication to the town being confined to the line wall. The troops were forbidden to enter the town, and even the main guard, which was augmented to one hundred and fifty men, was outside, the sentries only being brought within it. Stringent measures were adopted for cleaning the streets, and infected houses; and as public funerals were forbidden, the dead were buried by the agents of the police, who carried them out in carts every morning to the neutral ground. It required all the exertions of the Lieut.-Governor and the generals of brigades, and other superintendents, among whom Major-General Sir Montague Burgoyne, Bart., was most conspicuous for his zeal and energy, to enforce the necessary regulations. By great exertions, however, this dreadful scourge was partially restrained, and when the weather changed in the month of October, the malignity of the disease began to abate.

During the month of September, and beginning of October, the mortality was immense; and though the higher classes, by timely and well-judged precautions, were less exposed, they did not escape the pestilence. The troops experienced less proportionate loss than the inhabitants; for notwithstanding the nature of their duties, not always favourable to them, the enforcement of the necessary precautions was in their case easier to effect. They were all encamped, some on the Landport glacis, and some in the south.

The Cameronians had removed from Windmill Hill Barracks, which were turned into a hospital, to Europa;

1813. 1st Batt.

1813.
1st Batt.

where they encamped, and were restrained from communicating with other parts of the rock, except on duty. Although the disease was less fatal among the military,* yet, even among them, it prevailed to a most alarming extent, so much so, that the effective men were unequal to the duties of the garrison, which were diminished by the town being completely cut off, and all the guards and sentries withdrawn, but such as were necessary to exclude every communication with it, except when made by the authority of the police. At one period the daily number of fresh cases in the battalion was from twenty to thirty, but they did not lose so many men as other corps. When the great heat abated after the rains, the deaths sensibly decreased, and in November they became comparatively very few, till in December the usual state of health was restored. Whether this terrible visitation originated in local causes, or whether it was a contagion imported from Spain, where the disease had appeared at an earlier period, are points about which the medical profession differed.

2nd Batt.

The second battalion was quartered at Dumfries till about the 3rd of September, when it proceeded to Kilmarnock. It marched on the 23rd for Dumbarton, and remained there the rest of the year. Early in 1813, it furnished a draft of ninety-six rank and file, which reached Gibraltar in May; and another of forty-four rank

---

* During the year 1813, the 26th lost the following officers from fever, namely—Captain Robert Child, 29th of September; Lieutenant Maurice Mahony, 30th of September; Surgeon John Butt Taylor, 1st of October; Lieutenant Thomas Thomson, 2nd of October; Captain Thomas Best, 6th of October; and Ensign Thomas Clubbe, 2nd of December. The deaths amongst the men amounted to fifty-four, and many were sent home invalided.

and file, which arrived there in October. The first was commanded by Major Frederick Jones, and the second by Captain Thomas Shepheard. Besides the recruiting, about twenty volunteers were obtained from the Lanark, and thirty from the Dumfries regiments of militia.

1813. 2nd Batt.

In 1814 the Cameronians continued in the usual routine of garrison duties, which present but little variety. This summer there were again symptoms of the bilious remittent, though not in so aggravated a degree as last year.* Its partial appearance, however, excited great alarm, and immediate measures of quarantine were adopted; but as the symptoms did not increase very materially, these precautions were neither so numerous, nor so strict as before. The troops had been previously encamped, and they continued so until about October, when the battalion struck its tents at Europa, and occupied the south barracks, having a detachment in the town of the men who had suffered from the fever the year before.† The inhabitants, in great numbers, encamped on the neutral ground; and the more wealthy were permitted to erect wooden sheds for their occasional residence in the summer. As the disease did not assume its former malignant type, though the deaths were still numerous, both public and private business was still transacted. The disease abated as usual in the month of October, when the cold weather commenced.

1814. 1st Batt.

---

* Captains Charles Grant and Thomas Shepheard died at this period, the former on the 23rd of September and the latter on the 2nd of October, 1814; also twenty-three men of the Regiment.

† In March, 1815, a return was prepared of the number of men remaining in the corps who had passed the fever in 1813 and 1814, with a view to their being employed on particular duties, by which

1814.
2nd Batt. The second battalion continued at Dumbarton till March, when it removed to Glasgow. It was disbanded on the 24th of October, in consequence of the peace, which caused a general reduction in the military force of the kingdom. A detachment of one hundred and twenty-five rank and file left Dumbarton, on the 29th of February, and reached Gibraltar on the 19th of May, a period much too late for troops to arrive in that garrison with a due regard to their health. In December, the remaining effectives (one hundred and fifty) of the late second battalion arrived there. The Cameronians were thus reduced to an establishment of ten companies of one hundred rank and file each, and one recruiting company, which remained at Glasgow. When the effective men joined at Gibraltar in December, the Regiment became forty men above its establishment of one thousand rank and file, notwithstanding that sixty-five men had been sent home as invalids.

1815. In 1815 the Cameronians continued to be quartered in the south, and were then brigaded with the eighth battalion of the 60th Regiment under the command of Major-General Widdrington. The depôt company proceeded on the 24th of June, 1815, from Glasgow to Ayr, but as the Regiment was above its establishment, it was not required to recruit.

---

they would be more exposed to this disease, should it reappear in the garrison, as it was thought that it did not attack the same person a second time. This paper showed that sixteen sergeants, twenty-three corporals, two drummers, and three hundred and twenty-two privates remained who had had the fever, to which number, if fifty-four deaths in 1813 and twenty-three in 1814, be added, there will be a total of four hundred and forty who had the disease in the two years. This number was smaller than that of the other corps then in the garrison.

The Regiment in 1816 was removed from the south to barracks in the town. Being by this time accustomed to the climate, and so many having actually had the fever, the Cameronians continued in the town during the remainder of their stay on the rock. The fear of infection being over, the communication with Spain was open, except in the autumn of 1820 and that of 1821.

Gibraltar is, in many respects, one of the best stations, both for officers and men, which the British dependencies afford, when the communication with Spain is free; yet a residence there is attended with little variety of pursuits, except by excursions into the Peninsula. The communication after 1814 was wholly without interruption, except in those years when the gates were shut during three or four summer and autumn months. A cordon was at these times established across the isthmus, beyond the village and gardens, some of the troops being encamped on the neutral ground, and guard huts of wood were built in 1820, for the better accommodation of the men employed on the duty. Thus the place was most effectually put under quarantine on the land side; and the result was, that for this, or some other less obvious cause, the fever did not penetrate. With Barbary the communication was also open until the plague broke out at Tetuan in 1818; when the most strict prohibitory system was immediately enforced, and with complete success. The usual supplies of meat, vegetables, &c., for which the garrison mainly depended on the Moroqueens, were, however, if not wholly suspended, in a great measure interrupted. The indolent habits, the bad husbandry, and the enormous exactions to which the cupidity of a disorganised and starving soldiery subjected the Spanish peasantry, in addition to duties on the produce of the soil, which the

1816.

1820.
1821.

1821. impolicy of a needy government exacted, rendered the neighbouring districts of Spain unable fully to supply wants, which, under better fiscal and agricultural management, would have proved a source of emolument. The active exertions and encouragement of the Lieut.-Governor, General Sir George Don, G.C.B., who introduced great improvements in the cultivation of the gardens, and the low price at which Ireland and Jersey furnished potatoes, with such supplies as came from Spain, still placed it within the power of the soldiery to procure an adequate quantity of vegetables for their dinners; so that their diet, although only varied twice a week with fresh meat of indifferent quality, was wholesome, and their health never suffered. To this good result, the abundance of fruit, such as oranges, melons, figs, and grapes, greatly contributed.

The use of wholesome ordinary wine, instead of spirituous liquors, the sale of which was forbidden to the troops, though it did not suppress drunkenness, rendered its consequences generally less fatal. From this vice the Cameronians were comparatively free.

A general reduction having taken place in the army in 1821, the Regiment, which was then eighty-two men below its establishment, was reduced from ten to eight companies, and from thirty-five sergeants, twenty-two drummers, and six hundred and fifty rank and file, to twenty-nine sergeants, twelve drummers, and five hundred and fifty-six rank and file, by which twenty-eight non-commissioned officers and men were discharged as supernumeraries. After that period its strength was effectually maintained by the recruiting parties, and the highest deficiency at any time was in 1822, when thirty-six men were required to complete the establishment.

In May 1821, an order was received for the Cameronians to return to England, but by the next packet a counter order arrived, which created general disappointment; not indeed that a dislike was felt to the place, but men are generally eager for change, and a station nearer to their homes could not be otherwise than acceptable. The next spring, however, the order was renewed, and on the 19th of September, 1822, the "Success" transport, with two companies of the 43rd Light Infantry anchored in the bay. The head-quarters of the 26th embarked in that vessel at one p.m., on the 28th, and sailed with a fair wind the same evening. It lasted just long enough to enable the transport to weather Cape St. Vincent, and as the wind was generally unfavourable, she did not anchor in the Cove of Cork till late on the evening of the 16th of October.

A tedious quarantine ensued, owing to the necessity of referring to Dublin; but on the evening of the 24th, pratique was received, and a division of the Regiment arrived the next day by the steamer at Ballinacurragh; this was quartered at Middleton until the 26th, when it marched into Fermoy Barracks. The 2nd division joined there on the 1st, and the 3rd division on the 2nd of November, having embarked from Gibraltar on the 5th and 8th of October, and anchored in the Cove on the 28th. The correspondence relative to the "Success" saved the others the delay of awaiting pratique from Dublin.

During the rest of the year 1822 the Regiment continued in Fermoy Barracks, being joined by its depôt of forty men from the Isle of Wight on the 16th of December. This depôt had proceeded from Ayr to Edinburgh in March 1816, where it remained till the arrangement took effect, by which all the depôts in the army were assembled at Albany Barracks in the Isle of Wight. That of the

1822. Cameronians arrived there in May, 1820. The recruiting parties, however, remained in Edinburgh, Glasgow, and Dumfries.

The Regiment was inspected by Major-General Sir John Lambert, K.C.B., on the 18th of November, and by Lieut.-General Lord Combermere, G.C.B., on the 9th of March, 1823.

1823. The 26th marched into Cork Barracks on the 7th of April. During their stay at Fermoy they were in a body; all the detachments which the troubled state of the country required being furnished by the 71st Regiment, which was almost entirely dispersed in small parties through the villages, to restrain the excesses of the Rockites. The Cameronians were constantly called upon to furnish patrols to traverse nightly the roads about Fermoy. The knowledge that such parties were on foot might have operated to restrain the evil disposed, but in no one instance did they succeed in apprehending them. Every thing, however, was done which the nature of the circumstances permitted, and legal powers, under the Insurrection Act, were even virtually vested in the military by the presence of a police constable with each party. The troops were thus employed against the people, yet it was extremely rare for them to be ill used; an occurrence which, when it did happen, nearly always originated in the fault of the soldier. No accident of the kind occurred among the Cameronians. On their removal to Cork, several detachments were given in the country, which were stationed in hired houses. Their orders were to patrol, and to assist the police, on requisition, a duty which was very harassing in its nature, as it occurred commonly after dark, without regard to weather, and across country. During the whole period, however, no instance happened of any quarrel with the people, with whom the men, in the course of their duties, were constantly brought into contact; a proof, in no ordinary degree, of the good temper, and of the discipline and judicious arrangements made by their officers. This state of things lasted through the remainder of 1823, during which the head-quarters of the Regiment performed, with the 1st Royal Veteran Battalion, the duties of the garrison of Cork.

On the arrival of the Regiment in Ireland the situation of the soldiers became greatly changed, and their moral discipline sustained a shock which threatened to produce results permanently injurious to its welfare. In Gibraltar almost the whole population spoke a different language, which rendered their intercourse with the soldiery extremely limited. In Ireland, on the contrary, the people, who are naturally social, eagerly seek the acquaintance of the military. This transition from a state of restraint to one of more than ordinary freedom, brought with it inducements to mix with the inhabitants to a degree which was attended with unavoidable temptation. The danger was greatly augmented by the wretched moral condition of the lower orders in the towns, whose ignorance and profligacy rendered their society ruinous to all who kept it. These circumstances gave rise to an increase of military offences; but amidst all their errors, the genuine good sense and intelligence of the men, and the restraining influence of the excellent moral education which distinguishes their country, generally brought them back in the end to the path of duty, without the necessity of severe coercion; and it may be said to their honour, that desertion was as yet altogether unknown. Intemperance, at this period, was only too common amongst the peasantry of Ireland, and its influence could not but be productive of breaches of discipline in regiments quartered in that country.

1823. The Regiment was inspected by Sir John Lambert, on the 14th of June and the 11th of October.

1824. In January, 1824, the Cameronians were removed to Kinsale and out-posts, which extended southward to Bere Island, in Bantry Bay, and to Macromp westward.* These detachments were afterwards increased by a sergeant's party, which occupied Camden Fort, at the mouth of Cork harbour, shortly before the inspection by Sir John Lambert, on the 20th of May. On the 4th of September a captain's party of one hundred men was sent, for a short time, to do duty in Cork; and so great was then the dispersion of the Regiment, that when Sir John came, on the 1st of October, to make his half-yearly inspection, there were not one hundred men at head-quarters.

Though a wild and unfrequented part of this great country, the greatest tranquillity prevailed among the people, so that the men were rarely called upon for duty. They passed their time very quietly in these quarters, which were much liked; but the breaking up of a regiment in this way is adverse to the preservation both of military and moral discipline, as it tends to idleness, by withdrawing many of the ordinary occupations of the soldier, and encourages too free an intercourse with the people.

In October, the Cameronians relieved the 29th Regiment, at Tralee, having detachments at Killarney, Listowel, and Tarbert, and afterwards at Castle Island. The 26th remained in these quarters till August,

1825. 1825, and were inspected by Lieut.-General Sir John Lambert, K.C.B., in June, just before that officer quitted

---

* *Vide* Appendix 1.

the staff of Ireland, where he rendered good services to the country during a period of violent domestic agitation, by measures at once firm, but conciliatory, and repressive of party violence. The Regiment was thus under his orders nearly three years, and obtained frequent expressions of his approbation.

1825.

The augmentation of the establishment of the Regiment from eight to ten companies, took place from the 25th of March, 1825; six companies were fixed at four sergeants, one drummer, and eighty-six rank and file each, and four at three sergeants, one drummer, and fifty-six rank and file. Recruiting parties were immediately sent to Scotland in addition to those permanently stationed at Glasgow and Edinburgh. Owing to the very great distance at which the Cameronians were then placed from their resources, it was not practicable so promptly to complete their new establishment, as those corps did which recruited on the spot. This circumstance gave the latter an appearance of advantage; but the continued popularity of the Regiment in its own country is strongly shown by one hundred and forty-eight recruits having joined during the last eight months of 1825, and one hundred and thirty-six more in the first six months of 1826; so that a body of two hundred and eighty-four men were raised in fourteen months, who nearly all came from Scotland.

In thus applying to their countrymen to complete their ranks, the Cameronians, as they had not been in Scotland, as a regiment, since 1803, except the second battalion, which was disbanded there in 1814, had to contend against great disadvantages. The long period of their absence, the distance from their country when the recruiting commenced, the small number of men who had been able to obtain furloughs to see their

1825. friends, and the consequently very limited intercourse which had subsisted between them and their countrymen, were circumstances which could not but have a tendency to diminish local influence. Notwithstanding all these disadvantages, however, the established character of the Regiment operated so powerfully in its favour, that if there had not been a large proportion of old soldiers to discharge, which produced a continued diminution of numbers, the establishment would have been completed early in 1826.* Had not also the distance to which the parties were sent, been so great, which rendered the commencement nearly two months later than was the case with corps recruited in Ireland, the Cameronians would have probably been complete as early as any other regiment.

---

* The establishment being nearly completed in June, 1826, the recruiting was then confined to the higher standard of five feet eight inches; yet, before the end of the year, twenty-three more recruits had joined. The casualties, however, were that year large, being one hundred and thirty-five men, whilst the increase amounted to one hundred and eighty-six, which left a balance in favour of the Regiment of fifty-one. The next year, 1827, the recruiting was still very successful, and though dependent on the regular parties, after the additional ones had been withdrawn between May and July, it produced one hundred and twenty-nine men, whereby there was in December a surplus over the establishment.

From 1807 to 1817, only forty-seven recruits were obtained, its requirements being met by volunteers from the Army of Reserve and from the Scottish Militia; but from 1818 to 1827, seven hundred and eighty-four recruits joined. The number of casualties, from 1807 to 1827 inclusive, amounted to five hundred and sixty-one dead, one thousand three hundred and twenty-five discharged, and two hundred and thirteen deserted. Rejoined from desertion, one hundred and twenty-eight. The average strength in non-commissioned officers and men during these twenty-one years was seven hundred and seventy.

On the 1st of August the 26th commenced their march to Limerick, proceeding through Castle Island and Rathkeale. Their stay in Limerick was very short. A sudden order, which left barely time for their inspection, on the 1st of October, by Major-General Sir Charles William Doyle, C.B., caused them to commence their march for Naas, on the 3rd, where the head-quarters arrived on the 7th, relieving the 73rd. One company was detached to Wicklow, one to Trim, and three to Drogheda, with smaller detachments at Baltinglass, Rathangan, Robertstown and Kilcock.* At these stations the Regiment continued during the remainder of 1825, and until May of the following year. On the 27th of March, 1826, the detachment at Drogheda was withdrawn, and upon its return a company was sent to Carlow, one to Athy, and another to Maryborough, which somewhat diminished the number of men at head-quarters, and small parties were subsequently placed in the mountain barracks in Wicklow.

In consequence of the riots in Lancashire, the 73rd and 58th Regiments were suddenly ordered from Dublin to England, but they shortly afterwards returned to Ireland. The Cameronians, then at Naas, received a route at midnight on the 2nd of May, in conformity with which they marched the next morning, at six, to Dublin, and occupied the Royal Barracks. The other detachments came in as soon as relieved, except the company at Wicklow, which did not join till the 10th of August. The Regiment remained the rest of the year in the Irish metropolis, and was inspected on the 20th of May by Lieut.-General Sir George Murray, G.C.B., and on

---

* *Vide* Appendix 1.

1826. the 14th of September by Major-General Sir Colquhoun Grant, K.C.B.

After the removal of the Regiment to Naas, but in a still more striking degree whilst in Dublin, the crime of desertion, which had been always very rare, increased to a remarkable extent. During its stay at Naas, there were thirteen, and at Dublin, between May and November, twenty-one cases, of which several were immediately, and others more remotely, recovered to the service.* This can only be attributed to the state of demoralization produced by the society to which the men were exposed in places depressed by poverty, and the resort of the most profligate characters. To such, a soldier is always a prey of sufficient value to induce them to exert their arts for his ruin, to fully avoid which, required the exercise of prudence and self-government. In this way so many as thirty-eight were tempted to violate their oaths of allegiance, some of whom never repented of their crime and returned to their colours. With the increase of this most aggravated offence, others of a minor nature were also frequent, to the injury both of moral and military discipline. Some severe corporal punishments proved insufficient; and other measures were adopted which checked the growing evil. Notwithstanding this deterioration, the general conduct of the Regiment was highly creditable,

---

* From 1818 to 1825, only thirty-seven men deserted from the Cameronians, and twenty-two rejoined from desertion. The Regiment during these eight years averaged six hundred and sixty-five non-commissioned officers and men. From 1826 to 1827, forty-two men deserted, and twenty-seven rejoined from desertion, on an average strength of seven hundred and twenty-eight.

especially after its removal in January, 1827, from the Royal to Richmond Barracks; and it might, without partiality, be deemed equal, if not superior to that of most other corps.

In July the Regiment was removed to Waterford, Kilkenny, Wexford, Duncannon, Carrick, and Kilmackthomas, its head-quarters being at the first-named town. The three companies at Kilkenny were removed on the 14th of August to Waterford.

Towards the end of September, orders were sent from the Horse Guards for the removal of the 26th, 58th, 61st, and 72nd Regiments to England, with a view to their being held in readiness for colonial service. The Cameronians were gradually relieved at their several stations between the 19th of September and the 5th of October, on which day they were all assembled at Fermoy. On the 9th, they marched into Cork Barracks, and the first division embarked on the 19th in the "Stentor" transport; the second on the 26th, in the "Lord Suffield;" and the third division in the "Flora," on the 1st of November. The first two divisions landed at Gravesend on the 5th of November, and marched the same day into Chatham Barracks, where the third arrived on the 12th of that month: here the Regiment continued the remainder of the year.

The 26th had been reviewed by Lieut.-General Sir George Murray, G.C.B., on the 10th of April, and were inspected by Major-General Sir Colquhoun Grant, K.C.B., on the 7th of May, at Dublin, and at Cork, on the 13th of October, by Major-General Sir George R. Bingham, K.C.B., who severally expressed their approbation of the general conduct and appearance of the corps.

When the Regiment embarked at Cork, as its destination was supposed to be India, permission was given

1827. to take on board twelve women to each hundred men, whereby all but fourteen of the soldiers' wives were provided with a passage. Of these, some took the allowance to go home, and others made their way after their husbands, by Bristol to Chatham. It is always a most difficult point to prevent marriages in a regiment extending beyond the means of providing for the wives and families on embarkation for foreign service, but the Cameronians, from judicious management and careful superintendence, and their destination allowing a larger proportion of women, did not suffer materially in this respect.

During its stay at Chatham every effort was made to render the Regiment efficient by removing such of the older soldiers as were not likely to be fit for service in India, after which it was reported in November, 1827, as complete in numbers, and then all recruiting was forbidden, notwithstanding that every effort was made to obtain permission to increase the corps to its future Indian establishment. Sufficient recruits to complete the Regiment to this augmented strength could at once have been easily procured, had not the order in question been issued. Owing, however, to the discharge of men that afterwards took place, the order for recruiting was
1828. renewed in February, 1828.

Although there was little doubt of the 26th being embarked in the course of the spring, and that Madras would be the destination of the Regiment, yet the official intimation was not given till the 7th of February. This delay in the promulgation of the order arose from the unwillingness of the Court of Directors that any fresh regiment should be sent out. Their wish was to bring home the 30th, 47th, and 59th, without being replaced. It was, however, overruled by the Cabinet, which determined that the number of the King's regiments should not be diminished, but that their establishment should be lowered, whereby a reduction of expense to the India Company, though in a different mode, would be effected.

After this official notification, the Court of Directors appeared to entertain the hope of a change of counsels, as they did not take up tonnage for the conveyance of the Regiment till the month of April, when the four following ships were assigned for this service. The arrangements made for the distribution of the Regiment in these four vessels were two hundred and ten non-commissioned officers and men in the "Rose," one hundred and seventy in the "Prince Regent," one hundred and ninety-seven in the "Asia," and one hundred and ninety-six in the "Marchioness of Ely." The first two received their proportion on the 9th of May—the baggage, with a large guard, having been put on board the day previously. The total number embarked amounted to thirty-eight officers, thirty-nine sergeants, twenty drummers, and seven hundred and fourteen rank and file. The head-quarter division, under the command of Lieut.-Colonel Henry Oglander, proceeded in the "Rose" on the 22nd of May, and the "Asia" and the "Marchioness of Ely" sailed on the day following. The "Prince Regent" and "Rose" started together, but experienced a gale in the Bay of Biscay, when the two ships separated. On the 15th of July these vessels again came close to each other, but on the 30th once more parted company. On the 30th of August two large ships were in sight of the "Rose," which the next day proved to be the "Prince Regent" and the "Asia." On the 6th of September, the "Prince Regent" was again in sight, and early on the morning of the 10th the "Rose" anchored in Madras Roads a few hours after the "Prince Regent." The "Asia" and "Marchioness of Ely" had a better passage across the

1828. Bay, and, being superior in sailing to the other two ships, fairly beat them, and reached their destination first; but the arrival of the four divisions of the Regiment with an interval of only forty-eight hours, was, however, a very fortunate termination of their voyage, and rendered the arrangements for landing and the occupation of their quarters in Fort St. George most convenient. The division from the "Asia" landed on the 9th, that from the "Marchioness of Ely" on the 10th, and that from the "Rose" and "Prince Regent" on the 11th. Nothing could exceed the healthiness of the men, among whom there was no serious sickness, and but little of any kind. The only man that died was Mitchell Douglass, who was very ill of consumption on embarkation, and, being unwilling to be left behind, was allowed to try the effect of the voyage. He died, however, on the 23rd of June.

Thus the Cameronians for the first time in their career were brought on service in the East Indies. They landed later than European troops generally arrive in that country, as they usually embark in the early ships. The great heat had passed by, but September, October, and November, are not the healthiest months. Though a considerable number of men passed through the hospital, yet the cases would have been slight, but for the occurrence of cholera. This fearful disease was not then generally prevalent, and the cases which occurred in the 26th were considered as sporadic. Under all circumstances, the Regiment was deemed to be remarkably healthy, which may be attributed to the men being generally of sober and regular habits, to every precaution being used to check excesses (whether in liquor or in the use of fruits), and to ensure a regular diet of four meals a day—the first, a pint of coffee-water taken before any man turned out for duty, parade, or exercise; the second, a breakfast of tea or coffee at half-past seven; the third, a dinner of meat and vegetables at two; and the fourth, a supper of tea or coffee at half-past seven.

By a watchful superintendence, and an appeal to the soldier's reason, the flannel belt and woollen bedgown were worn with tolerable regularity; and their use proved a great preservative against disease. Much attention was given to prevent unnecessary exposure to the sun; and by limiting the hours, and seeking for shady places, even the drill of the recruits was carried on without any increased sickness being observable among them. To avoid wet feet, from the morning dew, is also of consequence, and therefore the evening was chosen for exercise in the field, whether of the squad or of the corps; and till the time of inspection, the 26th were rarely taken beyond the fort.

The recruiting, which had taken effect in March, was continued after the departure of the Regiment, and proved so successful, that sixty-eight men were raised before the 24th of July, when it ceased, the establishment having been exceeded. The depôt was thus rendered strong, and its appearance, and the conduct of the men, were stated to be very creditable; but unhappily they were not allowed to remain in the Regiment. Calculating on the effect of the volunteering from corps about to return home, to complete the deficiencies in the Cameronians, the Commander-in-Chief directed that the depôt should be drafted into regiments thus circumstanced, to effect which, a bounty was offered as an inducement to the men to change; so that the depôt, from which a fresh supply of good soldiers was expected, became reduced nearly to a skeleton, since there only remained a few undersized men, with some old soldiers, who were awaiting their discharge.

1828. In India, two hundred and thirty-four men were transferred from the 30th Regiment, a considerable proportion of whom were neither an acquisition either in appearance or in morals. These men joined on the 5th of November, which made the 26th the strongest corps in the Presidency. Immediate measures were adopted to supply the volunteers with clothing and accoutrements; this was effected partly before the end of 1828, and completed early in the following year, the stores of the Company furnishing a portion of the articles required, and the remainder being made according to pattern by native workmen. Though some articles were not of as good a quality, as they would have been if furnished from England, their average price was less, and the decided advantage of immediate equipment was gained, which could not have been otherwise effected in less than twelve months. The Regiment was inspected by Major-General Sir John Doveton, on the 8th of December.

1829. The Cameronians remained the whole of 1829 at Fort St. George, the year being passed in perfect tranquillity and without any remarkable occurrence. They were inspected on the 30th May, by Major-General Sir John Doveton, and on the 19th December, by Brigadier-General Andrew Macdowall, C.B.

Throughout the year the men were very healthy, the loss by death being only nineteen.

1830. From the 1st of January, 1830, to the 30th of September, the Cameronians remained in garrison in Fort St. George; their half-yearly inspection being made on the 24th of May, by Brigadier-General Andrew Macdowall, C.B., when the Regiment was commanded by Major Mountain. Various rumours had been some time current as to its removal to Bengal, but no certain information was received till July, when, besides the relief of 1830. the 89th and Royals by the 55th and 62nd, the Cameronians were directed, after the arrival of the 57th from New South Wales, to proceed to Calcutta, to replace the 14th Regiment.

It being the wish of Lieut.-General Sir George Townshend Walker, G.C.B., that the Cameronians should be removed to Bangalore, as it would have saved expense to have sent on the 57th to Bengal, whenever they might reach Madras Roads, application was made to General the Earl of Dalhousie, G.C.B., Commander-in-Chief in India, to authorise this deviation from the orders sent from home, and Bangalore continued therefore nearly to the last moment to be regarded as the future station of the Regiment; but as no reply was received from his lordship, then at Penang, the Governor in Council decided, on the arrival of part of the 55th, that the Cameronians should embark in the ships which brought that and the 62nd, as they arrived.

The head-quarter division accordingly embarked, on the 30th of September, in the Honourable Company's chartered ship "Malcolm," which sailing on the morning of the 2nd of October, reached Calcutta on the 10th. The second division, under Captain William Johnstone, embarked in the chartered ship "Lady Kennaway" on the 2nd and arrived at Calcutta on the 10th of October. These divisions were transhipped into two steamers on the morning of the 11th, and landed at Chinsurah at three p.m. of the same day. The third division, under Captain Michael Poynton, embarked in the ship "Protector" on the 6th of October, and reaching Calcutta on the 23rd, passed up the river in boats to Chinsurah, where it landed on the 25th of that month. The fourth division, under Major Armine Simcoe Henry

1830. Mountain, which quitted Madras Roads in the "Marquis of Hastings" on the 9th of October, arrived at Calcutta on the 30th of October, and Chinsurah on the 2nd of November. The last division, under Captain Henry Francis Strange, in the ship "Susan," was placed in boats at Calcutta on the 4th and joined the Regiment on the 5th of November. Thus, in the space of thirty-six days, the removal of the Cameronians from Fort St. George to Chinsurah was completed, with the loss of only two men, who died at sea. A small party of sick, and a few others, in number twenty-eight, remained at Madras.

On the return of the Earl of Dalhousie from Penang, after a short hesitation relative to the future station of the 26th, it was decided that they should march to Kurnaul, which, though a distance of nearly one thousand miles, would, after their long stay at Fort St. George, afford them a favourable change of climate. The 1st, 10th and 20th of November, and 1st of December, were successively fixed for the commencement of the march, and on the 7th of December, the Regiment actually moved from Chinsurah into camp at Tarragonee, where, however, it was detained till the 16th, owing to the Chowdry, who had contracted to supply two hundred and forty-one hackories for the conveyance of the baggage of the officers and men, proving deficient in about one hundred of that number. In the interval, the requisite supply was obtained through the commissariat, and the Regiment resuming its march on the 16th of December, proceeded by Burdwan to Bancoorah, and encamped at Arrard on the last day of the year, having then proceeded one hundred and twenty-six miles.

The loss suffered by death was this year greater than the last, being altogether thirty-one—thirteen died at

Madras, two on the passage, fifteen at Chinsurah, and one after embarkation on the river.

The sickness at Chinsurah was considerable, and, owing to the frequency of cholera in its worst form, it often proved fatal; yet no sooner was the Regiment encamped than it ceased, the whole number of admissions from the 7th to the 31st of December being reduced to twenty-four, and only seven were in the hospital tent on the latter day. Sixteen of the men left sick at Madras had been embarked, but were ordered ashore by the Inspector of Hospitals, owing to the crowded state of the ship. Most of these, shortly after, recovered.

On the 6th of January, 1831, the Regiment reached Chass, no considerable local difficulty having been experienced on the march, except the passage of the Dammoodah near Burdwan on the 22nd of December.

The country being flat and at this season dry, and not intersected with rivers and nullahs, the road, though often very inefficiently made and repaired, was practicable for the hackory, which is the sole mode of conveyance in Bengal. The ox of that presidency, though small, draws with ease the light country cart of bamboos, carrying a load of from six hundred and forty to eight hundred pounds.

During the nine following marches, which were attended with great difficulty, the Regiment passed through the beautiful and picturesque district of Ramghur. An extensive line of hills, which, in some places, rose three thousand feet above the sea, was passed over, and though the road had been made with skill, yet from its imperfect condition, and the frequency of the declivities, the baggage occasioned much delay. The oxen became unequal to the task of dragging the carts up the hills, and across the beds of the rivers and nullahs. From

1831. fatigue and sickness occasioned by the extreme cold, the thermometer having for many days been below freezing point, and once at twenty-four, so that these animals died in great numbers. Both the commissariat and private baggage suffered so much, that it was only by halts and by putting the whole resources of the district in requisition, and by the aid of constant and large fatigue parties, that the Regiment reached Hazareebagh on the 14th of January. Ramghur is a country which has little land reclaimed from jungle, though all very susceptible of cultivation; and the Saggur oxen are so small and wild as to be very unfit for the yoke in the Bengal hackory. Though two companies were at work on fatigue till past mid-day, the distress had become so serious at Chittroo Chuttee on the 11th, that one-half of the men's boxes were broken up to lighten the loads, and they marched to Hazareebagh with knapsacks. With every effort some of the baggage remained behind, which did not come up during the halt at Hazareebagh, and was therefore brought to Benares, where it was embarked in boats. At Hazareebagh some public draught oxen and a portion of pack bullocks were procured, with which the baggage was conveyed to Sheirgatty without much difficulty. At this place the Collector had procured a considerable supply of fresh hackories, which rendered the further progress to Benares a matter of comparative ease. No assistance from the fatigue parties was required after passing Hazareebagh, except at the Soane, where as at the Dammoodah, the whole Regiment was employed during the heat of the day and relieved at night by the coolies. The deep sandy beds of these rivers occasioned much more labour than the ferries. In the Dammoodah there was one stream only to be passed in boats, but in the Soane there were two. Many of the smaller streams which, would have occasioned great loss of time and of cattle, were made nearly as good as the highway, by the simple expedient of laying clay on the sand, which formed an excellent road. For this idea the Regiment was indebted to the Assistant-Collector, Mr. Neave, whose zeal and intelligence had greatly contributed to smooth the obstacles which impeded its progress through this difficult but beautiful country. At Benares, the passage of the river was a matter of comparative ease, as there was not much sand, and the river deep but not broad, with plenty of boats.

The Regiment encamped at Secrole from the 4th to the 6th of February inclusive. The new hackories, with the fine oxen of Cawnpore, which were ready for use at Benares, enabled it to move along the excellent broad road to Allahabad.without any difficulty, and the crossing of the Ganges was easily effected in one day, although there was a ferry and a large tract of sand to pass. On the 22nd, 23rd, and 24th of February some inconvenience was felt from the deep state of the road, occasioned by the heavy fall of rain on the three previous days, during which the Regiment halted at Chanby Serai. These rains had a very favourable influence on the weather, which continued cool till after the 26th reached Meerut. No obstacle occurred during the march, which was continued, with only the halt on Sundays, till the Regiment arrived at the barracks at that station on the morning of Saturday the 26th of March.

Thus was successfully terminated a journey of unusual length for a King's regiment in India. The total distance was nine hundred and five miles, which was performed in eighty marches, being somewhat over eleven and a half daily. The longest march was sixteen, the shortest under three, miles.

1831. The men were very healthy, especially during the first month, when the sick list fluctuated from six to eighteen, afterwards it increased to thirty, but never exceeded forty, and only two men died—one of cholera at Ranee-kee Tolea, and one of apoplexy at Bolundshuhur.

Supplies from the commissariat were excellent, and regular—one pound of biscuit, one and a half of beef, two drams of rum, were the daily allowance to Benares; thence, to Meerut, bread, which was generally of good quality, in place of biscuit.

The remainder of the year passed over without anything remarkable. The barracks afforded every comfort and accommodation; but after a fire in the cavalry line, the 16th Lancers were obliged to send a detachment, which occupied the four rear lines of the new, and the two rear lines of the old barracks from 1st June till October, which occasioned an uncomfortable crowding.

The detachment which left Chinsurah by the river on the 6th of December, 1830, and consisted of thirty-eight sick and forty-six married and weakly men, arrived at Meerut on the 16th of May, having lost one by disease and one by accidental drowning—seven were still sick. The difficulties and delays experienced by this small detachment afforded a strong example how much the march by land is preferable to the river navigation.

On the 2nd of May and the 22nd of November, the Regiment was inspected by Major-General Sir Samford Whittingham, K.C.B., K.C.H., who, on both occasions, expressed his full satisfaction with its appearance and conduct. General the Earl of Dalhousie, G.C.B., also visited the Cameronians in October. He arrived on the 24th and departed on the 29th of that month to rejoin his camp at Delhi.

During 1831 the Regiment was generally healthy; it

lost twenty-four men, of whom four died by accident; ten of the twenty-four were absent from the corps at the time of their decease. The total of admissions into hospital —including those from the river party, numbered seven hundred and seventy-nine, being fifty-one less than in 1830, and one hundred and sixty-nine less than in 1829. The other casualties amounted to ten—two sent home as invalids, five transferred, two discharged by purchase, and one on expiration of limited service.

The year 1832 was passed in undisturbed tranquillity at Meerut, and unmarked by any event of note. The successor to the Earl of Dalhousie, as Commander-in-Chief in India, General Sir Edward Barnes, G.C.B., reviewed the Regiment, with other corps, in line on the 14th of March, 1832, and again on the 3rd of December, when he inspected it separately. On both occasions he expressed his satisfaction at its appearance.

Brigadier David Ximines, Lieut.-Colonel of the 16th Foot, made the first half-yearly inspection of the Regiment, on the 7th of May, and Major-General Sir Samford Whittingham, the second; both signified their favourable opinion of its appearance and conduct.

In 1832, the health of the Regiment was not so good as in 1831, owing chiefly to an epidemic catarrh in April, and its sequence in the hot and rainy season. The admissions into hospital were nine hundred and ninety-five, being two hundred and sixteen in excess of the previous year. The deaths were, however, two less, all except three being at head-quarters, and, with two exceptions, from disease. The other casualties were twenty-six; of which twenty-three were discharges.

No material change in the situation or circumstances of the Regiment occurred during 1833. The Commander-in-Chief, Sir Edward Barnes, proposed its re-

1833. moval to Ghazeepore, to make way for the 16th Foot; but his recommendation was not acceded to by the Governor-General in Council, on account of expense, and the 26th therefore continued at Meerut, which was considered the best station in India. The first half-yearly inspection was made by Brigadier Sir David Ximines, K.C.H., on the 4th of May, and the second by Major-General the Honourable John Ramsay, on the 3rd of December; both these officers expressed their good opinion of the appearance, discipline, and conduct of the corps.

Notwithstanding the extraordinary heat of the summer and autumn, the admissions into hospital were three hundred and two less than in the previous year, and the deaths were diminished by seven, which, with due allowance for reduced numbers, proved a better state of health. It is remarkable, however, that both dysentery and hepatitis, two of the most ruinous enemies to the constitution with which Europeans have to contend in India, had considerably increased, although the total number of admissions were so greatly diminished. It is much to be feared that the use of ardent spirits, restricted as it was, contributed mainly to create a predisposition to these diseases. Besides the fifteen deaths, there were fifty other casualties, of which forty-six were from discharges, including four invalids.

From the 1st of January, of this year, the embroidery of the officers' uniform was changed from silver to gold, in conformity to the general orders from the Horse Guards on the subject, Nos. 495 and 503, dated 25th of September, 1830, and 18th of May, 1831.

1834. Meerut continued to be the station of the Regiment during the year 1834, with one short exception. On the 21st of August, a totally unexpected order of immediate preparation for service in the field was received, but no 1834. destination was stated. Report, however, indicated the Rajpoot principality of Marwar as the object of attack, which, in the result, proved correct. Subsequent orders intimated a delay in the march, which was fixed for the 24th of September, and it was further postponed to the 1st of October, on which day the Regiment left Meerut. Its progress was arrested by the receipt, on the night of the 11th, of a letter from Major Alves, the political agent in Rajpootana, in which he recommended the corps to be halted till instructions should be received from Brigadier-General Stevenson.

This change arose from the amicable arrangement of the differences with the Rajah of Joudpore, who had prudently yielded all the points in dispute. On the 14th, an order was received for the Cameronians and two squadrons of the 11th Dragoons to return to Meerut, where they arrived on the 25th. The country between that station and a village within six miles of Rewaree, the extreme point reached by the Regiment, presented few objects worthy of notice, except Delhi. In the advance, the road to the Sohulke Sevai left all the antiquities of Delhi unseen; but on the return, that through Maroulee afforded a complete view of them. The rendezvous assigned for the formation of the army was distant from Meerut two hundred and seventy-four miles, of which only eighty-seven were marched. The equipment was complete. The baggage of the officers and men was carried entirely on camels, of which eighty-four were employed for the former and one hundred and fifty-five for the latter. The average weight of each soldier's kit was twenty seers, in which were included his knapsack, coatee, and bedding. Each company had one camel for stores.

1834. The Regiment was inspected on the 5th of May and on the 5th of December by Major-General the Honourable John Ramsay, who on both occasions expressed his satisfaction with regard to its field discipline and internal economy.

Orders were issued from the Horse Guards, on the 17th March, for recruiting to recommence in Scotland, but as only one sergeant, one corporal, and five privates were employed, little progress was made therein.

1835. No change took place in the station of the Regiment during 1835; but it was included in the autumnal schedule of reliefs for removal to Ghazeepore, the 3rd Buffs having been appointed to replace it at Meerut.

The half-yearly inspections were made on the 8th of May and the 22nd of December, with the usual results, by Major-General the Honourable John Ramsay.

In November, sixty-two recruits and one old soldier landed at Calcutta, and in the following month they embarked in boats to join the head-quarters. Four men from the 38th, which regiment embarked for England, in December, volunteered for the Cameronians. Notwithstanding that the year was remarkably favourable to health, the deaths equalled those in 1834, but there was a decrease in the admissions to hospital. The number invalided was small, being only six.

As the arrival of the 3rd Buffs at Meerut had been fixed for the 5th of January, 1836, preparations were made for the 26th Cameronians to encamp at Kurkowda on that day, the two regiments passing each other on the road. The hospital was broken up on the 27th of December, and the detachment of sick, convalescent, and married men, under Captain William Cain, left Meerut for Ghurmuckliour, on the 28th. It consisted of five sergeants, eight corporals, one drummer, eighty-four privates, sixty-four women, and one hundred-and-twenty children. They embarked on the 31st December, and leaving the Ghauts on the 2nd of January, after a passage rendered tedious by the shallowness of the river and by contrary winds, arrived at Ghazeepore on the 8th of February. Here the recruits, who had embarked at Calcutta on the 6th of December, as a part of a large battalion of detachments, joined on the 10th of February.

The Regiment having proceeded into camp on the 5th of January, as previously arranged, was enabled to continue its march on the 9th, all its equipments and supplies having been completed on the previous day. The journey terminated on the 29th of February, after forty-five marches and eight Sabbath-days' halt, in addition to the three at the Camp of Kurkowda. The men of both the water detachments were very healthy, and but one died of cholera. The Regiment was also very healthy, the sick ranging only from five to twelve daily, with one death.

Having occupied its new station on the 29th of February, 1836, the Regiment expected to have remained therein for the usual period, but to its great surprise, was included in the change of quarters for the approaching cold season. The 44th Regiment, from Fort William, having been named to replace the Cameronians, the latter were finally ordered to commence their march to Calcutta on the 1st of December.

The recruits of 1835 who had joined at Ghazeepore, generally proved an acquisition to the Regiment, and only eighteen men left it; of these recruits eight died within twelve months.

As Brigadier-General White's health did not admit of his visiting Ghazeepore, the half-yearly inspection was not regularly made in May, neither was there any in

1836. November, previous to the march, but the Regiment was reviewed on the 10th of October, by General Sir Henry Fane, G.C.B., who was pleased to express his satisfaction at its general appearance and conduct.

During the nine months the 26th remained at Ghazeepore, the climate proved very unfavourable to health. In March, April, and May, the admissions into hospital were within the average of the seven previous years; but towards the end of May, three cases of cholera occurred, and this disease rapidly increased. The hospital became a scene of horror and distress, which demanded, and happily received, every exertion of moral courage and of medical skill, to meet its almost overwhelming duties. Some alarm was excited lest further injury should spring from the building being so crowded; but happily the disease abated with the setting in of the rains, and disappeared as the wet season advanced. During the continuance of cholera, there was little other disease; the admissions in July, August, September, and October, were beyond the usual average, and in the last half of September, and early in October, a severe but not fatal fever prevailed, so that when General Sir Henry Fane, G.C.B., Commander-in-Chief in India, visited the hospital at his inspection, there were one hundred and eleven patients. The men's health rapidly improved in November, and all those with the Regiment, on the 1st of December, were fit to march.

On the morning of the 1st of December, the 26th crossed to the right on the Ganges, and continuing their march, with only Sabbath-day halts, reached Ghyretty

1837. at half-past six a.m., on the 13th of January, 1837, when the men and baggage immediately embarked in the boats which brought up the 44th Regiment, and dropped down with the tide to Fort William, disembarking thereat during the evening of the same day; the men encamped on the glacis until the 17th, when, at sunrise, they marched into and occupied the fort barracks. As about one hundred and seventy camels had been procured from Agra, of which sixty-five were for the use of the non-commissioned officers and men, and the remainder for the officers, the difficulties encountered in 1830-31, on the same line of road in the march to Meerut, were not again experienced.

The greater part of those who proceeded by water were convalescent, and their health became so improved on the passage down the Ganges, that only seven were in hospital on the arrival of the corps at Fort William. The mortality during the preceding year was greater than any which had occurred during the service of the Regiment in India; of the fifty deaths, thirty arose from cholera, otherwise the difference, twenty, would have been two and a half below the previous annual average.

Colonel Oglander, who had held the command of the Regiment since March, 1818, having been appointed Brigadier at Cawnpore, resigned the command of it at Hazareebagh, while *en route* to Calcutta, on the 19th of December, 1836, to Lieut.-Colonel William James.

The year 1837 was passed in Fort William. The health of the Regiment, considering the general insalubrity of the climate of Bengal, and of that of Calcutta in particular, was good. The number daily in hospital amounted to sixty-one, which, out of an average strength of six hundred and eighty, was a higher rate than had been before experienced, but still much lower than was usual at the station, and the deaths, considered a large number elsewhere, constituted a moderate mortality for Calcutta. The average death-rate for eleven years

1837. amongst the regular army in this garrison was sixty-six. The deaths in the 26th, in 1837, amounted to thirty, three of which were from cholera. This more favourable state of health in the Regiment was partly due to the existence of a Temperance Society, which, though before attempted, had encountered so much opposition, that it failed; but happily, at Calcutta, circumstances occurred which favoured its formation.

The summer inspection was made on the 27th of May, by Brigadier-General Penny, and the winter one by Major-General Sir Willoughby Cotton, K.C.H., on the 15th of December, on which occasions Lieut.-Colonel James had the satisfaction of receiving those officers' approval of the appearance and conduct of the Regiment.

During the year, fifty-seven recruits and old soldiers joined from home, and twenty volunteers from the 20th and 45th Regiments. The recruits would have been eighty-two had not volunteering been authorised at Chatham, to fill up the former corps, to which twenty-nine of them transferred their services. The 26th had long been below their establishment, notwithstanding every effort having been made to recruit; but as men can only be enlisted after vacancies become known in England, a deficiency was almost inevitable; and the large number of men likely to be reported non-effective, rendered it desirable for the depôt to be excepted from this volunteering, which caused the loss of its best recruits.

Major-General Sir John Colborne (afterwards Lord Seaton), G.C.B. and G.C.H., was removed from the 94th to the colonelcy of the 26th or Cameronian Regi-
1838. ment on the 28th of March, 1838, in succession to General the Earl of Dalhousie, G.C.B., deceased.

No remarkable event occurred during 1838, to break the monotony of the duties of the garrison of Fort

William, where the Regiment continued throughout the year. Its health was good, notwithstanding an attack of cholera in March and April. The average strength was six hundred and thirty-six.

The Temperance Society still continued its operation, and though the number of members was fluctuating, yet its general result, as evinced by the improved health of the men, proved gratifying to its promoters.

Major-General Sir Willoughby Cotton, K.C.H., made the summer inspection on the 24th of May, and Major-General Faithfull the winter one, on the 28th of December. Both these officers expressed strongly their satisfaction with all which came under their notice.

Two enlistments at head-quarters, and ninety-eight men from England were insufficient to prevent the Regiment from experiencing a further decrease in its strength, but there were fewer ineffective soldiers in the ranks than formerly.

During the year 1838 the Regiment lost by death (including eight cholera cases) twenty-four men; these, with discharge and other casualties, made the decrease one hundred and thirty-seven.

Nothing of importance affecting the Regiment occurred during its continued stay at Fort William in 1839. It was only once inspected—namely, on the 30th of May—when Major-General Burgh bestowed the usual meed of praise.

The Temperance Society still maintained its firm footing, and may justly be deemed to have exercised a beneficial influence, not only with regard to morality, but also in respect of health. Many who did not adopt the pledge, doubtless, profited by an indirect influence which may have often checked the disposition to excess. The remittances to friends and the deposits in the savings' bank were this year of a respectable amount.

1839. By authority received from the Horse Guards and War Office, dated the 30th of March and the 3rd of April, 1839, the establishment of the nine companies of the Regiment in India was increased to forty-seven officers, fifty-one sergeants, eighteen drummers, and nine hundred and seventy-one rank and file; but the efforts of the recruiting parties, acting upon the popularity of the Cameronians at home, speedily produced the required supply of men, of whom one hundred and twenty-six joined in August, forty-five in November, and twelve in December, with three more at other dates. These, with five boys, enlisted at head-quarters, made an increase of one hundred and ninety-one. The casualties consisted of thirteen deaths and six discharges.

A question arose in the autumn of 1839, regarding the enlistment of Cosmo Cameron for the purpose of being employed as a Piper in the 26th Regiment. This recruit appears to have been below the standard, and a correspondence ensued on the subject, which resulted in authority being granted for his receiving the full bounty.*

1840. At the beginning of the year 1840 the Cameronians still remained at Fort William, but in February orders were received for them to prepare for active service. The Regiment having been inspected by the Commander-in-Chief in India, General Sir Jasper Nicolls, K.C.B., who spoke of it in the highest terms, embarked at Calcutta, on the 24th of March, nine hundred and two strong, namely, forty-four sergeants, sixteen drummers, and eight hundred and forty-two rank and file, leaving behind only six sick. The meritorious conduct of the

---

* The question of Pipers was also renewed in 1862, *vide* correspondence, Appendix II.

26th, whilst in garrison at Fort William, also called 1840. forth a very flattering order from the Right Honourable the Governor-General the Earl of Auckland.

A course of persecution had been pursued by the Government of China against the property and persons of British merchants trading with that empire, in consequence of the introduction by the latter of opium into that country, which, although admitted by the local authorities, was contrary to the Chinese laws; and when at length the Emperor resorted to summary measures, without sufficient notice, application was made to the Governor-General of India for assistance. The result was, that an expedition was fitted out, in order that the ruling powers of the Celestial Empire might be taught to acknowledge the principles of international law, as understood by civilized nations, and the 26th was one of the corps selected for this service.

The Regiment was commanded by Lieut.-Colonel James; but Colonel Oglander, relinquishing his sick leave and local rank as Major-General, with that zeal for the service which had always distinguished him, obtained permission to join, and overtaking it at Singapore assumed the command.

Twenty-eight officers embarked with the 26th, namely —*Lieut.-Colonel*, William James; *Captains*, William Johnstone (*Major*), James Paterson, James Piggott, George F. Mylius, John Shum; *Lieutenants*, Thomas Ffrench, William B. Staff, Edward Regan Gregg, Edmund Pomeroy Gilbert, John M. Daniell, John William Johnstone, Charles Cameron, John Rodgers, George Sweeny, Alexander Gordon Moorhead, Henry James William Postlethwaite, William Thomas Betts; *Ensigns*, John Cumming, Richard Palmer Sharp, Henry B. Phipps, Albany French Wallace, Robert Colville

1840. Jones; *Paymaster*, Richard Henry Strong; *Adjutant*, Alexander M'Donald; *Quarter Master*, Joseph Goodfellow; *Surgeon*, William Bell, M.D.; and *Assistant-Surgeon*, Chilley Pine.

The whole force (the naval portion of which was under Captain Elliot, R.N., the Queen's representative, and the military under Brigadier-General George Burrell, of the 18th Royal Irish regiment) was to rendezvous at Singapore, and the transports in which the 26th were embarked having reached Penang on the 16th of April, remained there for some days, and arrived at Singapore on the 6th of May. The entire fleet sailed for the China seas on the 30th of May, and now commenced the first of a series of misfortunes which rendered this year a most unfortunate one for the Corps. Colonel Oglander gradually sank, under an attack of dysentery which had assailed him, and died on the 22nd of June, when the ships were off the Canton river; in him the 26th lost an invaluable commanding officer, whose high talent and well-regulated mind were entirely devoted to the prosperity and happiness of the Cameronians, by whom his memory will ever be respected.

The last Memorandum dictated by this extraordinary man, on his death-bed, was to the following effect:—That with regard to the officers and men of the Regiment, they have now for so many years always had his best care, and on being removed from amongst them that feeling will accompany him as one of the sources of future enjoyment.

Chusan, the destination of the force, was reached on the 4th of July, and a landing being effected on the following day, possession was taken of Tinghae, the principal city, with scarcely any opposition on the part of the Chinese.

The 26th were encamped on a hill, within the city walls, and here the body of Colonel Oglander was deposited, none anticipating the number of his fellow soldiers by whom he was shortly to be surrounded. This hill was one mile and a half from the shore, the greater portion forming a very steep ascent, and the Regiment being without native followers had to carry their provisions and perform various other fatigue duties, which, coupled with those of a military nature, were so severe as not to give a single day of rest, and all were performed under a burning sun. Provisions (mostly salt) of the very worst description, and frequently so bad as not to be fit for use, a climate most inimical to the European constitution, and the irregularity of the ground, which would not admit of the tents being pitched so as to afford proper shelter, naturally produced fearful results— in the first six weeks this fine corps was reduced to a mass of debilitated dying soldiers. The sickness became so appalling that the Regiment was moved into the city of Tinghae in September, where the sick (over four hundred men) were placed in a large building, ill-adapted, from its site and want of glazed windows, for a hospital; here the mortality continued great, amounting in October to seventy-nine, and in November to eighty-four. An attempt had been made to re-embark the corps; this failed, from the transports which brought the 26th being filled with naval stores from Her Majesty's ship "Melville." A party was, however, actually embarked and sent to Manilla in November, and of these two hundred and sixty were Cameronians. They were selected from men who had been ill and were recovering, it being hoped that the voyage thither would benefit them; but this anticipation was, unhappily, not realized, as the mortality amongst them proved fearful. At the termi-

1840. nation of the year there were at head-quarters, Chusan, on the 31st of December, only two hundred and seventy-three men, and of them one hundred and sixty-three were sick.* The officers, though equally attacked, did not suffer in the same proportion as the men; but several contracted disease, which afterwards proved fatal; only one, however, (Lieut. John M. Daniell) died at this period.†

Whilst recording this great sickness and mortality, it may be well, in juxtaposition, to subjoin a copy of a most singular Memorandum from the Court of Directors, dated in November of this year, calling for all the details of the arrangements adopted for the internal economy of the 26th Foot, because they had noticed the comparative immunity which the Regiment had enjoyed from both :—

"*Adjutant-General's Office, Head Quarters,*
"*Calcutta,* 13*th November,* 1840.

"MEMORANDUM.

"The Honourable the Court of Directors having had

---

* The number of deaths amongst the non-commissioned officers and men, during 1840 and two succeeding years, amounted to seven hundred and seven—viz., in 1840, two hundred and forty; in 1841, two hundred and sixty-seven; and in 1842, two hundred. These were exclusive of casualties amongst those invalided home. In February, 1843, twenty-six died at Calcutta, seven on passage to England, and forty-eight at Chatham, during August.

† The following officers of the Regiment also died from disease contracted on this service. In 1841, Lieut.-Colonel William James (while on passage to England); Lieutenants William B. Staff and George Sweeny. In 1842, Major (Lieut.-Colonel) William Johnstone, Ensign Horatio De Quincey, and Assistant-Surgeon William Godfrey Bace, M.D. In 1843, Lieutenant Thomas Seccombe.

" under consideration the Report of the Medical Board 1840.
" on the health of the European troops of the Presidency,
" and having noticed the comparative immunity from
" mortality and sickness enjoyed by Her Majesty's 26th
" Regiment during the year 1838, the excellency of the
" system established in that Corps has impressed itself
" on the Honourable Court; and the Adjutant-General
" of the Army, in consequence, under instructions from
" Government, has been directed by His Excellency the
" Commander-in-Chief to request that the Adjutant-
" General, Queen's Troops, will have the goodness to
" obtain and forward to him the details of the arrange-
" ments adopted for the internal economy of Her
" Majesty's 26th Regiment, for transmission to the home
" authorities.

"(Signed)   J. R. LUMLEY,
" *Adjutant-General of the Army.*"

At the commencement of the year 1841 the Regiment 1841. was still at Chusan. The men sent to Manilla in search of health, arrived at the Canton River on the 2nd of January, but so far from being recovered they had there many deaths, and the survivors continued in a most wretched condition. One vessel, the "Defiance," having suffered in a gale of wind, was so leaky that the men had just been removed therefrom into the "Thetis." The sick and healthy were separated by putting the latter into Her Majesty's ship "Jupiter." A sudden order, however, was received on the night of the 5th of January to move up all the healthy men to the Bocca Tigris to assist in the attack upon *Cheumpee*. They at once proceeded in a steamer, reached the fleet on the evening of the 6th, and on the morning of the 7th of January were present at the attack and capture of the forts and batteries

1841. of the island. The detachments of the Queen's troops, the 26th and 49th Regiments, were under the immediate command of Brevet-Major William Johnstone, of the Cameronians; the whole force, amounting to one thousand four hundred and seventy men, were under that of Brevet-Major Thomas Simson Pratt, of the same corps, who, with those under him, was thanked in general orders, and for this service he was subsequently promoted to the rank of lieutenant-colonel in the army.

On the morning of the 8th, the troops and ships were again on the move to attack the principal forts, when the Chinese having struck their colours and begged for time to communicate with Keshen, the Imperial Commissioner, the assault was countermanded, even after a few shots had been fired, and negotiations again commenced. The result of these were that apparent peace was made, the Island of Hong Kong taken possession of by the English, and the forts at Cheumpee and Fycoctow delivered formally back. Chusan also was restored, and the whole force ordered down from the north; but either through the treachery of the Imperial Commissioner, or a change in the Emperor's council at Pekin, this treaty, which was equally disliked by the Government at home and the Chinese authorities, became null and void. Evident intentions having been displayed on their part to renew hostilities, the fleet and troops, on the 22nd of February, again moved to the Bocca Tigris, and on the 26th of that month, the formidable forts there were forthwith attacked, and carried by the combined force. Major William Johnstone again commanded the detachments of the Queen's regiments, and Brevet-Major Thomas Simson Pratt had once more the good fortune to command the land force. It being advisable to advance rapidly without awaiting the arrival of the troops from Chusan, in two days the expedition proceeded up the river, and arrived at Whampoa on the 2nd of March, when Major-General Sir Hugh Gough, K.C.B., joined, and assumed the command from that date. The troops continued to advance, and Howqua's Fort was taken possession of, without opposition, by the detachments under Major Pratt; but the progress of the force was arrested during a reconnaissance, within sight of the walls of Canton, by an announcement that negociations had again commenced.

1841.

Meanwhile the troops began to arrive from Chusan, and the head-quarters of the Regiment, joined by the detachments, were collected together with the rest of the force at the Bocca Tigris, on which all had fallen back. Here Lieut.-Colonel William James left on sick leave, and the command of the corps devolved on Brevet Lieut.-Colonel Pratt, to which rank he had been promoted on the 6th of May, of this year. The fleet having dropped down to Hong Kong Bay, preparations were being made for a move to the northward, when hostile feelings once more displaying themselves at Canton, the expedition again moved up the river on the 22nd of May, and arrived within a few miles of that place. The Regiment was ordered to land on the 24th, and take possession of the factories, and co-operate with the navy on the south side, whilst the main body, under Sir Hugh Gough, disembarked to the north of the city, and on the 25th took possession of the heights with the forts thereon. While the 26th were protecting the factories, an agreement had been made with the senior naval officer, for a simultaneous attack on the sea line; and the General having determined to escalade on the north front, sent orders for the Cameronians to join him without delay, which was

1841. effected on the 27th, and they were quartered in a joss house. Here the Regiment found, that pending certain negotiations, warlike operations had been stopped. On the morning of the 30th of May, however, the right wing was suddenly ordered out, in consequence of multitudes of armed men advancing from the interior, and collecting on every side around the British posts. The Major-General gave instructions for the 26th, with a party of the 37th Madras Native Infantry, and the Bengal Volunteers, to drive them from the opposite hills. This service was performed, the enemy retiring in all directions, and the 26th crowned the hills, the hordes of Chinese having retreated to another range. It being now nearly sunset, and a violent thunder storm setting in, directions were given for the troops to return. Some of the Chinese, thinking the firelocks would not go off from the violence of the rain (which was the case), made an attempt, by rushing at the rear of the column, to spear the men, and it became necessary to reform line, in the midst of the paddy cultivation, and use the bayonet, on which the enemy withdrew altogether.

This affair took place under a burning sun (so violent that Major Robert Becher, Deputy Quartermaster-General, dropped dead in the field), and continued from ten o'clock in the morning until eight o'clock at night, amidst perfect swamps; it was considered so creditable, that on the next day the following general order was issued by Sir Hugh Gough upon the subject.

" To the wing of the 26th Cameronians, the com-
" pany of Royal Marines, three companies of the 37th
" M. N. I., and detachment of Bengal Volunteers, who
" were engaged yesterday in repelling the advance of
" a large body of the enemy, Major-General Sir Hugh

" Gough, offers his best thanks for their steady and
" spirited conduct, which was as satisfactory to the
" Major-General as it was creditable to them.

"By order,
"A. S. H. MOUNTAIN,
"*Lieut.-Colonel, D. A. G.*"

1841.

From the 23rd to the 30th of May, during the operations before Canton, the 26th had three men killed and fifteen wounded. Lieutenant John William Johnstone was slightly wounded.

The troops were ordered out on the 31st, but no contest took place, a ransom having been offered for Canton, and a provisional treaty agreed to. On the 6th of June, the whole force re-embarked on board the several ships, which all dropped down to Hong Kong Bay, where they were subject to violent typhoons, which did much damage, but not to the vessels.

A Court of Inquiry was held this year to examine into the cause of the mortality at Chusan, of which Sir Hugh Gough was appointed president, and Lieut.-Colonel Pratt, a member.

In August, a move northwards having been determined upon, the main portion of the Cameronians was directed to continue and protect British interests in the Canton River; but three companies, under Major Johnstone, proceeded with the force to the attack of *Amoy*, situated in a fine gulf in the province of Fokien, the great tea district of China. In this they participated on the 26th of August. Major Johnstone also commanded the attack on the Island of *Koolangsoo*, and the conduct of the detachment was deemed most creditable. These companies remained in garrison there, until re-united to the head-quarters, which had been ordered up to join

o

1841. the force at Ningpo, and embarked for that purpose in Her Majesty's ship "Jupiter," on the 26th of December, having been increased in numbers by the arrival of two hundred and sixty-two recruits from England, which again raised the corps to five hundred and eighty-four men in China. Percussion muskets were issued to the Regiment immediately before starting, which were joyfully accepted, in lieu of the wretched flint-lock previously in use. Having regained health to a great extent during its stay at Hong Kong, the 26th proceeded to the north, in good heart and spirits. Lieut.-Colonel Mountain, who was with the force as Deputy Adjutant-General, and Lieut.-Colonel Pratt, were this year, for their services, appointed Companions of the most Honourable Order of the Bath.

1842. At the beginning of the year 1842, the Regiment was in the Formosa Channel, beating up to the northwards. It reached Amoy on the 9th of January, and the anchorage at St. Helen's, Chusan, on the 3rd of February, when disturbances being expected at Ningpo, the corps was suddenly ordered to proceed thither, and arrived there on the 7th of February. Here the Cameronians had an opportunity of being drilled to a certain extent, and were inspected by Sir Hugh Gough on the 1st of March, when much praise was bestowed.

About this time information was received of the death of Lieut.-Colonel James (succeeded by Lieut.-Colonel Pratt), at sea, while on passage home on medical certificate.

At dawn on the 10th of March, the Chinese, who had approached the place on the night of the 9th, attacked Ningpo, and were repulsed. The 26th, with the exception of a few men, were not engaged in this affair; but, on the 15th of that month, the head-quarters, and three companies, were directed, with other portions of the force, to proceed to Tsekee, a town about fifteen miles from Ningpo, on the hills, in the neighbourhood of which, the Chinese were stated to have a fortified camp, protected by the *élite* of their soldiery. They made rather a warm resistance, but were eventually driven off by the troops which headed the columns. A portion of the 26th Regiment was ordered to protect the guns; but the grenadier company succeeded in getting into contact with the enemy. The force advanced on the next day to the Chankee Pass, where another body was posted, and the Cameronians were on this occasion detailed to lead. On reaching the top, however, of this very formidable position, which might easily have been defended, it was found quite deserted, and the troops thereupon returned to cantonments in Ningpo.

No further operations took place until the 7th of May, when it was decided to evacuate Ningpo, and proceed northwards in order to attack *Chapoo*. The troops assembled off that city on the 17th of May, and landed on the following morning, the 26th forming the leading regiment of Colonel Schoedde's column,* and in a few hours the place was escaladed and taken. A

---

* The left column, under Colonel Schoedde (the late Lieut.-General Sir James Holmes Schoedde, K.C.B.), of the 55th Regiment, consisted of the following corps:—

	Officers.	Other Ranks.
26th Cameronians	27	521
55th Regiment	15	274
Sappers	1	25
	43	820

1842. number of Tartars retreating unto a joss-house* outside the walls, defended themselves to the last, and Lieut.-Colonel Mountain, C.B., Deputy-Adjutant General, received three severe wounds. Two men of the 26th were killed and three wounded. Lieut.-Colonel Pratt was named in the despatch.

The Regiment re-embarked on the 27th of May, and proceeded with the force to the Yangtse-Kiang, and rendezvoused off Woosung. On the 16th of June, the line of batteries there was principally taken by the naval force. The 26th landed with others and proceeded to the attack of Paoushan, a walled city, into which it was stated the Tartar soldiers had retired; the place was, however, undefended. The troops advanced, on the 19th, up the Woosung River to Shanghae, which city also offered no resistance, and remained tnere for some days, when on the 6th of July the force, now largely increased both from England and India, moved up the noble river Yangtse-Kiang, *en route* to Nankin. After sundry delays,

---

* "The rout of the Chinese soon became total, the fugitives " throwing away their arms. At this period, three hundred " Tartars, finding their retreat cut off by Her Majesty's 26th ' Regiment, threw themselves into a loop-holed joss-house, in one " of the defiles, and defended themselves a considerable time with " the most determined bravery. The artillery had no effect in " dislodging them. This check to the whole force by a handful " of men, could not be borne, and several runs were made at the " door, to burst it in and get amongst them, but without effect. " The gallant Colonel Tomlinson, of the 18th, was shot through " the neck in leading one of these assaults, and several other " officers and men fell at this spot. Ultimately, the place was " fired by rockets, and breached by bags of powder, placed under " the superintendence of Captain Pears, when about fifty of the de-" fendants were taken prisoners, but nearly all of them wounded."
—Hough's "Political and Military Events in British India."

caused by ignorance of the river, the troops reached the walled city of *Chin-Keang-foo*, one of the strongest and most important in China, situated at the entrance of the Grand Canal and having Golden Island in its neighbourhood. This place was defended by a strong body of Tartar soldiers. The troops landed on the 21st of July on different points of the city; the 26th on the north, as part of Major-General Lord Saltoun's brigade. The place was captured on both sides about the same time, the Cameronians entering by a gate which was blown in by the engineers; they had one man killed, and Ensign Charles Duperier, and seven men wounded; many, however, suffered from the extreme heat.

On the 3rd of August the Regiment again moved on to Nankin, and arrived before that city on the 7th, when the walls were seen covered with white flags, there appearing a great desire on the enemy's side to make peace. On the 11th of August the Regiment landed with the rest of Lord Saltoun's brigade, and the corps was posted in a joss-house on a hill to the northward of the city, and within one thousand yards of one of its gates, which was selected as the point of attack. The Emperor, seeing that it was impossible to offer further resistance, sued for peace, and a month was employed in drawing up the terms of a treaty, which met the most sanguine wishes of the British.

Peace being concluded, the 26th re-embarked on the 11th of September, being the last troops on shore. The whole force suffered from the intermittent and remittent fevers during its stay here, and passage down the river; but fortunately, from having plenty of native followers, and good food, the Regiment escaped the mortality which had so severely visited it in Chusan; indeed, the Cameronians were about the most healthy corps in the river. On the 5th of October they reached

1842. Chusan, and again starting from that place on the 22nd, arrived at Hong Kong on the 30th of that month: here, instead of the Regiment being joined by a body of healthy, well-drilled recruits, four hundred and thirty-nine having landed there in June, it found them a mass of emaciated dying lads; one hundred and twenty-seven had already died, whilst the survivors seemed fast following them. Immediate precautions were taken to arrest the progress of disease, by affording aid with native followers and increased medical attendance; ultimately, by a removal to hospital ships, these measures had effect to a certain extent, and though many were too far gone to recover, yet several lives were saved.

In commemoration of the services of the 26th during these campaigns, the word "CHINA" and the device of the "DRAGON" were authorised by Her Majesty to be inscribed on the regimental colour and appointments.*

---

* The following letter signified Her Majesty's authority for this additional inscription:—

"*Horse Guards,* 17*th January,* 1843.

"Sir,—I have the honour to acquaint you, by direction of the "Commander-in-Chief, that in consideration of the gallantry dis-"played by the 26th Regiment (Cameronians) when serving with "the troops recently employed under the orders of Lieut.-General "Sir Hugh Gough, upon the coasts and in the rivers of China, "Her Majesty has been graciously pleased to permit the Regiment "to bear upon its colours and appointments the word "CHINA" "and the device of the "DRAGON," in commemoration of its dis-"tinguished services.

"I have, &c.,
"JOHN MACDONALD,
"*A-G.*

"*Lieut.-General Lord Seaton, G.C.B.,*
"*Colonel of the* 26*th Regiment (Cameronians).*"

The 26th remained at Hong Kong until the 20th of 1842. December, when the portion of the force destined to return to India, embarked for Singapore, and on the last day of the year the vessel conveying it was at anchor in the roadstead of that place. Information was here received that Major Johnstone had been promoted to the brevet rank of Lieut.-Colonel for services in the Canton River, and on reaching Calcutta, it became known that this excellent officer and worthy man had died at sea on the 19th of October, 1842, when on leave on medical certificate, of disease contracted in China.

It was also on arrival at Singapore, that Lieut.-General Sir Hugh Gough, G.C.B., received a letter from the Commander-in-Chief in India, General Sir Jasper Nicolls, K.C.B., to the effect that, having to send two regiments home, he had been induced to fix on the 26th as one, because those before it on the roster were employed on the north-west frontier, and he imagined that the change to Europe would benefit the corps after the severe sickness with which it had been visited. This order was unacceptable to almost every individual in the Regiment, who, after much privation and confinement on board ship, looked forward with pleasure to return to Bengal; and, as it proved, was most unfortunate for the Cameronians, by excluding them from all participation in the future brilliant services of their heroic leader in China (who, in March, 1843, was appointed Commander-in-Chief in India), which gained for Sir Hugh Gough his peerage; while, on the other hand, a march to the upper provinces of India might have had as beneficial an influence upon the health of the men, as the long voyage to England.

The head-quarters of the Regiment arrived in Calcutta on the 7th of February, 1843, and the remaining divi-

1843. sions between the 7th and 10th, and the corps encamped on the glacis of Fort William on the 16th of that month. Lieut.-Colonel Mountain, who, on the termination of the war, had been struck off the staff, assumed command of the Cameronians on the 16th of February, and was immediately called upon to make arrangements for the embarkation of the Regiment, which was then upwards of one thousand strong, and the Governor-General's order against volunteering made it necessary to provide tonnage for all, with the exception of twenty-four left sick in hospital at Fort William.

Towards the end of the month the Gazettes arrived, containing the promotions and rewards granted by Her Majesty on the close of the China war. Captain James Paterson was promoted to a brevet majority, and Lieut.-Colonel Mountain was appointed Deputy-Adjutant General to the Queen's troops, Madras, but his Regiment being under orders for embarkation, he embarked with it.

Prior to the embarkation of the 26th for England, the following Government General Order was issued by the Honourable the President of the Council in India:—

" *Fort William,*
" *28th February,* 1843.
" No. 49 of 1843.

" Her Majesty's 26th and 49th Regiments, being
" about to return to England, the President of the
" Council of India in Council cannot permit them to
" leave the shores of India without some public ac-
" knowledgment of their gallant services.

" Both these corps had served many years in India,
" and were remarkable for exemplary conduct before
" their embarkation for China. During the protracted

"struggle in a country new to Europeans, where the 1843.
" troops were alternately exposed to great temptation
" and to harassing privations, these corps maintained
" their high character in all situations, from Canton to
" Nankin, in quarters and in the field, and they have
" now returned triumphant, having won the warm ap-
" proval of His Excellency Sir Hugh Gough, Bart. and
" G.C.B., by whom they were commanded.

" The President of the Council of India in Council,
" deeply sympathised in the sufferings and losses of
" these corps from the effect of sickness, arising from
" exposure and vicissitudes of climate upon the distant
" service on which they were employed; and now that,
" on their triumphant return to Bengal they are re-
" called to the United Kingdom, he begs thus publicly
" to assure the officers, non-commissioned officers, and
" soldiers, of both these distinguished regiments, that
" they carry with them the marked approbation of the
" Supreme Government.

" The President of the Council of India in Council
" would neglect a gratifying duty if he omitted to notice
" the report of the General in command upon the con-
" duct of the officers of the general staff of the army in
" China.

" To the heads of the departments struck off by
" general orders of the 13th instant—Lieut.-Colonel
" Mountain, C.B., Deputy Adjutant-General; Lieut.-
" Colonel Hawkins, C.B., Deputy Commissary-General;
" and Lieut.-Colonel Gough, C.B., Deputy Quarter-
" Master General;—the President of the Council of
" India in Council considers it due publicly to acknow-
" ledge their valuable and unremitting exertions.

" In thus taking leave of a body of men who, in
" conjunction with the rest of the forces serving in

1843. "China, have rendered such signal services to their "country, the President of the Council of India in "Council has the satisfaction of assuring them that "those services have been most highly appreciated, "not only by the Government of India, but by their "Sovereign, who has been pleased to direct that medals "be granted to the officers and men of Her Majesty's "and the East India Company's Naval and Military "Forces, without distinction, who took part in the "more prominent events of the war, in commemoration "of the success of Her Majesty's arms in China, and in "token of Her Majesty's high approbation.

"By order of the Honourable the President of the "Council of India in Council.

"(Signed) W. M. N. STURT, *Major,*
"*Offg. Secy. to the Govert. of India,*
"*Military Department.*"

The first division sailed in the "Auckland," under Captain Piggott, on the 26th of February, and the head-quarters in the "Queen" on the 2nd of March. The third division, in the "Maria," under Brevet Major Paterson; the fourth, in the "Bolton," under Major Strange; the fifth, in the "John Wickliffe," under Lieut.-Colonel Pratt, C.B.; and the last in the "Burrampooter," under Captain Ffrench, sailed a few days afterwards.

The "Queen" outstripped them all, and the head-quarters landed at Gravesend on the 3rd of July. This ship touched at St. Helena, and the Lieut.-Colonel landed the men for Divine Service, marching them afterwards to Napoleon's tomb, which pleased the soldiers, and made a sensation in the town, being the first time that a regiment had proceeded in a body to visit this celebrated spot. Most of the other vessels had long passages. The "Auckland" did not arrive until the 14th of August, and the "Bolton" not before the 23rd; the former was in great danger off the Cape. The "Queen" had the good fortune to arrive without the loss of a man. In the remaining ships forty-four men died on the voyage of disease contracted in China.

Before the landing of the head-quarters, the 26th had been ordered to Deal, and a route furnished accordingly; but on the following morning they were met a couple of miles from Gravesend by a staff sergeant, the bearer of a counter order, to march into Chatham Barracks, which they reached with only one case of drunkenness; this was regarded in the garrison as a creditable fact. The counter order had been given under an impression of facilitating the invaliding of the men, the Regiment being erroneously supposed to have a great number unfit for further service.

Edinburgh was fixed upon as the station of the Cameronians as soon as they should be assembled; in the meanwhile the corps took its share of garrison duties. The band, which had suffered severely in China, was sent off parade by the Commandant at Chatham, Colonel Sir Thomas Willshire, Bart., K.C.B., and to redeem its credit the officers shortly afterwards engaged Mr. Wallace, Bandmaster of the 58th, then under orders for embarkation. The first division proceeded to Edinburgh on the 2nd of August, 1843, under Captain Mylius; the second followed on the 16th of that month under Major Paterson; and the head-quarters on the 16th of September in the "Dee" steamer.

Major Hogarth, who joined at Edinburgh from Calcutta on the 15th of October, 1843, had been previously gazetted a Companion of the Order of the Bath.

1844. During the winter the corps made weekly marches, generally taking some gentleman's place, or remarkable spot, for its object. Arthur's Seat was one, and it was noticed at the time, that no regiment had been there for forty years.

The health of the men was now entirely established, care being taken to clothe them warmly, and every exertion was made to re-organize the corps, while sojourning in the capital of their native country, the best quarters in the United Kingdom.

There was, however, this drawback—several of the men, having plenty of money, and being within reach of friends, could not resist temptation; and although there was no other serious crime, absence without leave and desertion prevailed to an extent hitherto unknown. This dereliction of duty was mainly confined to the young soldiers, who, after being hastily recruited, and half drilled on board ship, were turned into the ranks to meet the exigencies of the service; these when brought home, after having endured much privation and confinement on board ship, had not sufficient moral training to withstand the surrounding allurements. This disposition to irregularity was further increased by the order to volunteer to the 53rd, then about to embark for India. Fifty-three men volunteered thereto during July, 1844. The greater portion of the old non-commissioned officers had been carried off by the mortality in China, and the young men necessarily brought forward to replace them, shared to a great degree in the general unsteadiness and love of pleasure, and were unavoidably reduced. To such an extent did irregularities prevail, that few of the officers could keep their servants, and it was difficult to find men willing to act in that capacity. By great exertion and continued attention, eventually a state of things more consonant with the old name of the Cameronians, was restored.

On the 3rd of May, 1844, when the new colours, granted by Lord Seaton, were presented by Lady Douglas on Bruntsfield Links, the Regiment turned out in a manner almost worthy of its former days, and the ceremony was thus noticed in the daily journals:—

" Bruntsfield Links presented, on Friday last, a most
" interesting and animating spectacle, being the day
" appointed for the presentation of new colours to the
" Cameronians, at present at the Castle.

" The circumstance of this gallant Corps having lately
" returned from China, where they bore a prominent
" part in the fatiguing and protracted warfare which has
" now happily been brought to a termination, and where
" they lost many of their brave companions, added addi-
" tional interest to this always attractive ceremony.
" Accordingly, by 11 o'clock, the hour at which the
" Regiment arrived at the Links, the most numerous
" concourse of people had assembled that has been
" witnessed on a similar occasion for a long time past,
" comprising all ranks — pedestrians, equestrians, and
" splendid equipages—and forming a living wall around
" the Corps during the time they remained on the field.
" About 12 o'clock, Sir Neil Douglas, commanding the
" forces in Scotland, appeared on the ground, surrounded
" by a brilliant staff, when the Regiment formed in line
" and saluted him. They then marched past, first in
" slow and again in quick time; after which, again
" forming line, the Regiment advanced and fired two
" rounds. Retiring again by files, they formed a square
" as preparing to receive cavalry, fired by files, and then
" a volley. After some other minor evolutions, all of
" which were executed with the utmost precision, and

1844. "called forth repeated expressions of admiration from
"several military gentlemen present, the Regiment again
"formed in line, and executed a brilliant charge; they
"again retired, formed in line, and the grenadier com-
"pany, commanded by Brevet-Major Paterson, stepping
"out and forming in front, the old colours, carried by
"Ensign Mountain and Ensign Cresswell, were borne
"along the line, the Regiment saluting as they passed.
"The appearance of these war-worn colours, with all
"their stirring associations, their tattered fragments
"streaming in the wind, excited much interest in all
"present. When this imposing ceremony was com-
"pleted, the Regiment again closed their ranks and
"formed three sides of a square, the drums placed in
"the centre; within the area of the square, Sir Neil
"Douglas, his staff, Colonel Mountain, Principal Lee,
"and a number of the friends of the officers, were placed.
"Major Hogarth and Major Strange brought forward
"the new colours, and consigned them to Sir Neil
"Douglas and Colonel Mountain, who placed them on
"the drums Principal Lee, then, proceeding to the
"ceremony of consecration, engaged in prayer. The
"General then raised the colours, and handed them
"to Lady Douglas, who addressed the Regiment as
"follows:—

"'Colonel Mountain and Cameronians,—It is with no
"'ordinary feelings of pride and satisfaction that I stand
"'before you this day, selected, as I have been, the
"'honoured instrument of presenting to you a new set
"'of colours. I need not tell you how bravely, how
"'gloriously, the Regiment has defended those which
"'are now about to be laid aside, and which, like
"'veteran warriors, have been borne and shattered in
"'their country's cause; nor need I remind you of the

"'gallant deeds achieved by the Regiment, in the old
"'German wars especially, under the renowned Marl-
"'borough, and subsequently in America, Egypt, Spain,
"'India, and lastly China, where your arms so essen-
"'tially contributed in subduing a mighty and almost
"'unknown empire—thus establishing the valour and
"'bravery of the Cameronians in the four quarters of
"'the globe. And should you, brave soldiers! be called
"'upon to unfurl these banners in defence of your
"'beloved Queen and country, O, remember! that the
"'God of Armies alone can render you invincible. To
"'your keeping, then, do I commit these colours. Take
"'them to your hearts; defend, protect, and guard
"'them—as I feel assured you will ever do—with that
"'devoted zeal and steady valour which have at all
"'times characterized the Cameronian Regiment.'

"At the conclusion of this address, her Ladyship
"handed the new colours to Lieutenant Wallace and
"Ensign Wallace (brothers), who received them kneeling.
"Lieut.-Colonel Mountain then addressed Lady Douglas
"as follows:—

"'Lady Douglas, in the name of the Cameronians,
"'officers, non-commissioned officers, and men, permit
"'me to offer you our warmest thanks. We thank you
"'for the honour you have conferred upon us in pre-
"'senting our new colours; we thank you for the
"'kindness with which you have spoken of the Regi-
"'ment; we thank you for the confidence which you
"'have expressed in our devotion to our duty.

"'It is my pleasing task, also, to offer the thanks of
"'the Regiment to Principal Lee for the eloquent and
"'impressive manner in which he has performed the
"'office of consecration, and invoked upon our banners
"'that blessing upon which all human success depends.

1844. "'These colours, granted to us by our most gracious Majesty the Queen, presented by your Ladyship, the wife of our General—a General so proudly distinguished by arduous and gallant services amid the unequalled triumphs of the Peninsula—and sanctified by the prayers of so eminent a minister of the Church of Scotland; these colours are committed to our keeping with all that can rouse the feelings of the subject, the soldier, and the Christian.

"'There cannot be, there is not, I am confident, a man in our ranks whose heart does not warm at this sight, who will not cheerfully give his life for his colours, and the cause of his country and his Queen.

"'You have reminded us, Lady Douglas, of the services of our old Corps in times gone by, and we acknowledge the obligation to support its character.

"'You have bid us awake to the spirit of chivalry, and bear in mind the true source of all strength, and we feel the sacredness of the summons.

"'You have kindly noticed the recent services of the Regiment, and we cherish the memory of the comrades whom we lost upon that service. Our ranks are now chiefly filled with lads, but they are lads who have begun their career amid stirring scenes, and who are, I hope, alive to the honour of their calling; and old soldier and young soldier, one and all, we will stand by our colours to the last, and never, so help me God, give you cause for regret that you have this day done us the honour to associate your name with ours.'

"While this impressive ceremony was proceeding the utmost order and decorum prevailed throughout: all seemed to feel the solemnity of the occasion, and many ladies were affected even to tears. When it was con-

" cluded the Regiment re-formed line, the new colours 1844.
" falling into their proper places in the centre, the old
" moving off to the right of the line of officers. In this
" position the Regiment advanced in open order, and
" after a general salute marched back to the Castle."

The Regiment appeared for the first time in the new hat recently ordered for the army, and which was of a much lighter construction than that hitherto worn.

On the 15th of May, 1844, a company was sent to Dunfermline, in consequence of some disturbance amongst the weavers, but happily no collision took place. With this exception, the Regiment remained together during its occupation of Edinburgh Castle, and Bruntsfields Links was the exercise ground, until Sir Thomas Dick Lauder, an old Cameronian, gave the Regiment a large field near his house for the purpose.

Major-General Sir Neil Douglas, K.C.B., K.C.H., who had inspected the 26th on the 14th of November of the previous year, again saw the Regiment on Bruntsfield Links upon the 7th of August, 1844, prior to its departure from Scotland, when the following general order was issued:—

" *Adjutant-General's Office,*
" *Edinburgh, 28th August,* 1844.

" The 26th Regiment having been ordered to the
" Northern District, Major-General Sir Neil Douglas
" cannot allow them to embark without expressing his
" great regret at losing their services.

" This corps, after a long residence in India and
" China, where their conduct was highly distinguished,
" came to Edinburgh, composed almost entirely of young
" soldiers and recruits; and arriving as they did,
" amongst their relations and friends, with large balances

P

1844. "to receive, a great deal of irregularity prevailed for a
"time amongst them; but it affords the Major-General
"much satisfaction to be able to add, that by the
"unremitting exertions of Lieut.-Colonel Mountain,
"this irregularity has very much disappeared, and that
"the 26th Regiment is now in all respects a well-
"conducted and highly efficient corps.

"The field movements are executed with great
"steadiness and precision; the arms, accoutrements,
"clothing, and necessaries, are in the most soldier-like
"condition, and the interior economy in a most satis-
"factory state.

"This reflects great credit upon the zeal, talent, and
"attention of Lieut.-Colonel Mountain, and every
"officer, non-commissioned officer, and soldier, in the
"26th Regiment; and the Major-General has no doubt
"that the future conduct of the Cameronians will justify
"the high character he has felt it his duty to give them
"to His Grace the Commander-in-Chief, and the Lieut.-
"General commanding the Northern District.

"By Order of the Major-General Commanding.

"JOHN EDEN,
"*Assistant Adjutant-General.*"

It may be remarked, that even during the continuation of the irregularities above referred to, there was good feeling amongst the men.

On the 19th of August, 1844, three companies, under Major Hogarth, embarked for Newcastle-on-Tyne; one of these, under Captain Layard, was destined for Thornley Hall and West Rainton; one, under Lieutenant Edgar, with the Major, for Durham; and one, under Captain Skinner, for Whitridge Farm. Another division, under Major Strange, embarked on the 22nd of August;

one of these companies was destined for head-quarters, 1844. one Tynemouth, and two to be stationed at Sunderland; the head-quarters embarked on the 30th, and arrived at Newcastle-on-Tyne on the same evening.

Lieut.-General Sir Thomas Arbuthnot, K.C.B., inspected the Cameronians on their arrival, and the half-yearly report was made by Major-General Brotherton, C.B., on the 21st of October, 1844. Early in April, the 1845. 26th received orders to proceed from Newcastle to Manchester, but the Regiment was detained in hourly expectation of the route until the 24th, when the whole corps, with the exception of detachments left at Sunderland and Tynemouth, was placed in one train and moved *viâ* York and Normanton to Manchester, where it arrived early the same evening, and marched at once into the Infantry Barracks. Here the Regiment was together again, and if more time had been allowed, great progress might have been made in the drill.

After the volunteering to the 53rd, the Regiment was brought considerably below its establishment. Head-quarter parties were sent out and the corps would soon have filled up had it not been removed from Scotland; but as the sergeants of these parties, who had been chosen for their fitness, were married men, they were ordered in, an order having been issued prohibiting the employment of non-commissioned officers thus situated on the recruiting service. Those who relieved them were less capable, and recruiting consequently flagged. The Lieut.-Colonel was informed that, unless the establishment was completed by the end of the year, the recruiting would be extended to England and Ireland; and as, unfortunately, the Regiment still continued deficient in numbers, instructions were issued, on the 3rd of May, to recruit for it, half-an-inch under the standard,

1845. throughout the United Kingdom. The result was, that in about six weeks the Regiment was nearly one hundred over its establishment, and that about two hundred recruits, mostly of a very inferior description, were poured in upon it from the districts in the course of a few days.

Sir Thomas Arbuthnot had the Regiment out twice, to practise for a brigade field-day, which took place on the 27th of May, 1845, on Kersall Moor, when he complimented the corps on its steadiness under arms.

Major-General Sir William Warre, C.B., held the half-yearly inspection on the 4th of June, and expressed himself much satisfied with the interior economy and general appearance of the men in the ranks, but he considered the recruits very inferior.

The first division, under Major Hogarth, was conveyed by rail to Liverpool on the 10th of June, 1845, and these embarked for Belfast, where it arrived on the following day, relieving a portion of the 5th Regiment. The head-quarters, under Lieut.-Colonel Mountain, C.B., proceeded to Liverpool on the 11th, and, embarking the same evening, arrived and disembarked on the 12th at Belfast. It had been utterly impossible to clothe the recruits in so short an interval, and their ragged appearance did not tend to give the Belfast authorities a pleasant impression of the corps.

Lieut.-General Sir Edward Blakeney, K.C.B., commanding the forces in Ireland, inspected the Regiment in August, and expressed himself satisfied with it, and encouraged the recruits, who had by this time attained some little progress.

Major-General Sir George Berkeley, K.C.B., made the half-yearly inspection on the 1st of October. The winter passed off quietly; there was no ground for drill

at Belfast, and, with the exception of one occasion, 1845.
when Sir George Berkeley had the Regiment out for a
sham defence of Shaw's Bridge, and on two others,
when the Lieut.-Colonel had it at Hollywood, and up
to Cave Hill, the manœuvring was confined to the
barrack yard.

Captain Carey's company, which had been detached
in the first instance to Carrickfergus, was relieved by
Captain Edgar's, on the 15th of October, and the latter
by Captain Johnstone's, on the 14th of February, 1846. 1846.

On the 31st of March, detachments were sent out,
under Brevet Major Whittingham, for Killashandra, and
Captain Rodgers, for Ballyconnell; on the 6th of April,
under Captain Gregg, for Ballyshannon, and Captain
Frend, for Belleek; and on the 7th, one under Captain
Layard, for Arvagh. The first division, under Major
Hogarth, marched for Enniskillen on the 11th, and the
head-quarters, under Lieut.-Colonel Mountain, on the
13th, arriving at that station on the 20th of April.
Enniskillen was a healthy and agreeable quarter. The
men enjoyed their country walks, but two lives were
unfortunately lost by indiscreet bathing in the lake.
Major-General Sir George Berkeley, K.C.B., inspected
the Regiment on the 13th of May, and expressed
himself satisfied with the progress which had been made.
On the 19th of June, Lieut.-Colonel Mountain, for his
services in China, was appointed aide-de-camp to the
Queen, with the rank of Colonel.

Major D'Urban who had exchanged on the 31st of
July, 1846, with Major Strange, was placed on half-pay,
and the step went in the Regiment; this occasioned the
promotion of Brevet Major Paterson, Lieutenant and
Adjutant Cameron, and Ensign Andrews. Lieutenant
Mountain was appointed to the adjutancy.

846. In August the Regiment received a route for Dublin. The detachments marched from their respective stations to the Royal Barracks and the head-quarters, in three divisions; the first under Major Paterson on the 14th, the second under Major Hogarth on the 15th, the third under Colonel Mountain on the 18th of that month. Officers and men were anxious to appear to advantage in Dublin, which garrison is generally considered in the light of an ordeal, and the spirit of emulation told favourably both upon the appearance and the conduct of the Regiment.

Lieut.-General Sir Edward Blakeney, K.C.B., reviewed the 26th in the Phœnix Park on the 18th of September, and expressed his satisfaction with the appearance and steadiness of the men, and particularly with their style f skirmishing.

Major-General Henry Wyndham made the half-yearly inspection on the 19th of October, and desired the Colonel to notify to the corps his satisfaction, but expressed regret at the number of courts-martial.

1847. In January, 1847, the Regiment came under the eye of Prince George of Cambridge in the Royal Barracks, and had the good fortune to receive at different times the approbation of his Royal Highness, which was renewed upon the Prince's half-yearly inspection on the 11th of May following.

It was anticipated that in Dublin at least, the Cameronians would remain together for a year; but owing to the call for troops, consequent upon their scarcity, the first detachment proceeded to Enfield for canal escort duty in January, and in February pushed on to Mullingar; in the middle of March the Regiment was ordered to take the detachment of the 68th, and furnish others, the head-quarters being removed to Ship Street Barracks.

Major Paterson went to Newbridge; Captain Edgar to Trim; Captain Johnstone to Athy; Captain Rodgers to Robertstown; Captain Frend to Oldcastle; Captain Nicholson to Rathangan; Lieutenant Wallace to Kells; Lieutenant Roberts to Maryborough; and Lieutenant Thomas William Andrews to Navan. Some of these detachments were subsequently reinforced, and another was sent out to Tullow under Lieutenant Thomas Andrews.

On the 15th of February, 1847, the Regiment received orders to recruit to one thousand rank and file, and to send out six additional recruiting parties; a like number being already so employed, each under a sergeant. Non-commissioned officers being very much required with the detachments for escort duty, it became exceedingly difficult to furnish all the duties required of the 26th, but this was accomplished. Meanwhile, the recruiting progressed rapidly, and before the 8th of April the Regiment was above the new establishment. The order for general recruiting was a third blow to the nationality of the corps, and was a matter of much regret; but the standard of the Regiment was in a great degree redeemed by the last recruiting, the fresh comers being generally of good appearance. Some difficulty arose in drilling the mass of recruits thus hastily collected, the larger portion having been forwarded to Newbridge, a part sent to Portobello, and the remainder continued with the head-quarters at Ship Street Barracks. The commanding officer hoped to have his recruits and the Regiment together in Dublin, but on the 6th of July orders were received to move to Buttevant. Captain Frend's company marched from Oldcastle, about one hundred and seventy miles, to Bruff; Captain Cameron to Hospital; Major Whittingham, with the

1847. grenadiers, marched to Ballingarry; and the remaining detachments to Buttevant; the head-quarters proceeding by steam *viâ* Cork. This march, with so many recruits who had never seen their companies and from so many detachments, to further outlying stations, was a great trial for the Regiment. Colonel Mountain issued an order, appealing to the officers, non-commissioned officers, and men, to assist him in this emergency—each by attention in his own sphere—and they did not disappoint their commanding officer.

The Regiment was called upon for further detachments immediately after its arrival at Buttevant; Captain Edgar's company marched to Charleville; Brevet-Major Mylius's, to Mallow; Lieutenant Park, with No. 1 company, to Kanturk; Captain Rodgers to Killarney; and Lieutenant Clerke, with a detachment, to Cahirciveen.

The grenadier company rejoined head-quarters at Buttevant in August; and the Cahirciveen detachment was in the following month removed to Mill Street. Captains Frend's and Cameron's companies also rejoined at Buttevant in November; during which month, a detachment commanded by Captain Johnstone was ordered to Liscarrol, about seven miles from Buttevant, as disturbances were apprehended in the neighbourhood. Nothing however occurred, and it returned to head-quarters in the course of a month, as no satisfactory accommodation could be procured for the men, who had been in most miserable billets. Shortly after this, the Charleville detachment was ordered to be increased to one hundred of all ranks, on account of the state of the country; and Major Whittingham, who had just been promoted upon the retirement of Major Davenport, was ordered to take command there.

In September, 1847, Colonel Mountain, C.B., quitted the 26th, to accompany the Earl of Dalhousie to Calcutta as his military secretary; that nobleman having just received the appointment of Governor-General of India, and the command of the Regiment devolved upon Major Hogarth.

The Regiment was inspected at Buttevant on the 8th of October, 1847, by Major-General Charles Turner, who expressed himself much pleased both with its appearance and steadiness.

The "Disarming Act" having come into force in January, 1848, another detachment under Captain Nicholson was ordered to Drumclogher, thirteen miles distant from Buttevant, there to be billeted and assist the police in their search for arms. This duty was only of a temporary nature, and it rejoined after a few days' absence.

In the beginning of 1848, there was a general relief of detachments—Captain Frend proceeding to Killarney; the grenadier company, under Captain Carey, to Charleville; and a detachment, under Lieutenant Park, to Kanturk; Captains Rodgers, Edgar, and Wallace, rejoining head-quarters with their respective companies. Towards the end of March, Captain Johnstone relieved Major Mylius at Mallow, and Captain Cameron with his company proceeded to Mill Street, replacing the detachment at that station under Lieutenant Clerke. The Regiment was also called upon about this time to furnish an additional detachment at Mitchelstown, of which Captain Nicholson took command.

In April, the head-quarters received a route for Cork, and marched in two divisions, on the 10th and 11th of that month. Upon arrival there, another detachment was ordered out to Middleton, of which Lieutenant

1847.

1848.

1848. Blackett took charge; this was subsequently reinforced, and the head quarters of No. 1 company, under Captain Wallace, proceeded thither.

On the 22nd of May, Major-General Turner made his spring inspection of the Cameronians, and again expressed his satisfaction, remarking, that he was persuaded they had used their time at Buttevant to the best advantage, and that all he had seen of them had given him much pleasure.

In the same month, two more detachments were sent out, one under the command of Brevet-Major Mylius to Spike Island, and the other under Captain Layard to Haulbowline; both these stations were subsequently reinforced, and the party at Spike Island was eventually increased to one hundred and seventy men.

About this time, intimation was received of the exchange of Lieut.-Colonel Andrew T. Hemphill, of the 29th Regiment, with Colonel Mountain, and on the 26th of July the former officer assumed the command of the Cameronians.

The Charleville and Kanturk detachments rejoined head-quarters in June and July, and were soon followed by those from Mallow, Killarney, and Mitchelstown. The Regiment furnished another detachment to Bandon in July, which was afterwards reinforced, and Major Hogarth, C.B., was ordered to take command at that station. In September the Mill Street detachment was ordered into Cork, and early in the following month Captain Rodgers's company relieved Captain Layard's at Haulbowline.

On the 17th of October the Cameronians were again inspected by Major-General Turner, and had still the good fortune to meet with his unqualified approbation.

Colour-Sergeant James Searson, of the grenadier

company, was, on the 11th of November, presented on parade, by Major George Hogarth, C.B., with the medal, which, according to the recent "Good Conduct Warrant" accompanied the annuity for "meritorious service," and that which he obtained was £20.

Towards the end of the year the Regiment was greatly scattered, having been called upon to furnish detachments at Bandon, Camden Fort, Mallow, and Castle Martyr, in addition to those previously sent to Spike Island, Haulbowline, and Middleton. On the 20th of December the head-quarters were removed to Ballincollig to make room for regiments embarking at Cork for India; they remained there for about a month, when they returned to Cork, and the several detachments rejoined the head-quarters in the early part of the year, the Regiment being eventually brought together again in June.

Major-General Turner made his spring inspection on the 18th of May, 1849, and again expressed himself much pleased with the Regiment.

On the 3rd of August the Queen landed at Cork, and a Guard of Honour, composed of the two flank companies, under Captains Layard and Carey, was furnished from the 26th to receive Her Majesty, the rest of the Regiment, conjointly with the other corps in garrison, lining the streets as the Queen went through. Brevet Major Mylius (who, at the particular request of Lieut.-General the Right Honourable Sir Edward Blakeney, K.C.B., was kept in command at Spike Island, after the relief of the detachment there,) received Her Majesty on her first landing in Ireland at Cove, since named Queenstown, in commemoration of the event.

In August, cholera made its appearance, and the Regiment lost about twenty men from this frightful disease, every case having proved fatal.

1849. On the 1st of October, Lieut.-General Sir Edward Blakeney, commanding in Ireland, inspected the Regiment, when it met with his entire approbation; and on the following day Major-General Turner made his autumnal inspection, and again expressed himself much gratified with the steadiness and appearance of the men.

Early in December, a notification was received ordering the Regiment to be held in readiness to proceed to Gibraltar, and arrangements were made shortly afterwards for forming a four-company depôt, to be left behind upon the embarkation of the six service companies; the latter, consisting of twenty officers and six hundred and four non-commissioned officers and men, embarked at Cork,

1850. on the 5th of March, 1850, under the command of Lieut.-Colonel Hemphill, on board the "Bombay" transport, which sailed from Queenstown on the 7th, and reached Gibraltar on the 20th of the same month. Nothing particular occurred during the voyage, and the conduct of the men was very satisfactory.

The depôt remained at Cork, although it had received orders to be held in readiness to proceed to Jersey.

On the 3rd of April, the Regiment was inspected by His Excellency Major-General Sir Robert Wm. Gardiner, K.C.B. and K.C.H., who expressed himself much pleased with its appearance and steadiness.

The Regiment underwent its half-yearly inspection on the 13th of May, when Sir Robert William Gardiner again stated that he was highly gratified with its general appearance.

On the 13th of May, the depôt companies, consisting of ten officers, and four hundred and sixty-two non-commissioned officers and men, embarked at Cork, under the command of Major George Hogarth, C.B., in the steam frigate "Birkenhead," and arrived at Jersey on the 15th 1850. of that month.

Another inspection of the Regiment was made by Sir Robert Gardiner on the 28th of October, when His Excellency was pleased to remark in complimentary terms upon its general appearance and interior economy.

On the 4th of March, 1851, the battalion companies, 1851. which, since the arrival of the Regiment at Gibraltar, had been stationed in the King's and Jumper's bastions, moved into the new casemates in the Wellington Front. The flank companies and head-quarters continued in the Town Range Barracks, which they had occupied from the date of their disembarkation at Gibraltar.

Major-General Sir Robert Gardiner, on the 26th of May, made his half-yearly inspection of the Regiment.

On the 25th of August, a draft, consisting of Lieutenant Thomas Andrews, Ensign William Mosse, two sergeants, and forty-nine rank and file, joined at Gibraltar from the depôt companies.

The Regiment was inspected by Sir Robert on the 14th of October, and again received the expression of His Excellency's entire satisfaction.

In May, 1851, the depôt companies were removed from Jersey to South Britain, and were afterwards stationed at Newport, Monmouthshire.

On the 11th of May, 1852, the Regiment underwent 1852. its spring half-yearly inspection by Lieut.-General Sir Robert Gardiner, who signified that he was highly pleased with its condition and appearance.

The autumn half-yearly inspection of the Regiment took place on the 12th of October following, when the Lieut.-General repeated his approval of its appearance and movements.

On the 19th of November, it appeared in garrison

1852. orders, that the Governor had received notice that arrangements were in progress for moving from Corfu to Gibraltar the 30th Regiment, to replace the 26th, ordered to proceed to the West Indies.

1853. Intimation was received on the 16th of February, 1853, that the arrangements for moving the Regiment to Barbadoes had been suspended, until more favourable reports should be received from the Windward and Leeward Colonies in regard to the health of the troops stationed in that command. On the 19th of March His Excellency the Governor announced in garrison orders, that he had received intimation that the service companies of the 26th were to embark for Canada upon the arrival of the 30th Regiment from the Ionian Islands. The Cameronians, mustering sixteen officers, twenty-eight sergeants, eleven drummers, and five hundred and forty rank and file, under the command of Lieut.-Colonel Hemphill, accordingly embarked on the 25th of April, on board the freight ships "Thomas Arbuthnot," "Joseph Somes," and "Santipore," which sailed on the following day. The head-quarters on board the "Thomas Arbuthnot" arrived off Quebec on the 28th of May, and the other ships about a week afterwards.

The head-quarters re-embarked on board the steamer "Montreal" during the evening of the 31st of May, disembarking and marching into Quebec Gate Barracks, Montreal, on the morning of the 1st of June, the companies on board the "Joseph Somes" and "Santipore" joining on the 7th of that month. On the 8th of July a detachment from the depôt, consisting of four officers, three non-commissioned officers, and twenty privates, arrived at the service companies.

On the 11th of July, Lieut.-General William Rowan, C.B., commanding in Canada, made his first half-yearly inspection of the service companies, and expressed his satisfaction at the appearance of the men on parade, and their steadiness under arms. This praise was re-iterated by the Lieut.-General at his autumnal inspection on the 14th of November.

A letter of readiness was received on the 17th of January, 1854, for the service companies to proceed to Quebec upon the opening of the navigation, which was then closed with ice, and another on the 15th of May, cancelling the former, and directing that they should prepare to embark for Bermuda.

Major-General Philip Bainbrigge, C.B., was appointed Colonel of the 26th Regiment, on the 31st of March, 1854, vice Lieut.-General Lord Seaton, G.C.B., removed to the 2nd Life Guards.

On the 17th of June, the Regiment was inspected by the Lieut.-General commanding, when its state and appearance again elicited his approbation.

The service companies embarked in two divisions at Montreal, the first on the 13th, and the second on the 15th of July, and disembarked at Quebec on the 14th and 16th of that month, from which they proceeded on the 9th of November, under Colonel Hemphill, in Her Majesty's troop-ship "Resistance," which, sailing on the day following, disembarked at St. George's, Bermuda, on the 3rd of December; upon landing, they were encamped until the 56th Regiment, which they had been sent to relieve, should leave for England.

The signal stations at Fort George, Mount Langton, and Gibbs' Hill were taken over by the Cameronians on the 8th of December, and on the 11th, Captain Chute, one sergeant, and twenty-one rank and file, occupied Fort Cunningham, and Fort George was allotted to

1854. Lieutenant Hardinge, one sergeant, and twenty-one rank and file; one corporal and three privates went to Ferry Point; and on the 14th, Captain Wallace, Lieutenant Colling, two sergeants, and thirty-one rank and file, of the grenadier company, proceeded to Hamilton; all these parties relieving detachments of the 56th Regiment. On the 13th of December the Regiment left the encampment, and marched into the Royal Barracks, six companies of the 56th having embarked on board Her Majesty's troop-ship "Resistance" the previous day.

1855. In January, 1855, the depôt companies proceeded from Newcastle-on-Tyne to Ireland, but returned to England in March following.

Captain Hopson, Lieutenant Lockhart, two sergeants, and forty-six rank and file, arrived from England on the 24th of March, 1855, in the transport "William," as a convict guard, and after giving over the prisoners at the dockyard, Ireland Island, they disembarked and proceeded to Hamilton, where they remained till the 7th of April, when they joined the head-quarters at St. George's, Bermuda.

On the 14th of April, Captains Kerrich's, Chute's, and Quartley's companies, proceeded to Ireland and Boaz Islands to relieve detachments of the 56th Regiment about to proceed to England in the transport "William," thus leaving the whole of the duties of the islands (which had hitherto been performed by one thousand rank and file) to devolve on about five hundred men of the Cameronians.

Brevet Lieut.-Colonel Whittingham, C.B., on the formation of the depôt into two companies, proceeded to Bermuda with the other two companies, consisting of one captain, six lieutenants, six ensigns, nine sergeants, seven corporals, three drummers, and two hundred and 1855. nine privates, arrived from England on the 30th of April in the freight ship "Walter Morris."

On the 13th of July, Lieutenant Mill, one sergeant, one corporal, and forty-nine privates also arrived in the transport "Emma Eugenia" from England, making a total increase this year from the depôt of three hundred and twenty-seven men; but owing to the war with Russia, the majority of these were young undrilled recruits, as nearly all the drilled soldiers belonging to the depôt had volunteered their services to regiments in the Crimea. A very watchful superintendence had, therefore, to be kept over them in such a climate as Bermuda, especially at this season of the year; great attention was given to prevent unnecessary exposure to the sun, and by limiting the hours and selecting shady places, even their drilling was carried on and completed without any sickness being observable among them.

On the 1st of August, the detachment at Ireland Island was reinforced by Captain Granville's company from head-quarters, and on the 12th of November Captain Clerke's company proceeded from St. George's to Ireland Island, in order to relieve Captain Quartley's, which joined head-quarters the same day.

Captain Chute, with Ensigns Bindon and Salwey, one 1856. sergeant, two corporals, and thirty-two privates, arrived from England on the 23rd of January, 1856, in the transport, "Castle Eden," in charge of convicts. On the 1st of February Captain Elderton's company relieved Captain Kerrich's at Ireland Island, and on the 29th of March that under Captain Hopson proceeded to Hamilton to replace Captain Wallace's, which on the same day joined head-quarters. About this time the Enfield Rifle was issued to the Regiment, and the whole of the

Q

1856. officers, non-commissioned officers and men, were put under a course of training according to instructions received from the School of Musketry at Hythe, for the purpose of making them proficient in the use of this formidable weapon.

Surgeon Coates, with Ensigns Franklin and Turner, arrived from England on the 11th of June, in the transport "St. Michael," in charge of a detachment of two sergeants and ninety-eight privates, all undrilled; consequently, the same precautions had to be taken that were adopted the previous year, and happily with success, as the drilling was carried on and perfected without the appearance amongst them of any sickness.

In August, yellow fever broke out in the Islands, and continued to exist till the end of December, but fortunately no case appeared at St. George's; the detachments at Ireland and Boaz Islands however, did not escape, as they had a number of men attacked; but owing to the successful treatment of the disease by the surgeons in the Naval Hospital, to which the men were admitted, only one man died. The detachment at Hamilton had also one death, namely, Lieutenant Hogarth, and it is remarkable that this officer was the only one belonging thereto attacked, although it was surrounded by the fever.

Brevet Lieut.-Colonel Whittingham, C.B., having been promoted to an unattached lieut.-colonelcy, Captain Hopson obtained the vacant majority on the 5th of September, and assumed the command of the detachment stationed at Ireland Island, on the 1st of December. On the 23rd of that month, Captain Clerke's company proceeded from Ireland Island to Hamilton, and replaced that under Captain Mosse, which joined the Ireland Island detachment the same day; and on the 24th,

OR CAMERONIAN REGIMENT.

Captains Granville's and Chute's companies returned to 1856. St. George's from Ireland Island, having been relieved from head-quarters by those under Captains Kerrich and Grantley.

Captain Mosse joined from England on the 26th of 1857. January, 1857, as Instructor of Musketry to the Regiment, having qualified himself for this appointment at the Hythe School of Musketry; and on the 29th of the same month, Captain Humbley's company relieved that under Captain Elderton at Ireland Island.

In April, 1857, the depôt, which had been stationed at Chatham for two years, was moved to Walmer.

A draft, consisting of Ensign Colebrooke, one sergeant, two corporals, and thirty-seven privates, arrived from England on the 16th of May, in the freight-ship "Agra," in charge of convicts.

On the 16th of October, Captain Chute's company relieved Captain Clerke's at Hamilton, and on the 9th of November, those under Captains Mosse and Betts proceeded from St. George's to Ireland Island, replacing Captains Humbley's and Calcott's, which, on the same day, joined head-quarters.

During the year, a commission was appointed by the Governor of Bermuda to inquire into the circumstances of the epidemic fever which prevailed in the Islands in the latter part of 1856, and the commissioners sent a number of questions to the officer commanding the Cameronians, requesting answers thereto at his earliest convenience, which information was accordingly given. As it is believed that the same may prove useful for future guidance, copies of the queries and replies are inserted in this Record.*

---

* *Vide* Appendix III.

1858. On the 2nd of January, 1858, Captain Chute's company, having been relieved at Hamilton by Captain Elderton's, from head-quarters, proceeded to Ireland Island, and replaced that under Captain Kerrich, which the same day joined head-quarters; Captain Quartley's company also returned thither on the 2nd of January, having been relieved at Ireland Island by the one under Captain Hardinge, from St. George's.

In February, 1858, the Captain in charge of the Depôt transmitted to the Officer commanding the Regiment the copy of a letter which he had received from the Adjutant-General, requesting him to state, for the General Commanding-in-Chief's information, whether a written authority existed for any deviation from the established pattern forage cap for the officers and men of the 26th Regiment. Immediately on receipt of this communication, Colonel Hemphill wrote to the Adjutant-General, informing him that there was no written authority with the Regiment, but that there was no doubt the same pattern forage cap had been worn by the "Cameronians" ever since their being raised in 1689; and that he trusted the General Commanding-in-Chief would sanction the continuance of a cap which had been of such a long standing in the Regiment, and His Royal Highness the Duke of Cambridge, K.G., was pleased to accede to this request.*

A draft, consisting of Brevet-Major William M'Donald, Ensign William Manjin, one sergeant, and forty-eight privates arrived, in charge of convicts, from England, on the 24th March, in the freight-ship "True Briton."

In March, 1858, the depôt proceeded from Walmer to

---

* *Vide* Copy of Correspondence on this subject in Appendix IV.

Ireland, and was stationed at Birr until July, when it 1858. was moved to Belfast, where it remained during the following year.

On the 7th of June, Nos. 2 and 5 companies proceeded to Watford Island, where they were encamped, the Governor being apprehensive of a rising amongst the convicts stationed at Boaz Island. These companies rejoined head-quarters on the 14th, but the civil authorities still remaining of opinion that the convicts would break out, applied to have the troops sent back, in consequence of which Captain Quartley's company proceeded to Watford Island on the 17th of June, where it remained encamped until the 13th of September, when it rejoined head-quarters at St George's.

A draft, consisting of Captain Kerrich, Ensign Wills, one sergeant, and forty-four rank and file, arrived from England on the 9th of November in the "True Briton," in charge of convicts; and on the 27th, the companies, under Captain Betts and Chute, returned to St. George's from Ireland Island, where they were replaced by those under Brevet-Major M'Donald and Captain Quartley from head-quarters. On the 4th of December, Captain Kerrich's company proceeded to Hamilton and relieved Captain Elderton's, which joined head-quarters the same day; and on the 17th, Captain Mosse's and Hardinge's companies returned to St. George's, having been relieved at Ireland Island by those under Captains Calcott and Colling from head-quarters.

On the 31st of August, 1859, a letter of readiness was 1859. received for the 26th to proceed to Portsmouth upon being relieved by the 39th Regiment from Canada. Her Majesty's steamship "Himalaya" arrived on the 12th of October with the latter corps, and on the 18th the head-quarters of the Cameronians embarked therein (the

1859. detachments at Hamilton, Ireland, and Boaz Islands, having gone on board on the 17th), and the vessel sailing for England the same day, reached Spithead on the 30th, where orders were received to proceed to Kingstown, Ireland. The "Himalaya" was, however, detained by a heavy gale of wind and coaling till the morning of the 3rd of November, when she again put to sea, and arrived at Kingstown on the morning of the 5th, when the Regiment, disembarking that day, was conveyed by railway to Dublin, the head-quarters and six companies marching into Linen Hall Barracks, one company to Aldborough House, and the remaining three to Naas.

Two companies proceeded on the 11th from Naas to the Curragh for rifle practice, which, on finishing, were relieved by others from head-quarters, and this was continued throughout the winter, two companies being continually stationed at the Curragh until the whole had gone through the annual course of musketry instruction.

The head-quarters and four companies removed on the 17th from Linen Hall to Ship Street Barracks, the company at Aldborough House joining the former the same day.

Major-General Cunynghame, C.B., commanding the second Infantry Brigade to which the Cameronians belonged, inspected the Regiment on the 21st, and expressed himself satisfied with the cleanly and healthy appearance of the men. On the 22nd, Major-General Gascoigne, commanding the Dublin division, inspected the 26th on the Esplanade, when their steadiness under arms, and cleanly appearance, elicited his approbation.

General Lord Seaton, G.C.B., commanding in Ireland, also inspected the corps on the 1st of December, at the same place, and signified his approval by repeating several times that "it was a very fine Regiment."

1860. On the 23rd of February, 1860, Major-General Cunynghame, C.B., again inspected the 26th previous to 1860. his departure for India, and passed a high eulogium on the corps; General Sir George Brown, G.C.B., who had been appointed Commander of the Forces in Ireland on the 1st of April, inspected the Regiment on the Esplanade, on the 12th of that month, when its state and appearance elicited his warm approbation.

On the 7th of May, Major-General Henry Keane Bloomfield, who on the departure of Major-General Cunynghame, C.B., for India, had succeeded to the command of the Second Infantry Brigade at Dublin, made his half-yearly inspection of the Cameronians.

. The head-quarters and six companies marched from Ship Street to Beggar's Bush Barracks on the 14th of June, into which the companies at the Linen Hall had moved the day before. On the 20th of the same month, the Regiment marched from Beggar's Bush Barracks to Naas, *en route* to the Curragh, there to be encamped till further orders, and on the 21st it proceeded from Naas and arrived at its destination the same day; but in consequence of the inclemency of the weather, the men were placed temporarily in huts until the 26th, when they went under canvas; the weather, however, continued very unsettled till the end of June.

On the 11th of July the Regiment removed into the huts vacated by the Louth Rifles, and on the 30th of that month, it marched to Maryborough Heath and encamped under canvas until the 1st of August, when it returned to the Curragh. It again went under canvas on the 6th, to make room for the 36th Foot, which, on that day, arrived in camp from England.

The Cameronians remained under canvas till the 30th of August, when, in consequence of the inclemency of the weather, it became necessary to move them again into huts.

1860. In May, the Enfield Rifles which had been supplied to the Regiment in 1856, were returned into store, and a superior weapon issued, named the interchangeable rifle. During the summer the whole of the men were completed with new accoutrements.

On the 28th of September, the Regiment marched from the Curragh to Naas, *en route* to Dublin, there to be stationed till further orders, and on the 29th it proceeded from Naas and arrived the same day at Beggar's Bush Barracks, Dublin.

Major-General Bloomfield made his half-yearly inspection of the Regiment on the 11th of October, and on the 24th of that month, Major-General the Honourable A. A. Dalzell, who had succeeded Lieut.-General Gascoigne in the command of the Dublin Division, inspected the Cameronians; these inspections proved satisfactory to both officers.

On the 15th of November, 1860, detachments from the depôt, consisting of forty men, joined the service 1861. companies, and on the 13th of February, 1861, another draft of thirty-five men joined from the depôt; but notwithstanding the arrival of these reinforcements the service companies, on the 31st of March, were still under their establishment, owing principally to the great number who obtained their discharge with pension at their own request, their twenty-one years' service having expired.

The Regiment, on the 21st of March, underwent its spring half-yearly inspection by Major-General Bloomfield, who expressed himself highly pleased with its condition and appearance.

Major-General Charles William Ridley, C.B., who had succeeded Major-General Hon. A. A. Dalzell in command of the Dublin division, inspected the Cameronians on the 15th of April, when he confirmed the praise 1861. bestowed by his predecessor.

On the 18th of April instructions were received to hold the Regiment in readiness to proceed to Glasgow, *en route* to Edinburgh. The Cameronians accordingly embarked in two divisions at the North Wall, Dublin, on the 2nd and 6th of May; arrived at Glasgow on the 3rd and 7th, and proceeded by rail the same days to Edinburgh Castle, detaching two companies as a guard over the military prison at Greenlaw.

Major-General Edward W. F. Walker, C.B., commanding the troops in North Britain, inspected the Regiment on the 14th of May in the Queen's Park, Edinburgh, when he requested the commanding officer (Lieut.-Colonel Carey) to inform the men that he was highly pleased with all he had seen, and more especially with their soldierlike appearance when walking in the streets.

The autumn half-yearly inspection took place on the 8th of October.

On the 21st of April, 1862, new colours were pre- 1862. sented to the Cameronians by Lady Belhaven, on the parade ground in the Queen's Park, in presence of the other troops in garrison, namely, the 2nd Dragoons or Scots Greys, and a battery of the Royal Artillery. The Regiment was drawn up in line under the command of Lieut.-Colonel Carey, on the north side of the ground facing St. Anthony's Chapel, and received Major-General Walker, commanding in North Britain, who arrived at two o'clock, with the usual honours. After he had inspected the corps a number of field evolutions were performed, and upon these being concluded, it again formed line on the same ground as before. The ceremony of presenting the colours then commenced; the

1862. old colours were trooped, and afterwards took up position on the right of the line. The latter was then formed into three sides of a square, in the centre of which a pile of drums was raised, against which the new colours were laid.

Lady Belhaven, accompanied by Lord Belhaven, Major-General Walker, and his staff, then advanced to them, and the Reverend James Miller, garrison Chaplain, having consecrated the colours, her Ladyship, on presenting them to Ensigns Buchanan and Eden, spoke as follows:—" I am proud of having the honour of presenting
" new colours to the brave Cameronians, and I feel more
" proud in consequence of my husband having served
" therein, it being the first Regiment in which he bore
" a commission. In delivering these colours into your
" hands, I feel that I am delivering them into the
" guardianship of men who will nobly do their duty to
" their Queen and country."

Lieut.-Colonel Carey then returned thanks to Lady Belhaven, in the name of the officers and men, for the honour she had done them. This concluded the ceremony. The 26th afterwards marched past in slow and quick time, and then returned home. The weather throughout was very fine, and the border of the parade ground was lined with a number of spectators, the heights overlooking it being also thickly covered.

On the 7th of May, orders were received for the Regiment to be held in readiness to proceed to Aldershot, and on the following day Major-General Walker made his half-yearly inspection. Previous to its departure from Edinburgh, he issued the following order:—

" In expressing his sincere regret at the departure of
" the 26th Regiment from Edinburgh (a feeling which
" he is assured is participated in by a large mass of the

" inhabitants of this city), Major-General Walker, in 1862.
" simple justice to Colonel Carey, the officers, non-com-
" missioned officers and men of the Cameronians, wishes
" to convey to them his best thanks for their admirable
" conduct during the period he has had the pleasure to
" have them under his command, and his sense of their
" high state of efficiency, reflecting as it does, great credit
" on all ranks of that distinguished corps, and he now
" takes leave of the Cameronians with every good wish
" for their welfare and prosperity."

The Regiment proceeded from Leith to Aldershot in four divisions, by steamers, to London, on the 14th, 17th, 21st, and 24th of May, and on their arrival were quartered in the West Block of the Permanent Barracks. Brigadier-General Brown, commanding the Second Infantry Brigade, to which it was attached, inspected the corps on the 29th of May. Lieut.-General Sir John Pennefather, K.C.B., commanding at Aldershot, also inspected the Regiment on the 2nd of June, and both were much pleased with its appearance and movements.

On the 6th of June, an official memorandum was received requesting to know whether any authority had been received for men being employed as Pipers in the Cameronians, and the result was that three were authorized.*

The Regiment, on the 1st of August, formed part of a flying column which marched from Aldershot to Ascot on that day, and encamped there. On the following morning a review took place, in which several Volunteer Corps participated. This column remained at Ascot until the 4th of August, when it returned to Alder-

---

* *Vide* Correspondence, Appendix II.

1862. shot. The autumn half-yearly inspection was made on the 2nd of October.

Major-General George Henry Mackinnon, C.B., was appointed colonel of the 26th on the 21st of December, in succession to General Sir Philip Bainbrigge, K.C.B., deceased.

1863. In January, 1863, the new pattern great coat was issued to the greater portion of the Regiment, and in April the new chakos were commenced to be worn.

The spring half-yearly inspection took place on the 5th of May, when Brigadier-General Bates, C.B., commanding the Second Infantry Brigade at Aldershot, inspected the Regiment.

On the 20th of May, the 26th were placed under orders to proceed to the under-mentioned places on the 27th of that month:—the head-quarters and three companies to Fort Grange, Gosport; three companies to Portland; one company to Weymouth; one company to Tipner, near Portsmouth; one company to Marchwood, near Southampton; and one company to Haslar. They accordingly left Aldershot on the day named. The head-quarters and Nos. 6, 8, and 9 companies proceeded to Fort Grange; Nos. 3, 7, and 10 companies to Portland; No. 1 to Weymouth, No. 5 to Tipner, No. 2 to Marchwood, and No. 4 company to Haslar. There being no room at Fort Grange for a number of the men, women, and children belonging to the head-quarter companies, they were also sent to Haslar.

The head-quarter companies and the detachment at Haslar were inspected on the 19th of June by Major-General Lord William Paulet, C.B., commanding the South-Western District. The autumn half-yearly inspection took place on the 6th of October, 1863, on which day his Lordship inspected the head-quarter com-

panies at Fort Grange and the detachment at Haslar 1863.
Barracks. Lord William Paulet had previously seen
those at Portland, Weymouth, and Marchwood, and expressed himself much pleased with everything.

On the 13th of November, the head-quarters and
Haslar detachment marched into the Clarence Barracks,
at Portsmouth; and, on the 16th and 17th, the detachments from Tipner, Marchwood, Portland, and Weymouth, were relieved by the 64th Regiment, when
they rejoined the head-quarters.

Major General Lord William Paulet, C.B., made 1864.
the usual spring half-yearly inspection on the 11th of
May, 1864, and the autumnal one on the 6th of October
following.

In February, 1865, the depôt companies were removed 1865.
from Belfast to Preston, in Lancashire.

A letter of readiness was received on the 30th of
April, for the Regiment to proceed to Bombay, to
relieve the 72nd Highlanders; and on the 1st of May,
the 26th were inspected by Major-General Lord William
Paulet, K.C.B., on Southsea Common. The following
order was received shortly before the Regiment embarked
for India, from the General Officer commanding the
South-Western District:—

"*Assistant Adjutant-General's Office, Portsmouth,*
"23rd *July,* 1865.
"*District Order.*

" The Lieutenant-General commanding cannot allow
" the 26th Cameronians to embark for India, without
" expressing his great satisfaction at the good conduct,
" orderly behaviour, and soldierlike appearance of this
" distinguished Corps, whilst in his command.

" The Lieut.-General having only recently assumed

1865. "the charge of this district,* speaks not so much from "his own experience, as from the opinion of his "predecessor, Major-General Lord William Paulet, "K.C.B.

"The greatest credit is due to Colonel Carey, Major "Henning, and the Officers and Non-Commissioned "Officers, for the high state of discipline in which "the Regiment now is; and the Lieut-General feels "that he cannot convey a better wish to the 26th, "when parting from them, than that they may continue "to preserve the unstained reputation with which they "now depart on foreign service.

"By order,
"A. ALISON, *Lieut.-Colonel*,
"*A.-A. General.*

"The Officer Commanding
"26th Regiment, Portsmouth."

On Monday the 24th of July, Nos. 7, 8, 9 and 10 companies, under Captain Charles Rowland Berkeley Calcott, in command; and Captains George Edmund Phipps Trent, James Armstrong, George John Hamilton, and Thomas William Lawson; Lieutenants Lewis Cubitt, and William Blakeway Burton; Ensigns George Henry Wilson, Livingstone Clarke, Frederick Samuel Alexander, James Bond Clarke, and John Macfarlane; and Assistant-Surgeon Joseph Johnston, M.D.; thirteen sergeants, thirteen drummers, fifteen corporals, and

---

* Lieut.-General Sir George Buller, K.C.B., succeeded Major-General Lord William Paulet, K.C.B., in the command of the South-Western District, on the latter being appointed Adjutant-General to the Forces, 1st July, 1865.

three hundred and seven privates, three officers' wives 1865. and two children, thirty-four soldiers' wives and forty-six children, embarked on board the "Cospatrick," which sailed from Spithead on the following morning.

The command of the Cameronians was, on the 25th of July, taken over by Lieut.-Colonel Shurlock Henning, who was promoted in succession to Colonel Carey, retired on half-pay. Captain C. R. B. Calcott succeeded to the vacant majority.

The head-quarters, consisting of Nos. 1, 4, and 6 companies, with Major Mosse in command, and Captains William Henry Salwey and Thomas Turner; Lieutenants Oswald Cresswell, Henry C. Sharp, William Barton Wade, Archibald Duffield Eden, and Charles H. Dougherty; Ensigns Henry FitzJohn Townsend and Edward M. Dougherty; Lieutenant and Adjutant Howard Molyneux Edward Brunker, and Surgeon-Major Richard Gamble; one officer's wife, twenty-two sergeants, fifteen corporals, two drummers, two hundred and eighty-nine privates, forty-eight soldiers' wives, and forty-six children, embarked on board the "Dilawur," which sailed on the 29th of July. The remainder of the Regiment, consisting of Captain Edward Archibald Collins, in command, with Captain William Beers, Lieutenants Philip Conway Story, Hercy P. Wolferstan, and James Ross Gray Buchanan, Ensign Charles William Hemphill, and Assistant-Surgeon William Carpenter, M.D., one officer's wife, nine sergeants, eight corporals, three drummers, one hundred and fifty-two privates, twenty-two soldiers' wives, and twenty-three children, embarked on the 9th of August on board the "Edwin Fox," which sailed on the 10th of that month.

The several ships arrived in Bombay harbour in the following order:—The "Dilawur," with head-quarters,

1865. on the 26th of October; the "Cospatrick" on the 28th of that month, and the "Edwin Fox" on the 9th of December. Two men and several children died on the passage out.

On arrival at Bombay, it was found that the Regiment was ordered to Belgaum. The head-quarters and detachment which had proceeded in the "Cospatrick" were embarked on board coasting steamers, and landed at Vingorla, where they remained encamped until the 8th of November, on which day the march up country commenced, and this portion of the 26th reached Belgaum on the 18th of that month.

The detachment, which had proceeded from England to Bombay in the "Edwin Fox," marched into Belgaum 1866. on the 1st of January, 1866. The strength of the Regiment on that day was—forty officers, forty-seven sergeants, forty corporals, nineteen drummers, and seven hundred and forty privates.

Brigadier-General A. T. Heyland, C.B., commanding the Belgaum brigade, made the half-yearly spring inspection of the Cameronians on the 15th, 16th, and 17th of March. He expressed his approbation in the following terms:—" I find the Regiment in exceeding good order " and very well drilled, and I shall have much pleasure " in making a most favourable report of them."

The autumnal inspection of the 26th was made at Camp Belgaum on the 20th, 22nd, and 23rd of October, by Brigadier-General Heyland, C.B., who again expressed himself pleased with the appearance, drill, discipline, and interior economy of the Regiment.

1867. At the conclusion of this Record, the service companies of the 26th Regiment continued at Camp Belgaum, under the command of Lieut.-Colonel Henning, and the depôt remained at Preston.

CONCLUSION OF RECORDS
OF
THE TWENTY-SIXTH, OR CAMERONIAN REGIMENT.

IN 1866 the Cameronians won the silver cup given by Sir R. Napier, Commander-in-Chief at Bombay, to be shot for by Non-Commissioned Officers of Regiments in the Presidency; and in 1867 they won the silver cup for the best contribution to the Soldiers' Industrial Exhibition at Poona. In 1868, the Regiment formed part of the Abyssinian Expedition. Leaving Belgaum 830 strong, they embarked at Vingorla on the 18th and 19th March, in the steamers "Queen" and "England," and anchored in Annesley Bay on the 30th and 31st. Landing at Zoulla, the Regiment was sent up country in detachments, the head-quarters starting April 11th. The heat at Zoulla was great, and the water supply limited. The Regiment was armed with the Snider breech-loading rifle, the old Enfield muzzle-loaders being given in. After a march of fourteen miles across the desert, the Regiment halted at Koomaylie, which is at the entrance of the great Rocky Valley, or ravine, nearly fifty miles long, which leads up to the plain of Senafe. In the rains this ravine is the central duct of a system of mountain streams, numerous valleys draining into it during its course. At this time it was a dry river bed up which a road had been made with great labour by the first native regiments which landed in the country. This ravine (commonly known as "The Passes,") is shut in by high rocks, and halting places were established at intervals where parties of two or three hundred men could pass the day after marching during the night. There were three halting places named Upper Sooroo, Undel Wells, and Raray Guddee.

The sanitary arrangements were carried out with great difficulty. The stench from dead camels, horses, and mules would have made The Passes uninhabitable, had not natives been actively employed in burning the carcases. The plain of Senafe, which is about 8,000 feet above the sea, was reached from Zoulla in five marches. Here the Regiment heard the news of the Battle of Arogee, and then of the release of the prisoners, capture of Magdala, and death of King Theodore. The campaign therefore was at an end. The camp at Senafe, commanded by General D. Stewart, was pleasant as to climate. The Regiment sent a detachment forward about forty miles to Adegarat. On the 10th May the Regiment began to move down country in parties. A railway had been made across the desert from Koomaylie to Zoulla. In the sailing ships "Trafalgar" and "Gavin Steel," the Regiment embarked on the 16th and 17th May. On the way down through the passes, the Regiment saw signs that there was no time to lose if the army was to get down from the highlands by that road. More than once in fine weather a wave some six or eight inches in depth flowed down the pass, the result of distant rain showers which had drained into the central channel. After these floods the road had to be repaired, and finally all the Regiments came down before the rains flooded the passes and made them finally impassable. Both ships reached Bombay on the 11th of June, and leaving behind a detachment to relieve the crowded state of the decks, sailed for Calcutta on the 26th, the detachment following in the "Malabar," a week later.

The Regiment proceeded to Dum Dum with a detachment in Fort William, Calcutta. The Indian Depôt, which had been left at Poona, rejoined the Regiment at Dum Dum. Here the Cameronians received an ornamental brass cross from Sir R. Napier, Commander-in-Chief of the Abyssinian Expedition. After the taking of Magdala, which was a natural fortress with a wooden town on its flat summit, the town was burnt, and the army at once marched for the coast. In the town were many small churches, and each of these contained a cross either of brass or silver. These crosses were probably carried in processions. The Abyssinian people had long been Christians. Sir R. Napier collected these crosses and sent one to every regiment that served in Abyssinia, as a memento of the campaign. At the end of 1868, the Cameronians marched from Dum Dum to Calcutta, and there relieved the 2nd Batt. 60th Rifles. In December, 1869, the Duke of Edinburgh brought his ship the "Galatea" up to Calcutta, and rode with Lord Mayo, the Governor General, from the landing place to Government House, the road being kept by the troops in garrison.

In January, 1870, the Cameronians proceeded by rail to Cawnpore, and thence marched through Lucknow to Fyzabad, which they reached January 12th. In April cholera broke out, but was at once stopped by sending a portion of the Regiment into cholera camps a few miles away. In July, 1870, the strength of the

Head Quarters was reduced from ten to eight Companies, letters I and K Companies being broken up.

In August, 1871, Colonel F. A. Willis, from the 38th Regiment assumed command of the Cameronians, having exchanged with Colonel Henning. While at Fyzabad the Cameronians were the best shooting Regiment in India, and second best in the army. The exertions of Lieutenant W. B. Burton, Musketry Instructor, contributed greatly to this result. In August, 1872, cholera again appeared, and the whole Regiment was broken up into camps, when the disease at once disappeared. In 1872, mounted Infantry Officers began to wear long boots and pantaloons. In December, 1872, the Cameronians marched to Cawnpore, went by rail to Agra, and marched to Morar Gwalior, which they reached December 28th, and relieved the 1st Batt. 11th Regiment. Morar is not a healthy station, but during the two years that the Cameronians were there they enjoyed most excellent health. Whilst at Fyzabad, the Regiment had won the prize for the best contribution to the Bengal Soldiers' Industrial Exhibition at Lucknow. In July, 1874, the Regiment having then received its orders for England, Colonel Willis received a letter in which Sir R. Napier, Commander-in-Chief in India, spoke in the highest terms of the Regiment and congratulated them on being the best shooting Regiment in the British Army. The Cameronians left Morar November 25th, reached Deolalee December 10th and 11th, embarked in H.M.S " Crocodile " (Capt. Hand), 17th, sailed 18th, and disembarked at Portsmouth, January 21st, 1875.

They marched into Clarence Barracks, Portsmouth, from which Barracks they had embarked for India in

1865. The Dragon for China was added above the number on the officers' forage caps. Martini-Henry rifles were received, and the valise equipment taken into wear. Lieut.-Col. Collins succeeded Colonel Willis in the command of the Cameronians in May, 1876. The Regiment embarked in H.M.S. "Orontes" 3rd August, 1876; disembarked at Greenock 7th, and occupied Gallowgate Barracks, Glasgow. They embarked at Greenock in the "Orontes" 22nd October, 1878, landed at Portsmouth, and reached North Camp, Aldershot, on the 26th. In March, 1878, this country had misunderstandings with Russia. The Cameronians being in the First Army Corps for foreign service, received 350 volunteers from 23 different Regiments.

On the 19th April the Army Reserve was called out, and about 230 joined the Regiment, making the strength of the Cameronians about 1,300 of all ranks.

The Regiment also received Regimental transport, consisting of 27 horses and 8 wagons.

In July the Army Reserve were sent back to their homes. January 8th, 1880, the Regiment moved to Chatham, and on the 6th and 7th August they embarked in the "Euphrates" and "Tamar" for Malta, and arrived there on the 18th and 19th. At Malta they were quartered successively at Pembroke Camp, Isola Gate, and St. Elmo. On the 22nd March, 1881, the Regiment embarked for active service at the Cape, on board the hired transport "Egypt," with the 2nd Batt. 10th Regiment. The Cape war with the Boers having come to an end the "Egypt" was stopped at Gibraltar, where they landed the 10th Regiment, and took on board the 93rd Highlanders, and reached Portsmouth April 5th. The Cameronians proceeded to Shorncliffe on the 6th. The married people and baggage did not arrive for some six weeks afterwards. Lieut.-Col. M. H. Hale succeeded to the command of the Regiment in May, 1881.

On the 31st May 300 men were sent to the 74th Highlanders, thus reducing the Cameronians to little more than a Depôt. On the 1st July, 1881, the re-organization of the British Army took place, and the 74th Highlanders ceased to be the linked Battalion. The 26th Cameronian Regiment and the 90th Perthshire Light Infantry were united as The Scotch Rifles Cameronians. This was soon altered to the Cameronians Scotch Rifles, and finally to The Cameronians Scottish Rifles. On the 1st July, 1881, therefore, the history of the old single Regiment, the 26th Cameronians, came to an end, the Battalion under its new title remaining at Shorncliffe, under the command of Lieut.-Col. M. H. Hale.

One more scene has to be described. On the 26th June, 1882, the Regiment being then clothed in their new rifle uniform, the Colours were carried to the Parade. The Regiment, under Lieut.-Col. Hale, marched past and saluted them, and then advanced in line and gave them a Royal Salute. The Cameronians then stood in line, and the Band played "Auld Lang Syne" whilst the Colours were marched off Parade for the last time.

SUCCESSION OF OFFICERS

OF

THE TWENTY-SIXTH

OR

CAMERONIAN REGIMENT.

Names.	Date of First Commission in the Regiment.		Highest Rank in the Regiment or the Army (* denotes the latter Rank).	Removed, Promoted, or Exchanged.	Dates of Removal, &c.	Died in the Regiment, &c.
EARL OF ANGUS	Colonel, 19 Apr. 1689		Colonel	..	..	Killed at Steinkirk, 3 Aug., 1692.
CLELAND	Lt.-Col.,	,,	Lt.-Col.	..	..	Killed at Dunkeld, 1689 (vide Record, p. 10).
ACLAND	,,	,,	,,	Half-pay	1690	Died of wounds received at Dunkeld, 21 Aug. 1689
HENDERSON	Major,	,,	Major	,,	,,	
KER OF KERSLAND ..	Captain,	,,	,,	..	..	Mortally wounded at Steinkirk.
MONRO	,,	,,	Captain	Half-pay	1690	
ROY CAMPBELL	,,	,,				
HAY	,,	,,				
DHU CAMPBELL	,,	,,	Colonel	..	1 Jan. 1706	Killed at Ramillies, 23 May, 1706
JOHN BORTHWICK ..	,,	,,				
HUME	,,	,,	Captain	Half-pay	1690	
CRAIGMOOR	,,	,,				
HALDEN	,,	,,				
HARRIS	,,	,,				
LINDSAY	,,	,,				
STEIL	,,	,,				
GILCHRIST	,,	,,	,,	,,	,,	
MATHISON	,,	,,	,,	,,	,,	
CALDWELL	,,	,,	..	..	..	Died of wounds received at Dunkeld.
STEPHENSON	,,	,,	Captain	Half-pay	1690	
GUNN	,,	,,	,,	,,	,,	
WALSH	Capt.-Lt.,	,,	Capt.-Lt.	,,	,,	
GILCHRIST	Lieut.,	,,	Lieut.			
STUART	,,	,,	..	..	..	Killed at Dunkeld
OLIPHANT	,,	,,				
DALZELL	,,	,,	,,	Half-pay	1690	
HUTCHINSON	,,	,,	,,	,,	,,	
FORRESTER	,,	,,	,,	,,	,,	
CATHCART	,,	,,	,,	,,	,,	

SUCCESSION OF OFFICERS OF

Names.	Date of First Commission in the Regiment.	Highest Rank in the Regiment or the Army (* denotes the latter Rank).	Removed, Promoted, or Exchanged.	Dates of Removal, &c.	Died in the Regiment, &c.
JOHNSTONE	Lieut., 19 Apr. 1689				
Wm. CAMPBELL	,, ,,				
VEITCH	,, ,,				
TATE	,, ,,				
BALLANTINE	,, ,,				
BLACKADER	,, ,,	Lt.-Col.			*Vide* Record, pp. 73 and 81.
CALDER	,, ,,				
CLARKE	,, ,,	Lieut.	Half-pay	1690	
HARKNESS	,, ,,	,,	,,	,,	
STEWART	,, ,,	,,	,,	,,	
AIKEMAN	,, ,,				
FAIRBORN	,, ,,	,,	,,	,,	
CRANSTON	Ensign, ,,				
PRINGLE	,, ,,				
BOYD	,, ,,	Ensign	,,	,,	
FERGUSON	,, ,,				
CAMPBELL	,, ,,	,,	,,	,,	
J. CAMPBELL	,, ,,				
NESMYTH	,, ,,				
LANG	,, ,,				
CLEGHORN	,, ,,	,,	,,	,,	
DENNISTON	,, ,,				
WILSON	,, ,,	,,	,,	,,	
KIRKLAND	,, ,,				
WILSON	,, ,,				
HISLOP	,, ,,				
M'CULLOCK	,, ,,	,,	,,	,,	
HAY	,, ,,				Killed at Blenheim 13 Aug., 1704.
STEPHENSON	,, ,,	Ensign	Half-pay	1690	
YOUNG	,, 1689	,,	,,	,,	
FULLARTON	Lt.-Col., 1690				Killed at Steinkirk.
GREEN	Lieut., ,,				
FERGUSON	,, ,,				
HALDEN	,, ,,				
MATHEWSON	,, ,,				
GILCHRIST	Ensign, ,,				
And. MONRO	Colonel, 1 Aug. 1692	Colonel			Died in the Camp at Halle, Aug., 1693.
Jas. FERGUSON	Lt.-Col., ,, ,,	*Br.-Gen-	Half-pay	25 Aug. 1693 1 Jan. 1704	Died in Brabant, 13 Sept. 1705.
LIVINGSTONE	,, 1704				
A. CAMPBELL	Captain, ,,				Killed at Blenheim.
SMART	,, ,,				
LAWSON	,, ,,	Major			
A. DOUGLAS	Lieut., ,,				Killed at Blenheim
G. SEATON	,, ,,				,, ,,
MONCRIEFFE	,, ,,				
Jas. HAY	Ensign, ,,				,, ,,
BARNARD	,, ,,				
M'LEAN	,, ,,				
OGILVY	,, ,,				
ROW	,, ,,				
DALRYMPLE	,, ,,				
OLIPHANT	,, ,,				
MARSHALL	,, ,,				
Earl of STAIR	Colonel, 1 Jan. 1706	Colonel *Lt.-Gen.	2nd Drs.	1 June, 1706	
DENNON	Captain, 1706	Captain			Killed at Ramillies.

THE TWENTY-SIXTH OR CAMERONIAN REGIMENT. 243

Names.	Date of First Commission in the Regiment.	Highest Rank in the Regiment or the Army (* denotes the latter Rank).	Removed, Promoted, or Exchanged	Date s o.* Removal, &c.	Died in the Regiment, &c.
G. PRESTON	Colonel, 24 Aug. 1706	Colonel *Lt.-Gen.	..	..	Lt -Governor of Edinburgh Castle. Died 7 July, 1748, aged 88.
CRANSTON	Lt.-Col., 1709	Lt.-Col.	..	..	Killed at Malplaquet.
Lord FORRESTER	„ „	„	..	..	
SHAW	Captain, „	Captain	..	..	Died„ of„ wounds received at Preston,12 Nov.1715.
PRESTON	„ „	„	..	..	
COCKBURN	Lieut.,				Killed at Malplaquet, 11 Sept. 1709.
INGLIS	Ensign, „	Ensign	..	..	
BURNET	„ „				11 Nov. 1760.
Philip ANSTRUTHER	Colonel, 3 May, 1720	Colonel *Lt.-Gen.	..	..	
John PRESTON	Chapln., 23 Feb. 1742				
Ed. SANDFORD	Colonel, 26 Nov. 1760	*M.-Gen.			
Rob. HASTINGS	Ensign, 8 Dec. „				Died Dec. 1775.
John SCOTT	Colonel, 14 Jan. 1763	..	..	..	
William ANSTRUTHER	Captain, 1 „ 1766	Captain	Retired	1777	
L. DALHUNTRY	Lieut., 18 Feb. „	„			
W. B. BOROUGH	„ 1 Apr. „	Lt.-Col. *Colonel	Sold out	1805	
Duncan CAMPBELL	Qr.-Mas.,13 July, 1767	Cap.&P.-M. *Captain	..	..	Died, 1806.
Dudley TEMPLAR	Lt.-Col., 7 Sept. 1768	Lt.-Col.			
Chas. PRESTON	Major, „	Major			
J. LESLIE	Ensign, „	„			
J. STRONG	Captain, 31 Oct. 1770	Captain	Retired	1777	
W. DELAPLACE	„ 25 Dec. „				
Ed. THOMPSON	Lieut., 1 Mar. „	Lieut.			
P. MONCRIEFFE	„ 2 „ „	„			
Wm. RICHARDSON	„ 31 Oct. „	„	43rd Regt	24 Apr. 1779	
George CUPPAIDGE	„ 25 Dec. „	„	17th Regt.	16 July. „	
Arch. CAMPBELL	„ 26 „ „		Retired	1779	
Wm. SMIBERT	Ensign, 12 Jan. „				
Rob. THOMAS	„ 2 Mar. „	„			
John HAY	„ 31 Oct. „				
James GORDON	„ „		..	..	Killed at Fort Clinton, America, Oct. 1777.
Francis STEWART	Captain, 27 Jan. 1772	Captain *Major			
J. LIVINGSTON	„ „	„			
D. M'DONALD	Lieut., 16 Nov. „	Lieut.	Retired	1777	
Row. SWAN	Captain, 11 May, 1774	Captain	„	1779	
Lord Adam GORDON	Colonel ,17 Sept. 1775				
W. DRAKEFORD	Captain, 17 Aug. „	„	Retired	1777	
E. P. WILLINGTON	Lieut., 19 June, „	Lieut.	71st Regt.	16 Oct. 1779	
Prins. HEWETSON	„ 17 Aug, „	„	„	„	
Tho. BOLTON	Ensign, 19 June, „	Ensign			
Alex. WALKER	„ 14 Aug. „	Lieut.	Indep. Co.	14 Feb. 1782	
D. ANSTRUTHER	„ 15 „ „	Ensign	31st Regt.	28 Dec. 1778	
John M'DONALD	Captain, 21 Feb. 1776	Captain			
Arch. WADMAN	„ „	„	Indep. Co.	2 Feb. 1790	
Lord LINDORES	Lieut., „ „				
J. DRUMMOND	Ensign, 22 „ „				
Wm. DACRES	„ 23 „ „	Lt.-Col. *M.-Gen.			
P. JOHNSTON	„ 24 „ „	Ensign	77th Regt.	1 May, 1783	Died in 1801.
B. WHITELOCK	„ 31 Oct. „	Lieut.	101st Regt.	29 July, 1784	
Hon. Charles STUART	Lt.-Col., 26 „ 1777	Colonel *Lt.-Gen.			
And. GORDON	Major, 18 Jan. „	Colonel *Lt.-Gen.	..	..	17 Apr. 1806.

R 2

SUCCESSION OF OFFICERS OF

Names.	Date of First Commission in the Regiment.	Highest Rank in the Regiment or the Army (* denotes the latter Rank).	Removed, Promoted, or Exchanged.	Dates of Removal, &c.	Died in the Regiment, &c.
John ANDRE†	Captain, Jan. 18 1777	Captain *Major	44th Regt.	9 Sept. 1779	Executed in America, 2 Oct. 1780.
Wm. MYERS	,, 19 Feb. ,,	,,	15th Regt.	25 ,, 1803	Died 29July,1805.
Wm. DUFFE	,, 9 Apr. ,,	*Lt.-Gen. Major	Retired	1783	
J. FELTHAM	Capt.-Lt., 7 Oct. ,,	Captain	,,	,,	
Jas. FITZGERALD	Lieut., ,, ,,	Lieut.			
Wm. KEELING	Ensign, 5 June, ,,	Ensign			
— MILLAR..	Surg., 21 May, 1777	Surgeon			
Chas. GORDON	Captain, 8 Jan. 1778	Captain			
Geo. INMAN	Lieut., 29 June ,,	Lieut.	Half-pay	1787	
Wm. PEMBLE	,, 2 Nov. ,,	,,	104th Regt.	6 May, 1782	
Henry GAGE	Captain, 24 Apr. 1779	Captain	99th Regt.	17 Jan. 1783	
Sir W. ANDRE, Bt.	,, 6 Sept. ,,	,,	Retired	1783	
Geo. DUKE..	,, 10 ,, ,,	*Lt.-Col.	65th Regt.		
Chas. MARTIN	,, 14 ,, ,,	Captain	99th Regt.	8 Aug. 1782	
Sir Jas. AFFLECK, Bt.	,, 15 ,, ,,	,,	16th Drs.	6 June, ,,	
Pat. STUART	Lieut., 1 Aug. ,,	*General Lieut.	Half-pay	1788	
— GREEN ..	,, 1 Sept. ,,	Captain	Sold out	1799	
Jas. SETON ..	,, 16 Oct. ,,	*Lt.-Col. Lieut.			
H. SCOTT ..	Ensign, 30 July ,,	Captain			
Walter LITTLE	,, 1 Aug. ,,	Lieut.			
R. ELSDEN ..	,, 9 ,, ,,	Ensign	101st Regt.	25 Aug. 1781	

† This unfortunate officer was appointed second lieutenant in the 23rd Royal Welsh Fusiliers, on the 2nd of April, 1771 ; and was promoted lieutenant in the 7th Royal Fusiliers, on the 24th of September, following. He served during the gallant but unsuccessful defence of St. John's, and became a prisoner of war with the garrison and its brave commander, Major Preston of the Cameronians (vide Record, p. 86), in which regiment he obtained a company, on the 18th of January, 1777. Captain André next served as aide-de-camp to Major-General Sir Charles (Earl) Grey, and subsequently on the staff of General Sir Henry Clinton, by whose influence he was appointed Adjutant-General to the Forces serving under his command in North America. On the 9th of September, 1779, he was removed to the 54th Regiment; and on the 5th of August, of the following year, whilst holding this important staff situation, he received the brevet rank of Major. The American General Arnold, who commanded a large force at West Point, having agreed to violate his trust, Major André was selected by Sir Henry to carry on the secret correspondence. The latter having had an interview with the traitor, was, on his return, taken, and the papers found on his person led to his trial as a spy, by a Court-Martial, of which the celebrated Marquis La Fayette was one of the members, and the decision was that he must, according to the laws of war, be hanged. Washington has been censured for directing this ignominious death, but can scarcely be condemned in the matter, although the amiable qualities of Major André occasioned great commiseration for his unhappy fate, which was shared in by the members of the Court, who wept while sentence was being passed upon him. Forty-one years afterwards, his remains were disinterred, brought to England, and buried in Westminster Abbey, where a marble monument has been erected to his memory. The figures were cut by Van Gelder. On a moulded panelled base and plinth stand a sarcophagus, on the panel of which is inscribed:—" Sacred to the memory " of Major André, who, raised by his merits, at an early period of his life, to the rank of Adjutant-General " of the British Forces in America, and employed in an important but hazardous enterprise, fell a " sacrifice to his zeal for his King and country, on the 2nd October, 1780, aged twenty-nine, universally " beloved and esteemed by the army in which he served, and lamented even by his foes. His gracious " Sovereign, King George III., has caused this monument to be erected ;"—and, on the plinth :—" The " remains of the said Major André were deposited, on the 28th of November, 1821, in a grave near his " monument." The sarcophagus has projecting figures; one of them (with a flag of truce) presenting to General Washington a letter which André had addressed to his Excellency the night previous to his execution, worded thus:—" Sir, buoyed above the terror of death, by the consciousness of a life " devoted to honourable purposes, and stained with no action which can give me remorse, I trust that " the request which I make to your Excellency at this serious period, and which is to soften my last " moments, will not be rejected; sympathy towards a soldier will surely induce your Excellency, and a " military tribunal, to adopt the mode of my death to the feelings of a man of honour ; let me hope, Sir, " that if aught in my character impresses you with esteem towards me—if aught in my misfortunes " marks me as the victim of policy, and not of resentment, I shall experience the operation of those " feelings in your breast, by being informed I am not to die on a gibbet. I have the honour to be, your " Excellency, John André, Adjutant of British Forces in America."

THE TWENTY-SIXTH OR CAMERONIAN REGIMENT.

Names.	Date of First Commission in the Regiment.	Highest Rank in the Regiment or the Army (* denotes the latter Rank).	Removed, Promoted, or Exchanged.	Dates of Removal, &c.	Died in the Regiment, &c.
Chas. DUKE	,, 18 Sept. 1779	Captain *Lt.-Col.	Sold out		
H. G. GRAY	,, 17 Oct. ,,	,,			
Arch. CUMINE	Lieut., 23 Apr. 1780	Captain	Half-pay	1789	
Robt. CRANFORD	Ensign, ,,	Lieut.	13th Regt.	14 Aug. 1782	
J. BRANTHWAYTHE	,, ,,	,,			
Aaron TOZER	,, 18 May, ,,	Ensign			
Sir W. COCKBURN, Bt.	,, 26 ,, ,,	,,	1st Regt.	1 Oct. 1783	
John TIDY	,, 13 Oct. ,,	Lieut.			
Thos. H. TIDY	Chaplain,16 May, 1781				
Geo. BERRY	Ensign, 15 Sept. ,,	Ensign			
B. Ford BOWLS	,, 25 Oct. ,,	Lieut. *M.-Gen.	6th Regt.	1783	Killed atSalamanca, 25June,1812.
Sir Wm. ERSKINE, Bt.	Colonel, 16 May, 1782	Colonel *Lt.-Gen.	..	..	Died 21 Mar. 1795.
W. A. BYGRAVE	Captain, 16 Feb. ,,	Captain *Lt.-Col.	65th Regt.	2 Sept. 1795	
John CLUNES	Ensign, 2 Jan. ,,	Ensign	} Retired	1783	
Jas. OGILVIE	,, 3 ,, ,,	,,			
Rich. RIMINGTON	,, 12 Mar. ,,	Lieut.	Half-pay	1786	
Holt M'KENZIE	,, 13 ,, ,,	Ensign	97th Regt.	19 Sept. 1794	
Chris. DAVIDSON	,, 28 May, ,,	Major	..	..	Drowned, 1805.
John CRAWFORD	,, 15 Oct. ,,	Ensign			
Thos. DALZELL	,, ,, ,,	,,	50th Regt.	7 Sept. 1785	
M. E. LINDSAY	Captain, 31 Dec. 1784	Captain *Ensign	Indep. Co.	20 Feb. 1790	
Saml. CROOKE	Ensign, 19 Jan. ,,	Ensign	22nd Regt.	31 May, 1791	
Hump. FOSTER	,, 29 July, ,,	,,			
W. WHEELER	,, 1 Oct. ,,	,,			
C. Stuart CAMPBELL, C.B.	Qr.-Mas., 25 Dec. ,,	Lt.-Col. *M.-Gen.	1st Foot	24 Jan. 1829	Died 30 August, 1854.
M. MONEYPENNY	Ensign, 30 Sept. 1785	Captain	78th Regt.	6 Aug. 1794	
Jos. WIGGLESWORTH	,, ,,	,,	Half-pay	1786	
John DANIEL	,, 4 Jan. 1786	Ensign			
H. H. MITCHELL	Lieut., 23 May ,,	Lt.-Col. *Colonel	51st Regt.	25 Mar. 1811	
Jas. BALFOUR	Ensign, 10 Apr. ,,	,,			
Thos. BOYES	Lieut., 5 Feb. 1787	P.M.&Cap.	Half-pay	1809	
John BAINBRIDGE	Ensign, 31 Mar. ,,	Lieut.	Indep. Co.	13 Aug. 1793	
Wm. ERSKINE	Lieut., 6 June,1788	,, *Lt.-Gen.	7th Regt.	9 Jan. ,,	
Jas. ERSKINE	Ensign, 26 Feb. ,,	Ensign *Lt.-Gen.	7th Regt.	20 Feb. 1791	
Ersk. HOPE	Captain, 20 Apr. 1789	Lt.-Col.	Sold out	..	Dec. 1805.
Geo. LEASON	Ensign, ,,	Ensign	101st Regt	11 Mar. 1794	
J. Thos. EYRE	,, 5 June ,,	Lieut.	Indep. Co.	6 Sept. 1793	
Hon. Hy. SAFTON	,, 19 May, 1790	Ensign	7th Regt.	11 May, 1791	
E. J. J. BYNG	,, 18 Aug. ,,	,,	Half-pay	29 June,1826	
Fred. JONES	,, 2 Mar. 1791	Major *Lt.-Col.	Sold out		
Geo. JONES	Lieut., 31 May ,,	Lieut.	Indep. Co.	14 ,, 1793	
Jas. F. ERSKINE	Ensign, 16 Mar. ,,	,,	Scot. Brig.	21 Oct. 1795	
Thos. BATT	,, 13 July, ,,	Captain	..	..	1806.
Jas. MILLAR	,, 20 Nov. ,,	Ensign			
Jephson G. FORTH	,, 2 Apr. 1793	Captain			March, 1809.
Geo. BILLINGHURST	,, 4 Sept. ,,	Ensign	7thLt.Drs.	11 Aug. 1794	
Pat. M'NEIGHT	,, 17 ,, ,,	Lieut.	93rd Regt.	3 ,, 1795	
Jas. LLOYD	,, 8 Oct. ,,	Ensign			
H. M. SCOTT	,, 16 ,, ,,	,,	6th Regt.	7 Oct. 1794	
Ed. O. EYRE	,, 1 Mar. 1794	Captain *Lt.-Col.	H. Guards		
John MIDGLEY	,, 12 Nov. ,,	Ensign *Lt.-Col.			Died 9 Sept. 1822.
Hild. OAKES	Lt.-Col., 1 Sept. 1795	Lt.-Col. *Lt.-Gen.			
W. GIFFORD	Captain, 30 Dec. ,,	Captain *Lt.-Col.	43rd Regt.		

246 SUCCESSION OF OFFICERS OF

Names.	Date of First Commission in the Regiment.	Highest Rank in the Regiment or the Army (* denotes the latter Rank).	Removed, Promoted, or Exchanged.	Dates of Removal, &c.	Died in the Regiment, &c.
Ed. JAMESON	Lieut., 27 May, 1795	Lieut.			
John PERRY	„ 3 Sept. „				
A. W. WAINHOUSE	„ 4 „ „	Captain	..	..	Dismissed the Service.
Charles STUART	„ 5 „ „	Lieut.	28th Regt.	18 Jan. 1799	
W. A. GORDON	„ 6 „ „				
Fred. ADAM	Ensign, 4 Nov. „	„			
Ed. SHEARMAN	Ensign, „	*Lt.-Gen. Major *Lt.-Col.	..	..	Feb. 1820.
Thomas AHMUTY	„ „	Ensign			
James CONOLLY	„ 16 Dec. „	Major	2nd Regt.	1816	
Wm. CONOLLY	„ „	Lieut.	15th Regt.	5 Aug. 1804	
F. HOGG	„ „	*Major Lt.-Col.	Sold out.		
W. HOGGINS	„ „	Captain	..	..	Drowned, 25 Dec. 1805.
James BOWIE	„ „	Lieut.	Sold out		
John BOYES	„ 2 Feb. 1796	„			
George GIFFORD	„ 20 „ „	„			
— OGLEVY	„ 8 June „	„			
Thomas MATHEWS	„ 29 July „	„			
Jno. ROBERTSON	Qr.-Mas., 7 Dec. „	Qr.-Mas.	..	..	„
— MITCHELSON	Surgeon, 15 Aug. 1797				
Lord ELPHINSTONE	Lt.-Col., 11 July, 1798	Colonel *Lt.-Gen.			21 May, 1813.
Thomas J. WARDE	Lieut., 25 „ „	Lieut.			
Rob. SKOTTOWE	„ 15 Aug. „	„ *Captain	4th Regt.	Jan. 1801	
Sam. NICOLL	Ensign, 8 Mar. „	„			
Alex. PROUDFOOT	„ 22 „ „	Lieut.	40th Regt.	8 Nov. 1799	
C. F. TOLFREY	„ 15 Aug. „	„			
Adam G. CAMPBELL	„ 22 Nov. „	Captain *Major	Half-pay	1826	
W. GARSTIN	Captain, 30 Dec. 1799	Captain	..	..	Drowned, 25 Dec. 1805.
W. WALKER	Ensign, 19 Oct. „	„	Sold out	13 July, 1813	
H. DABSAC	„ 11 Jan. 1800	Lieut.	..	..	„
J. A. HOPE	„ 12 „ „	Captain *Lt.-Col.	3rd Ft Gds.	July, 1814	
Pat. GRAHAM	„ 24 July, „	Captain	..	..	Sept. 1813.
Henry EYRE	„ 21 Aug. „	„	Half-pay		
Rob. CHILD	„ 4 Sep. „	„	..	..	Died at Gibraltar, 29 Sept. 1813.
Jas. HUNT	„ 9 Oct. 1801	„	40th Regt.	1811	
N. SAVAGE	Capt.-Lt.,26 Mar. „	Major	..	..	Superseded in 1809.
Alex. TOFFMEY	Ensign, 25 „ „	Lieut.			
Duncan CAMPBELL	P.-Mas., 3 Apr. „	Pay-Mas.	..	..	Died in Apr. 1806
Fran. GLASSE	Ensign, 14 Aug. „	Lieut.			
T. Owen JONES	„ 21 Mar. „	Captain	72nd Regt.	1810	
Sir W. MAXWELL, Bt.	Major, 9 July, 1803	Lt.-Col.	Sold out	1812	
Hugh ANTROBUS	„ 23 Nov. „	Major *Lt.-Col.	„	1807	
Sir Jas. DALZELL	Captain, 9 July, „	Captain	„	5 Jan. 1805	
A. CAMERON	„ „	„	..	..	Drowned, 25 Dec. 1805.
N. LAMONT	„ „	„	Sold out	1806	
R. DEWAR	Surgeon, „	Surgeon			
J. COLDSTREAM	As.-Sur., „	„	..	..	Retired on Full Pay, 1825.
Jas. MAITLAND	Captain, „	Captain *Colonel	Ceyl. Reg.	1807	
Wm. FOTHERINGHAM	„ „	Captain	..	..	died Aug. 1809.
G. H. DUNDAS	„ „	„	Sold out	..	
J. CAMPBELL	Lieut., „	Lieut.	..	..	Drowned, 25 Dec. 1805.

THE TWENTY-SIXTH OR CAMERONIAN REGIMENT. 247

Names.	Date of First Commission in the Regiment.	Highest Rank in the Regiment or the Army (* denotes the latter Rank).	Removed, Promoted, or Exchanged	Dates of Removal, &c.	Died in the Regiment, &c.
J. ZOBELL	Lieut., 9 July, 1803	Captain	66th Regt.	July, 1811	
— M'MILLAR	" "	"	Sold out	7 Mar. 1814	
C. B. MARSHAM	" "	Lieut.	..	..	Drowned, 25 Dec. 1805.
James CRAMPTON	" "	"	90th Regt.	..	Died at Gibraltar, 23 Sept. 1814.
Charles GRANT	" "	Captain	..	..	
Edw. WHITTY	" "	"	Half-pay	12 June, 1826	Died, 16 Dec. 1835, at Calcutta.
		*Major			
Charles ADDISON	" "	Captain	Half-pay	1817	
		*Major			
D. DOOLITTLE	" "	Lieut.			
H. BALNEAVIS	" "	"	27th Regt.	Sept. 1804	
W. BROWNE	Lieut., 31 Dec. "	"	..	..	Drowned, 25 Dec. 1805.
J. DUNDAS	Ensign, 9 July, "	"			
J. CHRISTIE	" "	Captain	27th Regt.	25 Mar. 1810	
R. HAGGERSTONE	" "	Lieut.	6th Drags.	1805	
— HAMILTON	" "	"	93rd Regt.	1806	
J. CLARKE	" "	"	81st Regt.	1805	
Wm. BYGRAVE	" "				
Wm. HOPKINS	" 25 Aug. "				
J. SCAULAR	" 25 Oct. "				
Wm. CHARTRES	" 22 Nov. "	Captain	Portg. Ser.	11 July, 1811	
		*Major			
John OGILVIE	" 16 Feb. 1804	Captain			
P. PYM	Captain, 15 June, "	"	Half-pay	1810	
Ar. ARMSTRONG	As.-Sur., 14 May, "	Surgeon	"	1814	
F. LIVINGSTONE	Ensign, 1 June, "	Lieut.	90th Regt.	1806	
		*Captain			
R. DAWSON	As.-Sur., 24 " "	As.-Sur.	3d Gr.Batt.	"	
W. MAYBEN	" "	"	Half-pay	1814	
Jas. NASH	" 14 May, "	"	..	..	Died, 23 Aug.1812
John CONNELL	Qr.-Mas., "	Qr.-Mas.	..	..	
John BROOKS	Ensign, 3 Aug. "	Captain	Sold out	1822	
— SNOW	" 4 " "	Ensign	"	"	
Joseph SMITH	" 28 " "	Captain	10th Regt.	1814	
And. LETT	" 5 Oct. "	"	R. Vet. Ba.	1816	
Sampson FRITH	Major, 27 Mar. "	Major			
		*Colonel			
R. L. PARKER	Lieut., 14 May, "	Lieut.			
Geo. HERIOT	" 5 July, "	"			
		*Captain			
Thos. L. DICK	" 6 " "	"	Sold out		
Thos. HOPKINS	P.-Mas., 29 Aug. "	Pay-Mas.			
R. IRELAND	" 22 Oct. "	"	..	Nov. 1817	
F. SHEARMAN	Ensign, 14 May, "	Captain	Half-pay	1817	
Jas. STEDMAN	" "	"	..	..	Killed at Corunna, 2 Oct. 1813.
Joseph NUNN	" "	Lieut.	..	..	
Thos. THOMSON	" 2 Apr. " "	"	1st Foot	11 July, 1816	Died 18 Sept.1861
Rob. SMITH	" 4 " " "	"	Half-pay		
L. CHEVERS	" 1 Aug. 1805	"	..	..	Killed at Corunna, 16 Jan. 1809.
Edw. DUPRE	" 2 " "	"	96th Regt.	July, 1810	
John WESTLAKE	" 12 Sept. "	Captain	50th Regt.	1828	
Jas. DUNN	" 8 Oct. "	"	Half-pay	1821	
Thos. MURRAY	" 10 " "	"	"	1825	
Hamilton MAXWELL	" 30 Jan. 1806	Lieut.	42nd Regt.	19 May, 1812	
J. SHEARMAN	" 19 Feb. "	"	62nd Regt.	Nov. 1806	
Jas. HERVEY	" 20 " "	"	22nd Regt.	" 1807	
Thos. G. MARSHAM	" 27 " "	"	3 Gn. Batt.	" "	
John LAW	" 13 Mar. "	"	Sold out	1809	
Mat. MOLE	" 3 Apr. "	"	1st Regt.	Aug. 1807	
Geo. PIPON	" 17 " "	Major	6 Dr. Gds.	7 Mar. 1819	
H. McLATCHIE	" 19 June, "	Captain	..	8 Apr. 1825	Died at Meerut, 26 June, 1833.
John ELLIOT	Qr.-Mas., 20 Feb. "	Qr.-Mas.	R. V. B.	1808	
H. MESSITER	Surg., 10 Apr. "	..	..	..	1809.

SUCCESSION OF OFFICERS OF

Names.	Date of First Commission in the Regiment.	Highest Rank in the Regiment or the Army ("denotes the latter Rank).	Removed, Promoted, or Exchanged.	Dates of Removal, &c.	Died in the Regiment, &c.
Henry MAXWELL ..	Ensign, 19 June, 1806	Lieut.	..	..	Died of wounds, Walcheren, Sept. 1809.
J. E. HUNT ..	Lieut., 26 Feb. ,,	,,	7th Regt.	1807	
P. ESPY ..	,, 27 ,, ,,	,,	..	..	Dismissed the Service.
Ar. BLAKE.. ..	,, 2 Apr. ,,	,,	Superseded	..	
Geo. PLATT ..	,, 3 ,, ,,	,,	Sold out	1813	
W. H. VERGO ..	,, 9 Oct ,,	,,	60th Regt.	1810	
H. C. E. V. GRAHAM ..	Capt., 6 Mar. ,,	*Captain ,, *Lt.-Col.	66th Regt.	18 June, 1811	
Hugh LAW ..	Ensign, 20 Nov. ,,	Lieut.	..	..	September, 1809.
Donald M'COLMAN ..	,, 4 Dec. ,,	,,	Half-pay	1817	
A. C. HOPE ..	,, 8 Jan. 1807	Ensign	Rifle Brig.	1808	
Jesse COLLINS ..	,, 15 ,, ,,	Lieut.			
J. Q. SHORT ..	Surg., ,,	Surgeon *Dep.-Ins.			
F. C. HEATLEY ..	Ensign, 18 Mar. ,,	Lieut. *Captain	50th Regt.	8 Apr. 1825	
Rob. ROBERTSON ..	,, 19 ,, ,,	Lieut.	Half-pay	1827	
J. MAXWELL ..	,, 30 Oct. ,,	,,	..	..	19 Sept. 1823.
A. F. TAYLOR ..	Major, 29 ,, ,,	Major	Sold out	1810	Died at Gibraltar.
Thos. BEST.. ..	Capt., 20 Nov. ,,	Captain	..	..	6 Oct. 1813.
Colin CAMPBELL ..	Ensign, 17 Dec. ,,	Lieut.			
Hugh POLLOCK ..	,, 31 ,, ,,	Pay-Mas.			
Thos. ARCHER ..	,, ,,	Ensign			
Hon. H. MURRAY..	Major, 26 Nov. ,,	Major *Lt.-Col.	18 Lt. Dra.	2 Aug. 1810	
Thos. E. SCARISBRICKS ..	Lieut., ,,	Lieut.	Sold	1807	
W. KEARY	Ensign, 11 Feb. 1808	*Captain	5 Dr. Gds.	25 Oct. 1810	
W. LAWRIE ..	,, 18 ,, ,,	Lieut.	..	..	Taken at Corunna
W. JOHNSTONE ..	,, 25 ,, ,,	Major *Lt.-Col.	..	26 May, 1841	Died on passage from China, 19 Oct. 1842.
J. F. ROSS ..	,, 26 ,, ,,	Lieut.	Half-pay	19 Oct. 1818	
P. J. ROBERTSON ..	,, 12 May ,,	,,	,,		
J. WRIGHT.. ..	Lieut., 3 Aug. ,,	,,	Sold out		
S. LOWCAY	,, 5 ,, ,,	,,	..	..	Dismissed the Service.
H. ROBERTS ..	,, 7 ,, ,,	,,	..	..	30 July, 1824.
J. CROTTY	,, 9 ,, ,,	,,	Superseded	..	
Ed. JORDAN ..	,, 10 ,, ,,	,,	Half-pay	Oct. 1817	
John MARSHALL ..	,, 11 ,, ,,	Captain	2 W.I. Reg.	..	12 March, 1829.
Thos. HAY.. ..	Ensign, 8 ,, ,,	Lieut. *Captain	..	2 June, 1814	
J. KIRK	,, 9 ,, ,,	Lieut.	Half-pay	..	
Geo. BRAY	,, 10 ,, ,,	,, *Captain	6 Dra. Gds.	20 Feb. 1812	
J. GRIMSHAW ..	,, 11 ,, ,,	Lieut.	103rd Regt.	7 Mar. 1811	
G. W. CHARLETON ..	,, 29 Dec. ,,	,,	..	..	Walcheren, 13 Sept. 1809.
E. J. WHITE ..	,, 30 Mar. 1809	,, *Captain	70th Regt.	25 Mar. 1811	
F. R. MASTERS ..	,, 25 Apr. ,,	Lieut.	..	..	29 Nov., 1814.
Robt. ROBSON ..	,, 26 ,, ,,	,, *Captain	Half-pay	30 Apr. 1826	
A. ARNOTT.. ..	,, 27 ,, ,,	Lieut.	.	.	
Pat. CARROLL ..	Surg., 11 May, ,,	Surgeon	..	..	Of fever, Walcheren, 25 Sept. 1809
G. ANDERSON ..	Ensign, 25 ,, ,,	Ensign	..	1811	Died in Portugal.
J. WILKINSON ..	,, 22 June ,,	Lieut.	Sold out	1813	
W. LAFOREST ..	P.-Mas., 3 Aug. ,,	Pay-Mas.	Resigned	,,	
Thos. TAYLOR ..	Ensign, 26 ,, ,,	Lieut.	Half-pay	25 Oct. 1814	
J. B. TAYLOR ..	Surgeon, 12 Oct. ,,	Surgeon	..	..	Died at Gibraltar, 1 Oct. 1813.
Tho. SHEPHEARD ..	Captain, 9 Nov. ,,	Captain	..	..	2 ,, 1814.

THE TWENTY-SIXTH OR CAMERONIAN REGIMENT. 249

Names.	Date of First Commission in the Regiment.	Highest Rank in the Regiment or the Army (* denotes the latter Rank).	Removed, Promoted, or Exchanged.	Dates of Removal, &c.	Died in the Regiment, &c.
T. W. Boyes	Ensign, 16 Nov. 1809	Lieut.	Paymaster 1 R.Vet.Bt.	1815	2 March, 1829.
W. Graham	,, 24 May, 1810	,,	,,	,,	
D. Black	,, 26 July, ,,	,,	Half-pay	25 Oct. 1814	
L. W. Otway, Bart.	Major, 2 Aug. ,,	Major *Colonel			
Jas. Lowrey	Captain, 30 ,, ,,	Captain	40th Regt.	14 Mar. 1811	
M. Poynton	Adjutant, 4 Oct. ,,	Lieut. *Captain	Retired		
Rob. Wrixon	Lieut., 25 ,, ,,	Lieut.	Half-pay		
J. Kyle	Ensign. 29 Nov. ,,	Captain	50th Regt.	3 Sept. 1824	
Lord Belhaven	,, 24 Jan. 1811	Lieut. *Captain	2 Life Gds.		
John Perkins	As.-Sur.,14 Mar. ,,	As.-Sur.	Half-pay	25 Oct. 1814	
James Brady	,, 19 Dec. ,,	,, *Surgeon	2nd Foot	30 July, 1829	
Wm. Ross	Ensign, ,, ,,	Lieut.	Half-pay	25 Oct. 1814	
B. Jackson	,, 11 July, ,,	Ensign	R. Stff.Cps.	23 Oct. 1811	
J. M'Entagert	Captain, 18 ,, ,,	Captain	Half-pay	1814	
J. M. Edgar	Lieut., 8 Aug. ,,	Lieut.	,,	,,	Died at Gibraltar, 30 Sept. 1813.
Maurice Mahony	Ensign, 17 Oct. ,,	Ensign	..	..	
Wm. Ross, jun.	,, 31 ,, ,,	Lieut. *Captain	R.A.Corps.	24 June, 1814	
W. H. Scott	Captain, 28 Nov. ,,	Captain	Half-pay	25 Oct. 1814	Died at Gibraltar, 2 Dec. 1813.
Thos. Clubbe	Ensign, 23 Jan. 1812	Ensign	..	19 May, 1814	
Ed. Warner	Major, 30 ,, ,,	Major *Lt.-Col.	Half-pay	25 Oct. 1814	
J. Farquharson	Captain,15 ,, ,,	Major	..	..	May, 1820.
W. Beetham	,, 16 ,, ,,	Captain *Major	Half-pay	8 April, 1826	
J. Hogg	,, 30 ,, ,,	Captain	,,	24 ,, 1816	
Serj. Buchanan	Qr.-Mas., 6 Feb. ,,	Qr.-Mas. *Ensign	2 Vet. Batt.	1821	
M. M'Donough	Ensign, 13 ,, ,,	Lieut.	Half-pay		
Wm. Clarke	,, 7 May, ,,	,,	,,		
— Torrens	,, 4 June, ,,	Ensign	Portg. Ser.	25 Oct. 1814	
Flem. Smith	,, ,, ,,	Lieut.	Half-pay	,,	
Hon. H. R. Pakenham	Lt.-Col., 3 Sept. ,,	Lt.-Col.	3rd Ft.Gds.	25 July, 1814	
J. Laidlaw	Ensign, 24 ,, ,,	Lieut.	Half-pay	27 Sept. 1833	
J. W. Graham	,, 12 Nov. ,,	,,	2 Vet. Batt.		
Al. Calder	,, 3 Dec. ,,	,, *Captain	Half-pay		
G. G. L'Estrange	Lt.-Col., 10 ,, ,,	Lt.-Col.	31st Regt.	8 June, 1815	
Simon Nehl	Captain, 28 Jan. 1813	Captain	72nd Regt.		26 Feb., 1813.
— Miller	Qr.-Mas., 4 Feb. ,,	Qr.-Mas.	..	..	
Chas. King	Ensign, 25 ,, ,,	Ensign	..	..	26 May, 1825.
— M'Gregor	Qr.-Mas., 11 Mar. ,,	Qr.-Mas.	..	..	
Chas. Barr	Ensign, 8 April, ,,	Ensign	..	..	16 June, 1814.
Jas. Dunlop	Captain, 13 May, ,,	Captain	..	..	27 Mar. 1838.
Earl of Dalhousie	Colonel, 21 ,, ,,	Colonel *General			
Robt. Maxwell	Ensign, 6 Aug. ,,	Lieut.	11Lt.Drag.	24 Oct. 1821	
A. G. Boyes	,, 9 Dec. ,,	,,	64th Regt.	,,	
— Jeffrey	Captain, 25 Dec. ,,	..	..	..	Only temporary rank, and reduced 25 Oct. 1814.
A. Cummings	Ensign, 27 Jan. 1814	,,	Half-pay	25 Oct. 1814	
T. S. Pratt	,, 2 Feb. ,,	Lt.-Col.	Dy.As.Gen. Madras	5 Sept. 1843	
H. Babington	,, 3 ,, ,,	Captain	Half-pay		
R. Carruthers	,, 19 May ,,	Ensign	2nd Regt.	25 Jan. 1825	
James Foot	,, 11 Aug. ,,	,,	Half-pay	25 Feb. 1819	
W. Glennie	,, ,, ,,	,,	,,	1817	
J. C. Browne	,, 9 Nov. ,,	,,	,,	14 May, 1818	
Thomas Tripp	Captain,14 Sept. 1815	Captain	Sold out	1822	

250 SUCCESSION OF OFFICERS OF

Names.	Date of First Commission in the Regiment.	Highest Rank in the Regiment or the Army (* denotes the latter Rank).	Removed, Promoted, or Exchanged.	Dates of Removal, &c.	Died in the Regiment, &c.
J. WAUCHOPE	Lt.-Col., 8 June „	Lt.-Col.	Half-pay	3 Oct. 1817	
James DONALD	Ensign, 19 Nov. „	Ensign		20 Nov. „	
J. F. CREWE	Captain, 25 Apr. 1816	Captain	3rd Ft.Gds.		
W. N. DOUGLAS	Lieut., 26 „ „	*Lt.-Col. Lieut.	Half-pay	1816	
J. G. POWEL	„ 10 July, „	„	„		
Step. COLLINS	„ 11 „ „	„	„	24 Mar. 1817	
E. J. CLAYFIELD	„ Apr. 1817	„	„	28 Mar. 1822	
Rob. BYERS	„ 21 Aug. „	Ensign	„	21 Aug. 1817	
H. OGLANDER	Lt.-Col., 23 Oct. „	Lt.-Col.			22 June, 1840, on the Coast of China
W. JAMES	Captain, 6 Nov. „	*Colonel Lt.-Col.			
H. F. STRANGE	Ensign, 20 „ „	Major	25th Regt.	16 Dec. 1845	
Thomas M'NIVEN	Lieut , 5 Mar. 1818	Lieut.	29th Regt.	29 Aug. 1825	
A C. DRAWATER	Captain, 23 July, „	Captain	P.M.64Rgt.		
J. MAULE	„ 30 Sept. 1819		Half-pay	12 July, 1826	
W. N. SITWELL	Ensign, 20 Apr. 1820	*Maj. & Lt. Col. Captain	„	23 Mar. 1832	
J. BROOKSBANK	Captain, 20 Oct. „	„	„	24 Dec. 1825	
W. E. HAY	Ensign, 10 May, 1821	Ensign	„	10 May, 1821	
P. P. BREHAUT	„ 28 Mar. 1822	Captain			26 Oct. 1825, on passage to Europe
Geo. PIGOT	„ 25 Sept. „	Lieut.	90th Regt.	13 Apr. 1826	
R. E. Rich	„ 12 Aug. 1824	„	Half-pay		
Lord RAMSAY	„ 25 Jan. 1825	*Captain Lieut.			
D. PERSTON	Surg., 17 Feb. „	*Captain Lieut.			27 Oct. 1832.
Mat. M'INNES	Lieut., 8 Apr. „	Captain	„	15 Feb. 1839	
Jas. FRASER	„ 9 „ „	„	4th Lt.Dra. 55th Regt.	20 Feb. 1835	
Jas. PIGGOT	„ 9 „ „		St.Hel.Rgt.	15 Mar. 1844	
D. C. CAMPBELL	Ensign, 8 „ „	Ensign			Resigned,20June, 1825.
John MAULE	„ 9 „ „	Lieut.			
Geo. SINCLAIR	Lieut., „ „	„	Half-pay	24 Nov. 1825	
R. M'DONALD	Ensign, 7 „ „	Ensign	3rd Regt.	20 June, „	
W. RODGERS	Qr.-Mas., 18 May, „	Qr.-Mas.	Half-pay	1 May, 1828	
J. R. VERNON	Ensign, 30 June, „	Lieut.	69th Regt.	8 „ „	
T. J. CAMPBELL	„ 21 July, „	Ensign *Lieut.	46th Regt.	1 „ 1830	
W. HAGART	„ 17 Sept. „		Half-pay	13 July, 1826	
J. GUTHRIE	„ 29 Oct. „	Lieut.	„	9 July, 1829	
An. M'DONALD	Lieut., 24 Nov. „	„	„	11 „ „	
A. D. COLLEY	Ensign, 11 Feb. 1826	Lieut. *Captain	Ex. 11 Foot	26 „ 1828	
C. P. BOWLES	Captain, 8 Apr. „	Lieut.	Half-pay	29 June,1826	
C. W. THOMAS	Lieut., 13 „ „	Lieut.	„	30 Aug. „	
Geo. HOGARTH	Captain, 18 May, „	Major			Died at Quebec, 25 July, 1854.
W. STEWART	„ 8 June, „	*Lt.-Col. Captain	71st Regt.	31 Aug. 1826	
J. PRINGLE	Major, 29 „ „	Major	Half-pay	29 „ „	
Thomas SECCOMBE	Ensign, 6 July, „	Lieut.			19 March, 1843.
T. E. WELBY	„ 11 „ „		13Lt.Drag.	14 Oct. 1830	
Robert BROOKES	Captain, 13 „ „	Captain	69th Regt.	30 Aug. 1826	
A. MUNRO	Ensign, „ „	Ensign *Lieut.	16th Foot	25 Apr. 1828	
J. W. BATHE	„ 29 Aug. „	Ensign *Lieut.	30th Regt.	24 „ „	
C. W. COMBE	„ 30 „ „	Ensign *Lieut.	20th Regt.	15 June,1830	
Thomas PARK	Captain, 31 „ „	Captain			10 Oct. 1832.
W. CROKE	Lieut., 30 Apr. 1827	Lieut.	56th Regt.	21 June,1827	
Lord A. CONINGHAM	„ 21 June, „	„	Half-pay	7 Aug. „	
R. H. STRONG	Ensign, 7 Aug. „	..	„ 30th Regt.	17 Mar. 1829	

THE TWENTY-SIXTH OR CAMERONIAN REGIMENT. 251

Names.	Date of First Commission in the Regiment.	Highest Rank in the Regiment or the Army (* denotes the latter Rank).	Removed, Promoted, or Exchanged.	Dates of Removal, &c.	Died in the Regiment, &c.
C. H. PEIRSE	Ensign, 22 Nov. 1827	Lieut.	Half-pay	15 Feb. 1830	
G. B. HILDEBRAND	Lieut., 31 Dec. ,,	,,	Adj.76Reg.	26 ,, 1828	
W. THOMPSON	As.-Sur.,24 Jan. 1828	As.-Surg.	13Lt.Drag.	26 Oct. 1830	
J. A. CAMPBELL	Lieut., 21 Feb. ,,	Lieut.			
Thomas FITZGERALD	Captain, 20 Feb. ,,	Captain	Retired		
Edward C. THOMPSON	Lieut., 25 Apr. ,,	,,	Half-pay	15 Sept. 1832	
Waldron KELLY	,, ,, ,,	Lieut.	..	..	Cashiered, Nov. 1830.
William Ker THOMSON	,, 26 ,, ,,	,,	1st Royal 21st Regt.	18 Mar. 1830 25 Apr. 1845	
Thomas FFRENCH	,, ,, ,,	Captain			Madras Road, 24 Feb. 1837.
J. B. HEMING	,, ,, ,,	Lieut.	..	..	
Wm. Foster HANNAGAN	,, ,, ,,	,,	Half-pay	29 Oct. 1829	
A. E. SHELLY	Ensign, 25 ,, ,,	,,	,,	11 Sept. 1835	
Gerald S. FITZGERALD	,, 26 ,, ,,	,,	Capt.Unatt	24 Mar. 1837	
Richard CHERNLEY	,, 24 ,, ,,	Ensign	88th Foot	19 Aug. 1828	
James RODGERS	Qr.-Mas., 1 May, ,,	Pay.-Mas.	38th Regt.	7 Oct. 1836	
Richard THOMPSON	Lieut., 8 ,, ,,	Captain	51st Regt.	12 Sept. 1813	
John SHUM	Ensign, 19 Aug. ,,	,,	..	..	9 Dec. 1844, at Restward.
W. R. STAFF	Lieut., 3 Dec. ,,	Lieut.	..	..	On passage from China, 14 June, 1841.
E. R. GREGG	,, 24 Jan. 1829	Captain	96th Foot	22 May, 1846	
Jno. Money CARTER	Ensign, 31 ,, ,,	Ensign	..	..	Appointment cancelled.
Anthony FORBES	,, 1 Feb. ,,	,,	..	..	Appointment cancelled.
Richard AMSTRONG	Lt.-Col., 24 Jan. ,,	Lt.-Col. *Colonel	Half-pay	13 Feb. 1835	
John LAURIE	Ensign, 13 Mar. ,,	..	..	..	Appointment cancelled.
Octs. G. PERROTT	,, 23 Jan. ,,	Lieut.	15 Lt.Drag.	15 June,1849	
A. S. H. MOUNTAIN	Major, 25 Dec. 1828	Lt.-Col. *Colonel	29th Regt.	8 Mar. 1848	
D. McDONALD	Ensign, 10 Oct. 1829	Ensign	..	..	Appointment cancelled.
James Wm. BOYD	,, 25 June, ,,	Lieut.	..	..	Died at Urrool, 16 Oct. 1832. 2 Oct. 1832.
A. M. ROBINSON	Lieut., 29 Oct. ,,	,,	,,	,,	
Alex. M'DONALD	Ensign, 13 Mar. ,,	Lieut.	Half-pay	4 Sept. 1843	
James SWEENEY	Lieut., 19 Nov. ,,	Captain	Unattachd.	15 Feb. 1839	
W. F. P. WILSON	Ensign, 15 June,1830	Ensign *Lieut.	39th Regt.	5 May, 1832	
Norman M'CLEAN	Captain, 10 Mar. ,,	Captain	..	..	Appointment cancelled.
Donald M. Ross	Lieut., 13 ,, ,,	Lieut.	2W.I.Regt.	24 July, 1835	
Chas. W. SIBLEY	,, 1 May ,,	,,	62nd Regt.	19 Aug. 1842	
P. P. NEVILLE	,, 14 Oct. ,,	,,	63rd Regt.	27 Nov. 1835	
W. R. L. BENNETT	Ensign, 30 June, 1831	Ensign	16th Regt.		
Allan MENZIES	,, 26 Apr. 1832	,,	3rd Regt.		Appointment cancelled.
Thomas Foss	As.-Sur., ,, ,,	,,	..	..	
J. C. MINTO	,, 26 Oct. 1830	As.-Sur.	The Staff	1833	
Peter BAIRD	,, 3 Dec. 1830	,,	11 Lt.Drag.	11 Jan. 1838	Exchanged to the 11th Lt. Drag., cancelled 2 Feb. 1838. To 45th Regt. 23d Nov. 1838.
George FORBES	Ensign, 10 ,, ,,	Lieut.	4 Lt. Drag.	24 Mar. 1837	
William BELL	Surgeon,13 Mar. 1831	Surgeon	Staff Surg.	7 June,1844	
R. H. STRONG	Lieut., 9 Dec. 1831	Pay Mas.	Half-pay	18 Aug. 1843	
H. W. CAULTMAN	Ensign, 20 Jan. 1832	Ensign	63rd Regt.	20 Sept. 1833	
Richard PRICE	Captain, 23 Mar. ,,	Captain	41st Foot	27 Oct. 1833	
J. T. BOURCHIER	Ensign, 5 May, ,,	Ensign	..	..	12 April, 1835, at Landour.

SUCCESSION OF OFFICERS OF

Names.	Date of First Commission in the Regiment.	Highest Rank in the Regiment or the Army (* denotes the latter Rank).	Removed, Promoted, or Exchanged.	Dates of Removal, &c.	Died in the Regiment, &c.
R. C. Hamond	Lieut., 28 Sept. 1832	Lieut.	67th Foot	25 Oct. 1833	
A. H. Bernard	Ensign, 13 Nov. ,,	Ensign	..	..	3 July, 1834, a Meerut.
William Senhouse	Captain, 15 Feb. 1833	Captain	12th Foot	31 Dec. 1833	
Christopher Savage	Ensign, 19 Apr. ,,	Ensign	Sold out	1839	
A. F. Evans	,, 10 May, ,,	Lieut.	,,	15 Nov. 1838	
Thomas Price	,, 24 May, ,,	Ensign	,,	1833	
John W. Johnstone	,, 31 Mar. ,,	Captain	..	..	Died at Montreal, C.E. 7 July,1858.
Chilley Pine	As.-Sur., 30 Aug. ,,	As.-Sur. *Surgeon	58th Regt.	12 Dec. 1843	
Henry Edgar	Ensign, 27 Sept. ,,	Captain	Sold out	21 Jan. 1855	
B. R. S. Hutchison	Lieut., 25 Oct. ,,	Lieut.	31st Foot	12 Oct. 1836	
William Caine	Captain, 27 ,, ,,	Bt.-Maj. *Major	Unattachd.	29 Nov. 1844	
James Paterson	,, 31 Dec. ,,	Major	94th Regt.	30 Apr. 1847	
John M'Daniel	Ensign, 14 Feb. ,,	Lieut.	..	..	At Chusan, 27 Nov. 1840.
Edmund P. Gilbert	Lieut., 28 Mar. 1834	Lieut.	..	..	At Singapore, on board the "Defiance,"23d May, 1840.
Charles Cameron	Ensign, 16 May ,,	Captain	Sold out	28 Apr. 1854	
Walter B. Park	,, 26 Dec. ,,	Lieut. *Captain	Unattachd.	15 June, 1849	
Marcus Beresford	Lt.-Col., 13 Feb. 1835	Lt.-Col.	3rd Regt.	25 Dec. 1835	
Dobson Young	Captain, 20 Feb. 1835	Captain	29th Regt.	17 Apr. 1843	
William L. Robson	Ensign, 24 July, ,,	Lieut.	..	..	Promotion cancelled, 11 Aug. 1837.
Hon. W. G. Osborne	,, 11 Sep. ,,	,,	Retired	27 Sept. 1842	
W. E. F. Barnes	Lieut., 24 July, ,,	,,	3rd Lt.Dra.	30 June, 1837	
Donald Robertson	,, 11 Dec. ,,	,,	Retired		Never joined.
Joseph Goodfellow	Qr.-Mas., 25 Sept. ,,	Qr.-Mas.	10th Regt.	27 Feb. 1243	
William T. Betts	Ensign, 24 Nov. ,,	Major	88th Foot	5 Nov. 1861	
Wm. H. James	,, 25 Dec. ,,	Ensign	..	..	At Fort William, 22 Jan. 1838.
William Maule	Lieut., 12 Oct. 1836	Lieut.	..	..	4 April, 1838, at Fort William.
George Sweeney	Ensign, 25 Nov. ,,	,,	..	..	At sea, on passage to England, 11 July, 1841.
John Rodgers	,, 31 Mar. 1837	Captain	..	..	Retired 14 Oct. 1851.
Edw. B. Parker	,, 1 July, ,,	Ensign	..	..	At Fort William, 5 Aug. 1838.
John Miller	Lieut., 24 Mar. ,,	Lieut.	66th Foot	30 June, 1837	
Chas. S. Teale	,, 30 June, ,,	,,	4th ,,	7 July ,,	
James W. Gryles	,, 7 July ,,	,,	Sold out		
Wm. Postlethwaite	Ensign, 11 Aug. ,,	,,	,,	27 Dec. 1838	
Arthur Wood, M.D.	As.-Sur., 11 Jan. 1838	As.-Sur.	..	..	Appointment cancelled by G. O. of 27th June, 1838.
John Cumming	Ensign, 23 Sept. 1837	Lieut.	4th Foot	2 Feb. 1844	
Sir John Colborne	Colonel, 28 Mar. 1838	Colonel	2 Life Gds.	24 Mar. 1854	
George Mylius	Captain, 2 July, ,,	..	Town Maj. Dublin, H.-pay, unat.		
Eyre Lynch	Lieut., 11 May, ,,	Lieut.	Retired	22 Feb. 1850	
Richard Palmer Sharp	Ensign, 18 ,, ,,	,,	72nd Regt.	18 May, 1838	
Alfred Rob. Margary	,, 26 June, ,,	Ensign *Lieut.	54th Regt.	16 Dec. 1840	
Henry B. Phipps	,, 17 Aug. ,,	Lieut.	86th Foot	18 Feb. 1842	
Wm. G. Bace, M.D.	As.-Sur., 23 Nov. ,,	As.-Sur.	..	..	At Hong Kong.
Fred. Hovenden	Captain, 15 Feb. 1839	Captain *Major	Retired	22 Feb. 1839	

THE TWENTY-SIXTH OR CAMERONIAN REGIMENT. 253

Names.	Date of First Commission in the Regiment.	Highest Rank in the Regiment or the Army (* denotes the latter Rank).	Removed, Promoted, or Exchanged.	Dates of Removal, &c.	Died in the Regiment, &c.
Alex. G. MOORHEAD	Lieut., 15 Feb. 1839	Lieut.	Adjt. of a Recruiting district.	6 Feb. 1846	
Alex. MILLER	Ensign, 15 Mar. ,,	,,	22nd Foot	17 Nov. 1843	
Albany F. WALLACE	,, 5 April, ,,	Captain	7th Foot	1 Oct. 1847	
Wm. Le Poer FRENCH	Lieut., 14 June, ,,	..	Retired		
Maurice CANE	Ensign, 14 ,, ,,				
Rob. C. JONES	,, 9 Aug. ,,	Lieut.	22nd Regt.	23 Aug. 1844	
Edward G. WHITTY	,, 29 Nov. ,,	,,	25th Regt.	26 Apr. ,,	
Gaskin ANDERSON	,, 8 May, 1840				
Henry L. BYRNE	,, 16 ,, ,,				
Chas. H. RHYS	Ensign, 26 June, 1840	Lieut.	Sold out	19 May, 1846	
Robert SYNGE	,, 20 Oct. ,,	Ensign	Half-pay	18 Oct. 1843	
R. E. De MONTMORENCIE..	,, 17 Nov. ,,	,,	7th R. Fus.	12 Jan. 1844	
H. D. WILLIAMS	Lieut., 16 Dec. ,,				
Barth. O'BRIEN	,, ,, ,,				
Charles DUPERIER	Ensign, 29 Dec. ,,	,,	80th Reg.	26 July, 1844	
Wm. W. TURNER	,, 19 Feb. 1841	..	Half-pay	4 Sept. 1843	
Horatio De QUINCY	,, 30 Apr. ,,				
Ferd. WHITTINGHAM	Captain, 18 May, ,,	Major *Lt.-Col.	Unatt.	29 Aug. 1856	
John PIPER	Lieut., ,,	Lieut.	Cashiered	14 Oct. 1843	
John R. BRUSH	As.-Sur., 8 June, ,,	As.-Sur.	St.Hel.Cps.	4 Aug. 1843	
Rob. M. DICKENS	Ensign, 18 ,, ,,	Lieut.	R.Can.Rfls.	26 ,, 1853	
Patrick DUFF	Lieut., 23 July, ,,		Retired	12 Nov. 1847	
Geo. N. BREDIN	Ensign, 6 Aug. ,,	Ensign	14th I. Reg.	30 Sept. 1843	
C. S. J. WALLACE	,, 3 Dec. ,,	Lieut.	25th Reg.	3 Jan. 1845	
G. W. M. LOVETT	Lieut., 18 Feb. 1842	,,	Half-pay	26 Oct. 1843	
Fran. J. CRESSWELL	Ensign, 27 Sept. ,,	,,	Retired	19 Mar. 1847	
Jacob G. MOUNTAIN	,, 25 Oct. ,,	Lt. & Adjt.	..	..	Died at Gibraltar, 17 June, 1850.
Sir G. F. R. WALKER, Bt.	,, 27 Dec. ,,	Ensign	Coldst.Gds.	28 Mar. 1844	
Charles DAINES	Qr.-Mas., 27 Feb. 1843	Qr.-Mas.	Half-pay	2 Apr. 1847	
Bernard G. LAYARD	Captain, 17 Apr. ,,	Captain	Half-pay	15 Mar. 1830	
Francis CAREY	,, 12 Sept. ,,	Lt.-Col. *Colonel	,,	25 July, 1865	
Rob. C. CRAIGIE	P.-Mas., 3 Nov. ,,	P.-Mas.	To a District	23 Oct. 1856	
Arthur A. LONGMORE	Lieut., 17 ,, ,,	Captain	Retired	11 May, 1858	
Kenneth MENZIES	As.-Sur.,12 Dec. ,,	As.-Sur.	Resigned	23 Feb. 1844	Retired,11th May, 1855.
W. M. CAMPBELL	Lieut., 2 Feb. 1844	Lieut.	2 W. I. Reg. Retired	9 Apr. 1847 15 Nov. 1850	
Thomas W. ANDREWS	Ensign, ,, ,,	,,	Staff Sur.	13 Nov. 1846	
William HORNE, M.D.	As.-Sur.,23 Feb. ,,	As.-Sur.	2nd class		
Fred. N. SKINNER	Captain, 15 Mar. ,,	Captain	Half-pay 55th Foot	4 Apr. 1845	
Rich. W. CLERKE	Ensign, 12 Apr. ,,	Major	..	..	Drowned at Fort Gomer, near Gosport, 3 Apr. 1864
H. E. S. RUDYERD	Lieut., 26 ,, ,,	Lieut.	Retired	22 Dec. 1846	
John STEWART	Surgeon, 25 June, ,,	Surgeon	Removed to the Staff Pay.-Mas.	13 July, 1847	
Charles E. PRESTON	Ensign, 26 July, ,,	Lieut.	18thR.Irish Retired	30 Mar. 1855	
Thomas ANDREWS	Lieut., 23 Aug. ,,	Captain	91st Foot	29 Dec. 1848	
A. E. G. SINCLAIR	Ensign, 20 Dec. ,,	Lieut.	93rd Foot	4 May, 1849	
Charles E. BLACKETT	,, 21 Dec. ,,	,,	28th Mar. 1855		
Bertie M. ROBERTS	Lieut., 3 Jan. 1845	Captain	94th Regt.	31 Dec. 1847	
David H. BLAIR	Ensign, 4 Apr. ,,	Lieut.	Retired	30 Oct. 1854	
George FREND	Captain, 25 ,, ,,	Captain *Major			
Willm. J. D'URBAN	Major, 16 Dec. ,,	,,	Half-pay Sold out	31 July, 1846 2 Mar. 1849	
Wm. R. BELL	Ensign, 19 May, 1846	Ensign	,,	7 Apr. 1854	
Wm. S. NICHOLSON	Captain, 22 ,, ,,	Captain	Retired	22 Nov. 1850	
Henry J. NOYES	Ensign, 26 June, ,,	Lieut.	Sold out	26 Mar. 1852	
Rodney MYLIUS	,, 14 Aug. ,,	,,			

SUCCESSION OF OFFICERS OF

Names.	Date of First Commission in the Regiment.	Highest Rank in the Regiment or the Army (* denotes the latter Rank).	Removed, Promoted, or Exchanged.	Dates of Removal, &c.	Died in the Regiment, &c.
Duncan MACINTYRE	As.-Sur., 27 Oct. 1846	As.-Sur.	Staff	27 Oct. 1848	
Henry V. STEWART	Ensign, 22 Dec. ,,	Ensign	Sold out	15 ,, 1847	
Wm. E. THOMAS	,, 19 Mar. 1847	Lieut.	,,	5 Dec. 1851	
Chas. KENT	Qr.-Mas., 2 Apr. ,,	Qr.-Mas.	Half-pay	2 Oct. 1857	
Chamb. HINCHLIFFE	Ensign, 9 ,, ,,	Lieut.	64th Regt.	21 May, 1850	
W. D. DAVENPORT	Major, 30 ,, ,,	Major	Retired	30 Sept. 1847	
James JOHNSTONE	Surgeon, 13 July, ,,	Surgeon	Resigned	3 Feb. 1848	
W. E. WALLACE	Ensign, 1 Oct. ,,	..	7th R. Fus.	9 Nov. 1849	
J. B. YOUNG	,, 15 ,, ,,	..	85th Regt.	9 Feb. ,,	
S. W. F. M. WILSON	,, 12 Nov. ,,	Ensign	83rd Regt.	11 May, ,,	
R. T. HEARN	Lieut., 31 Dec. ,,	Lieut.	Appointed P.-Mas. 76th Regt.	30 Sept. 1851	
W. A. HEISE, M.B.	Surgeon, 4 Feb. 1848	Surgeon	Resigned	18 Oct. 1849	
A. T. HEMPHILL	Lt.-Col., 8 Mar. ,,	Lt.-Col. *M.-Gen.	Half-pay	29 June,1860	Died at Dublin, Mar. 30, 1863, in command of the 1st Infantry Brigade at the time of his decease. Appointed Brigadier-General,29 June, 1860.
Fredk. CLARKE	As.-Sur.,17 Oct. ,,	As.-Sur.	25th Regt.	30 Mar. 1849	
Wm. HOPSON	Captain, 1 Dec. ,,	Major	Retired	7 Jan. 1858	
Count Geo. RIVAROLA	Lieut., 29 ,, ,,	Lieut.	,,	3 Aug. 1849	
Fredk. THISTLETHWAYTE	Ensign, 9 Feb. 1849	Ensign	,,	15 Mar. 1850	
R. C. GRANVILLE	,, 2 Mar. ,,	Captain	Sold out	28 Jan. 1862	
Fredk. DOUGLAS	As.-Sur., 30 ,, ,,	As.-Sur.	Staff-Sur. 2nd Class	2 Oct. 1857	
W. T. H. ELLIOT	Lieut., 4 May, ,,	Lieut.	Retired 38th Foot	7 June,1849 Apr. 1852	Never joined.
John STRATTON	Ensign, 11 ,, ,,	..	Retired	14 Mar. 1851	
Fredk. A. CARRINGTON	,, 8 June, ,,	Ensign	Unattach.	30 July, 1852	
F. T. LYSTER	Lieut., 27 July, ,,	Lieut.	Staff	14 Nov. 1851	
William MOSSE	Ensign, 21 Aug. ,,	Surgeon	Retired	2 June,1859	
Andrew FERGUSON, M.D.	Surgeon, 19 Oct. ,,	Captain	,,	11 Mar. 1855	
Rich. CHUTE	Ensign, 15 Jan. 1850	,,	,,	23 Jan. 1852	
W. B. PARK	Captain, 22 Feb. ,,	Ensign	Retired	17 Nov. 1854	
Chas. Lord LURGAN	Ensign, 11 Mar. ,,	Captain	Staff	25 Jan. 1856	Back to Regt.from Staff Surgeon, 25 April, 1856.
W. H. HUSSEY	Captain,15 ,, ,,	As.-Sur.			
John COATES, M.D.	As.-Sur., 2 Apr. ,,				
Wm. E. WALLACE	Lieut., 21 May, ,,	Captain	Appd. Adj. DepôtBatt.	3 Jan. 1859	
W. F. KERRICH	Ensign, 12 July, ,,	,,	Retired	18 Sept. 1863	
C. F. ELWES	,, 22 Nov. ,,	Lieut.	Sold out	28 Apr. 1854	
E. H. P. ELDERTON	,, 13 Dec. ,,	Captain	,,	12 June,1860	
Henry Chas. HARDINGE	,, 14 Mar. 1851	,,	Retired	21 Feb. ,,	
William John NUNN	Lieut., ,, ,,	Lieut.	Sold out	3 Oct. 1855	
Thos. W. H. HUTCHINSON	Ensign, 12 Dec. 1851	Captain	9th Lt.Dra.	18 Jan. 1856	Killed in India.
John COLLING	,, 13 ,, ,,	,,	..	..	Accidentally shot at the Curragh Camp, 18 May, 1860.
Edw. Arch. COLLINS	,, 23 Jan. 1852	,,			
Wm. Elliott LOCKHART	,, 17 Aug. ,,	,,	74 Highlrs.	2 June,1865	
Estcourt DAY	,, 22 Apr. 185?	,,	Sold out	8 July, 1865	
Matthew Holford HALE	,, 13 May, ,,	,,			
Geo. Wm. NORTHEY	,, 27 Sept. ,,	,,	Adj. 18th DepôtBatt.	18 Oct. 1864	
G. E. Phipps TRENT	,, 17 Mar. 1854	,,			
L. Sherwood KING	,, 7 Apr. ,,	Ensign	56th Regt.	3 Aug. 1855	
J. GIVINS	,, 6 June, ,,	Lieut.	Retired	23 Apr. 1858	
James ARMSTRONG	,, 7 ,, ,,	,,			
George MELDRUM	,, 11 Aug. ,,	,,	..	..	Died,Mar.29,1862, at Edinburgh, of rheumatic fever.

THE TWENTY-SIXTH OR CAMERONIAN REGIMENT. 255

Names.	Date of First Commission in the Regiment.	Highest Rank in the Regiment or the Army (*donotes the latter Rank).	Removed, Promoted, or Exchanged.	Dates of Removal, &c.	Died in the Regiment, &c.
George W. APPLEBY	Lieut., 18 Aug. 1854	Captain	31st Foot	Jan. 1865	
Joseph LOWNDES	,, 24 ,, ,,	,,	Sold out	,, ,,	
William BEERS	Ensign, 25 ,, ,,	,,			
George HOGARTH	,, 13 Oct. ,,	Lieut.	..	..	Died, 28 Oct.1856, of yellow fever, at Bermuda.
Edward KEMPSON	,, 27 ,, ,,	,,			
Henry A. BARTON	,, 10 Nov. ,,	,,	Sold out	8 Oct. 1861	
Morris ROBINSON	,, 1 Dec. ,,	,,	95th Foot	26 ,, 1860	
C. R. B. CALCOTT	Lieut., 12 Nov. 1852	Major	..	25 July, 1865	Exchanged to 28 Batt.27July,1866
C. H. PAYNTER	Ensign, 28 Apr. 1854	Ensign	..	..	Killed at the explosion at Newcastle-on-Tyne, 6 Oct. 1854.
F. Du Bois LUKIS	,, 30 Mar. 1855	,,	64th Foot	28 Dec. 1855	
W. McDonald MILL	Lieut., 28 Jan. ,,	Lieut.	6th Foot	30 Oct. 1857	
C. H. BINDON	Ensign, 15 Dec. 1854	Ensign	78th Foot	25 June,1858	
G. W. H. WARDELL	Ensign, 3 Aug. 1855	Ensign	83rd Foot	23 Oct. 1855	
W. H. SALWEY	,, 10 ,, ,,				
W. FRANKLIN	,, 14 Sept. ,,	,,	24th ,,	16 Apr. 1858	
A. KERSHAW	,, 4 May, ,,	,,	1st Royals	22 June, 1855	
H. GANDY	,, 23 Oct. ,,	,,	83rd Foot	18 Apr. 1856	
J. E. MARSDEN	,, 7 Dec. ,,	,,	Resigned	18 ,, ,,	
Thomas TURNER	,, 28 ,, ,,				
W. W. W. HUMBLEY	Captain, 18 Jan. 1856	Captain	Half-pay	23 Oct. 1857	
J. A. COLEBROOKE	Ensign, 18 Apr. ,,	Lieut.	83rd Foot	5 Mar. 1858	
W. MANJIN	,, 18 ,, ,,	Ensign	..	..	Died at Dublin, 15 Feb. 1860.
J. COATES	Surgeon, 23 ,, ,,	Surgeon	24th ,,	4 Aug. 1865	
F. A. QUARTLEY	Lieut., 8 June,1852	Captain	..	..	Drowned 27 Jan. 1859, at Bermuda.
A. HALL	Qr.-Mas., 2 Oct. 1857	Qr.-Mas.	75th ,,	5 July, 1864	
W. McDONALD	Captain, 23 ,, ,,	Captain *Lt.-Col.	72nd ,,	23 Oct. 1860	
James BRIDGE	Pmas., 24 ,, 1856	..	28th ,,	11 July, 1865	
W. F. CULLEN	As.-Sur., 1 Dec. 1854	As.-Sur.	Staff	10 Sept. 1858	
G. P. FAWKES	Ensign, 8 July, 1856	Captain	83rd ,,	12 ,, 1865	
P. C. STORY	,, 5 Sept. ,,				
J. McLETCHIE	As.-Sur., 28 ,, 1857	As.-Sur.	..	..	Services dispensed with, 16 Jan. 1863.
L. A. GREGSON	Ensign, 18 Dec. ,,				
Hon. W. H. B. OGILVY	,, 15 Jan. 1858	Lieut.	Sold out	26 Oct. 1860	
C. H. WILLS	,, 16 Mar. ,,	,,	,,	13 Jan. 1862	
O. CRESSWELL	Ensign, 23 Apr. 1858				
H. P. WOLFERSTAN	,, 25 June, ,,				
H. C. SHARP	,, 2 July, ,,				
J. DAVIDGE	As.-Sur.,10 Sept. ,,	As.-Sur.	Staff	24 May, 1861	
W. B. WADE	Ensign, 11 Mar. 1859				
George DOUTHWAITE	,, 3 June, ,,				
J. R. G. BUCHANAN	,, 14 ,, ,,				
Arch. D. EDEN	,, 21 Feb. 1860				
Hon. G. G. CRAVEN	,, 9 Mar. ,,	Ensign	S. Fus. Gds.	12 June,1860	
Simeon Harrison HARDY	,, 12 June, ,,	Lieut.	74 Highlrs.	11 Apr. 1865	
James YOUNG	Captain, 31 July, ,,	Captain	Sold out	30 Nov. 1860	
Wm. Blakeney BURTON	Ensign, 3 ,, ,,				
A. Des Montiers CAMPBELL	,, 24 Aug. ,,	Ensign	Sold out	29 July, 1862	
Edw. Jas. UPTON	Captain, 23 Oct. ,,				
Lewis CUBITT	Lieut., 26 ,, ,,				
H. M. E. BRUNKER	Ensign, 26 ,, ,,				
James Samuel GREER	,, 21 Dec. ,,				
Godfrey Stuart HUGHES	,, 9 Oct. 1861	Ensign	Sold out	25 July, 1865	
Shurlock HENNING	Major, 5 Nov. ,,	Lt.-Col.			

SUCCESSION OF OFFICERS OF THE TWENTY-SIXTH.

Names.	Date of First Commission in the Regiment.	Highest Rank in the Regiment or the Army (*denotes the latter Rank).	Removed, Promoted, or Exchanged.	Dates of Removal, &c.	Died in the Regiment, &c.
Vivian DAVENPORT	Ensign, 14 Jan. 1862	Lieut.	..	25 July, 1865	
George GOSLING	,, 28 Jan. ,,	Ensign	S. Fus. Gds.	10 July, 1863	
Charles W. HEMPHILL	,, 30 Mar. ,,				
William A. GLYNN	,, 8 July, ,,	Ensign	Sold out	4 July, 1865	
G. H. WILSON	,, 29 ,, ,,				
Joseph JOHNSTON, M.D.	As.-Sur., 6 Feb. 1863				
J. E. Northmore WHITLOCK	Ensign, 28 Aug. ,,	Ensign	,,	21 June, 1864	
Livingstone CLARKE	Ensign, 18 Sept. 1863				
Chas. Cecil HAZLERIGG	,, 26 Feb. 1864	Ensign	Sold out	4 July, 1865	
Wm. Henry TOPP	Qr.-Mas., 5 July, ,,				
H. FitzJohn TOWNSEND	Ensign, 21 June, ,,				
William EVERETT	,, 28 ,, ,,	,,	33rd Regt.	24 Aug. 1864	Never joined 26th Cameronians.
Fred. Samuel ALEXANDER	,, 23 Aug. ,,				
Edward Lyster GREEN	Bt.-Maj., 11 Oct. ,,	Captain *Major	..	23 Dec. 1864	
Augustus R. DAVIES	Ensign, 30 Dec. ,,	Ensign	61st Foot		
James Bond CLARKE	,, 3 Jan. 1865				
Geo. J. HAMILTON	Captain, 24 ,, 1865				
Charles H. DOUGHERTY	Lieut., 11 Apr. ,,				
John MACFARLANE	Ensign, 2 June, ,,				
Thomas W. LAWSON	Captain, 2 ,, ,,				
Edward M. DOUGHERTY	Ensign, 2 ,, ,,				
Wm. CARPENTER, M.D.	As.-Sur., 9 ,, ,,				
Wm. HIGGENS	Ensign, 4 July, ,,				
Henry A. BERRY	P.-Mas., 11 ,, ,,				
Rob. A. GILCHRIST	Ensign, 4 Aug. ,,				
Richard GAMBLE, M.D.	Sur. Maj., 4 ,, ,,	..	Half-pay	11 Jan. 1867	
T. G. COOTE	Captain, 12 Sept. ,,				
S. HACKETT	Major, 27 July, 1866	Major	..	27 July, 1866	
T. MOORHEAD, M.D.	Surgeon, 11 Jan. 1867				

Positions held by the Cameronians for the last twelve years that Regiments were classified according to their figure of merit in Rifle Shooting:—

Year ending			Position in the Army.
31st March,	1872		2nd.
,,	,,	1873	3rd.
,,	,,	1874	1st.
,,	,,	1875	not exercised.
,,	,,	1876	3rd.
,,	,,	1877	1st.
,,	,,	1878	8th.
,,	,,	1879	13th.
,,	,,	1880	5th.
,,	,,	1881	5th.
,,	,,	1882	3rd.
,,	,,	1883	1st.

SUCCESSION OF OFFICERS—*continued.*

J. de W. Jebb	Ensign	14 Sept. 1867.
W. Bolton	Ensign	5 Nov. 1867.
E. P. Benn	Ensign	20 Nov. 1867.
J. Gray, M.D.	Ass.-Surg.	23 Oct., 1867.
G. Winter	Ensign	22 July, 1868.
P. J. Hughes	Ensign	8 July, 1868.
T. W. Conran	Ensign	8 July, 1868.
T. C. Jameson	Ensign	29 Oct., 1868.
L. T. Bishop	Ensign	2 Dec., 1868.
H. C. Lamb	Ensign	5 May, 1869.
T. E. Blomfield	Major	14 June, 1869.
J. R. Mecham	Lieut.	14 July, 1869.
F. H. Carleton	Lieut.	
F. Goldney	Ensign	10 Nov. 1869.
D. A. Thuillier	Ensign	9 Feb., 1870.
P. H. Drayton	Ensign	
S. G. C. Greenaway	Ensign	7 May, 1870.
F. M. Skues	Surgeon	

8 THE TWENTY-SIXTH, OR CAMERONIAN REGIMENT.

SUCCESSION OF OFFICERS, *continued.*

F. A. Willis...............	Colonel	31 May, 1871.
A. H. Ratigan	Ass.-Surg.	
W. Carpenter	Ass.-Surg.	19 Aug., 1871.
C. T. Barrow	Sub.-Lieut.	3 July, 1872.
H. E. Railston	Lieut.	14 Oct., 1873.
D. Creagh	Paymstr.	26 Oct., 1873.
L. R. Phillips............	Captain	24 Jan., 1874.
W. C. Anton	Sub.-Lieut.	28 Feb., 1874.
C. W. Atkinson.........	Lieut.	30 June, 1874.
C. M. Smyth	Captain	20 Aug., 1874.
J. Bridge	Paymstr.	23 Oct., 1875.
A. McClintock	Lieut.	20 Nov., 1875.
F. B. Bleazby	Captain	5 Jan., 1876.
G. S. Douglas	Sub.-Lieut.	12 Feb., 1876.
E. Cooke..................	Sub.-Lieut.	15 July, 1876.
E. D. Kennedy	Sub.-Lieut.	15 July, 1876.
L. F. Knollys............	Captain	15 Aug., 1877.
J. D. M. Guthrie	2nd Lt.	8 Dec., 1877.
L. W. de M. Thuillier	2nd Lt.	30 Jan., 1878.
A. W. Ranken	2nd Lt.	1 May, 1878.
C. C. Douglas	2nd Lt.	1 May, 1878.
S. G. Grant...............	2nd Lt.	1 May, 1878.
F. H. W. Fetherstonhaugh	2nd Lt.	11 May, 1878.
C. B. Wood	2nd Lt.	11 May, 1878.
C. G. B. Saunders ...	2nd Lt.	12 June, 1878.
F. S. Le Fanu	2nd Lt.	13 Aug., 1879.
A. P. D. Lushington...	2nd Lt.	11 Aug., 1880.
F. J. Nason	2nd Lt.	11 Aug., 1880.
H. E. Wise...............	2nd Lt.	25 Aug., 1880.
T. T. Macan	2nd Lt.	23 Oct., 1880.
E. Johnson...............	2nd Lt.	22 Jan., 1881.
A. R. Dick	2nd Lt.	22 Jan., 1881.
A. V. Ussher............	2nd Lt.	19 Feb. 1881.

APPENDIX.

I.

Stations and Out-Posts of the 26TH REGIMENT, whilst in Ireland, between October, 1822, and October, 1827.

Head Quarters of the Regiment.	Period.		Out Posts.	Period.		Consisting of		
	From	To		From	To	Officers.	Sergeants.	Rank and File.
Fermoy ..	25 Oct. 1822	6 Apr. 1823	None.					
			Garacloyne ..	8 Apr. 1823	16 Jan. 1824	1	1	25
			Newgrove ..	8 ,, ,,	16 ,, ,,	1	1	25
			Cloyne	10 ,, ,,	10 May, 1823	–	1	8
Cork ..	7 Apr. 1823	15 Jan. 1824	Fermount ..	8 May ,,	16 Jan. ,,	1	1	30
			Glenville ..	15 ,, ,,	16 ,, ,,	–	1	15
			Watergrasshill ..	24 Oct. ,,	16 ,, ,,	1	1	25
			Dripsey	4 Nov. ,,	16 ,, ,,	–	–	7
			Macromp ..	16 Jan. 1824	6 Oct. 1824	2	1	31
			Inchegeela ..	16 ,, ,,	8 ,, ,,	1	1	14
			Ballyvoorney .	16 ,, ,,	8 ,, ,,	1	1	18
			Bandon	16 ,, ,,	5 ,, ,,	2	1	37
			Dunmanway ..	16 ,, ,,	5 ,, ,,	1	1	19
			Bantry.. ..	16 ,, ,,	17 ,, ,,	1	1	29
			Cloghnakilty ..	16 July, ,,	29 Aug. ,,	2	2	21
Kinsale ..	16 Jan. 1824	4 Oct. 1824	Rosscarbery ..	16 ,, ,,	5 Oct, ,,	1	1	17
			Skibbereen ..	16 Jan. ,,	19 ,, ,,	1	1	18
			Charles Fort ..	16 ,, ,,	10 ,, ,,	2	1	51
			Ballinhassig ..	26 ,, ,,	16 Feb. ,,	–	1	13
			Bere Island ..	2 March ,,	18 Oct. ,,	1	1	29
			Widdy Island ..	2 ,, ,,	18 ,, ,,	–	–	11
			Camden Fort ..	28 Feb. ,,	29 Aug. ,,	–	1	10
			Cork	4 Sept. ,,	10 Oct. ,,	3	4	98
			Killarney ..	7 Oct. ,,	31 July, 1825	1	1	20
			Listowel.. ..	9 ,, ,,	24 Apr. ,,	1	2	30
			Tarbert	25 Apr. 1825	2 Aug. ,,	1	1	23
Tralee ..	8 Oct. ,,	31 July, 1825	Carrig Island ..	25 ,, ,,	2 ,, ,,	–	–	4
			Tarbert Island ..	25 ,, ,,	2 ,, ,,	–	1	12
			Castle Island ..	14 Jan. ,,	1 ,, ,,	1	1	30
			Drogheda ..	18 Oct. ,,	27 Mar. 1826	6	9	114
			Trim	17 ,, ,,	3 May, ,,	2	3	51
			Garristown ..	19 ,, ,,	27 Mar. ,,	1	1	16
			Wicklow ..	17 ,, ,,	9 Aug. ,,	2	2	42
			Kilcock	15 ,, ,,	3 May, ,,	1	1	44
			Baltinglass ..	30 Mar. 1826	9 ,, ,,	1	1	25
			Rathangan ..	30 ,, ,,	18 Apr. ,,	–	1	11
			Robertstown ..	30 ,, ,,	20 May, ,,	–	1	11
Naas ..	7 Oct. 1825	3 May, 1826	Athy	29 ,, ,,	8 ,, ,,	1	2	41
			Maryborough ..	30 ,, ,,	4 ,, ,,	2	2	48
			Carlow	30 ,, ,,	8 ,, ,,	3	2	63
			Glenmalure ..	11 Apr. ,,	11 Aug. ,,	1	1	7
			Leitrim	11 ,, ,,	29 May, ,,	–	–	4
			Glencree.. ..	11 ,, ,,	26 June, ,,	–	–	4
			Aughravanagh ..	11 ,, ,,	29 May, ,,	–	–	4
			Gold Mines ..	11 ,, ,,	8 Aug. ,,	–	–	4
			Laragh	11 ,, ,,	10 ,, ,,	–	–	4
Dublin ..	4 May, 1826	26 July, 1827	Wexford.. ..	27 July, 1827	27 Sept. 1827	3	4	78
			Duncannon Fort	2 Aug. ,,	24 ,, ,,	2	1	38
			Kilkenny ..	1 ,, ,,	14 Aug ,,	6	8	130
Waterford	2 Aug. 1827	24 Sept. ,,	Carrick-on-Suir	2 ,, ,,	22 Sept. ,,	1	1	26
			Kilmackthomas	21 ,, ,,	22 ,, ,,	1	1	24
			Callan	30 July, ,,	12 Aug. ,,	1	1	20
Fermoy ..	27 Sep. ,,	8 Oct. ,,	} None.					
Cork ..	9 Oct. ,,	24 ,, ,,						

II.

Correspondence regarding the PIPERS *of the* 26TH *or* CAMERONIAN REGIMENT.

Recruiting Department.

Horse Guards,
24*th September,* 1839.

MEMORANDUM for the information of the Assistant Adjutant-General in North Britain.

Under the circumstances stated in an application from the officer commanding the depôt of the 26th Regiment, the General Commanding-in-Chief will approve of Cosmo Cameron, the lad alluded to, being enlisted for the above corps to be employed as a Piper, provided he is found on inspection to be surgically fit for the service.

JOHN MACDONALD,
A.-G.

Recruiting Department.

Horse Guards,
11*th October,* 1839.

MEMORANDUM for the information of the Assistant Adjutant-General in North Britain.

With reference to Lord Robert Kerr's letter of the 5th inst., the General Commanding-in-Chief is pleased to confirm the enlistment of Cosmo Cameron into the 26th Regiment, and to approve of his receiving the full bounty under the circumstances stated.

JOHN MACDONALD,
A.-G.

APPENDIX. 259

Copy of a Reply to a Memorandum received on the 6th June, 1862, requesting to know whether any authority existed for men to be employed as PIPERS *in the* 26TH *or* CAMERONIAN REGIMENT.

Aldershot,
June 6th, 1862.

SIR,—In reply to your memorandum of this day, referring to the Pipers of the Cameronians, I have the honour to state that the Regiment has had them for so many years that no trace of the original authority or date of their formation exists; the Band-Master of the Regiment who has been in it for five and thirty years, states that, at his enlistment, nothing was known of their origin, but about the year 1839, the casualties of Indian service appear to have reduced them so as to make it necessary to enlist men for the purpose as acting Pipers, and the fact of a man being below the standard, brought the matter before the General Commanding-in-Chief, whose sanction was given, as shown in the correspondence annexed, which was attached to the attestation of an undersized Piper recently discharged. There has, since then, been no interruption to the existence of a body of Pipers, whose number has varied from *three* to *five,* according to the number of men qualified; they have been returned as rank and file.

I have, &c.,
F. CAREY, *Lieut.-Colonel,*
Commanding 26*th Cameronians.*

The Brigade-Major,
2nd Brigade, Aldershot.

Copy of Answer to the preceding Letter.

Horse Guards,
June 13th, 1862.

SIR,—I have laid before the General Commanding-in-Chief your letter of the 7th instant, with its enclosures, relative to three Pipers, who are borne as Privates by the 26th Regiment, and am directed by His Royal Highness to acquaint you that, under the circumstances therein stated, no alteration as to these Pipers is required.

I have, &c.,
J. YORKE SCARLETT,
A.-G.

Lieut.-General
   Sir John Pennefather, K.C.B.,
      &c. &c. Aldershot.

Copy of authority for employment of a Piper at the Depôt of the 26th or Cameronian Regiment.

(26th Cameronians.)

Horse Guards, S.W.,
7th August, 1865.

SIR,—I have the honour, by desire of the Field Marshal Commanding-in-Chief, to acknowledge the receipt of your letter of the 31st ultimo, and to acquaint you that His Royal Highness approves of a Private of the Depôt, 26th Regiment, being employed as a Piper, on the same conditions as those under which the Pipers of the service companies are employed.

I have, &c.
A. HORSFORD,
D.-A.-G.

Lieut.-Colonel Henning,
   Commanding 26th Regiment, Portsmouth.

APPENDIX. 261

III.

Questions and Replies relating to the Epidemic Fever at Bermuda in 1856.

(Addressed to the Military, Naval, and Convict Departments.)

1. What was the mean strength between the 1st June and the 31st December, 1856, of your Regiment, Corps or Establishment, including women and children, and distinguishing Natives from Europeans?   1,052. No Natives.

2. How many of your Corps, Regiment or Establishment, were attacked with yellow fever during the late epidemic, and of those how many expired?   35 attacked, including one officer. 2 died: one officer and one private.

3. To what extent was your Regiment, Corps or Establishment, increased between the 1st June and the 31st December, 1856?   113 officers, men, women, and children.

4. Of the new arrivals in your Regiment, Corps or Establishment, how many were attacked with yellow fever between the 1st June and the 31st December, and of these how many died?   2, both of whom arrived in January, 1856. No deaths.

5. How was your Regiment, Corps or Establishment, distributed between the 1st June and the 31st December, 1856?

6. What was the mean strength at each station during that period?

7. How many were attacked at each station during the same period, and of those how many died?

8. What sanitary and precautionary measures are habitually adopted in your Regiment, Corps or Establishment?

Head-quarters at St. George's; Detachments at Hamilton, Gibbs' Hill, Mount Langton, Prospect Hill, Ireland and Boaz Islands, and Ferry Point.

At Head-quarters, 685; Hamilton, 42; Gibbs' Hill, 4; Mount Langton, 12; Prospect Hill, 1; Ireland Island, 276; Boaz Island, 22; and Ferry Point, 10.

Hamilton, 3 attacked, 1 died; Gibbs' Hill, 3 attacked, 1 died; Mount Langton, 1 attacked; Ireland Island, 26 attacked; Boaz Island 2 attacked.

The Barracks are whitewashed annually, and there is a thorough cleaning of Barracks and the bedding taken out and well aired once a week. During the hot weather the drains, privies, &c., are sprinkled with lime twice a day, the men are not allowed to quit the Barracks till after the supper hour, viz., 5 p.m., nor are they even permitted to expose themselves to the sun or be employed on any fatigue duties between 8 a.m. and 5 p.m.

The Royal Barracks are, during the hot months, thinned, nearly half of the men usually occupying the rooms, being encamped at the Naval Tanks. The Barracks at Ireland Island are thinned in like manner, and the men encamped on the Glacis.

9. What special measures were resorted to on the first alarm and during the progress of the epidemic of 1856, and with what apparent results?	The men of the Regiment were inspected daily by the Surgeon during the existence of the epidemic, and any cases having the slightest tendency to fever were immediately sent to Hospital. Disinfecting fluids were freely used for the deodorization of the privies and urinals; the results were favourable, no cases of the epidemic having occurred at the Head-quarters of the Regiment, and the cases of common continued fever which were treated in Hospital were, I am informed by the Surgeon, with one exception, of a mild nature.
10. Can you give any other information relative to the special objects of this inquiry, viz., the introduction or first appearance of the epidemic of 1856, and the manner of its diffusion in the Colony?	None.

IV.

Correspondence relative to the PLAID FORAGE CAP *worn by the* 26TH *or* CAMERONIAN REGIMENT.

                                      Horse Guards,
                                     15*th January*, 1858.

SIR,—With reference to a letter from the War Office, dated 13th instant, I have it in command to request that you will state, for the General Commanding-in-Chief's information, whether any written authority exists for any deviation from the established pattern Forage Cap for officers and men of the 26th Regiment.

                                 I have, &c.,
                                      T. TROUBRIDGE,
                                                      D.-A.-G.

The Officer Commanding
   Depôt 26th Regiment.

                                St. George's, Bermuda,
                                  24*th February*, 1858.

SIR,—In acknowledging the receipt of a copy of your letter of the 15th ultimo, addressed to the Officer commanding the Depôt of the Regiment under my command, I have the honour to acquaint you, for the information of the General Commanding-in-Chief, that there is no written authority with the Regiment for any deviation from the established pattern Forage Cap for the Army being worn by the officers and men of the 26th Regiment; but the present Bandmaster (a man of the highest respectability) states that the officers and men wore the same pattern Forage Cap as they now do when he joined the "Cameronians," in the year 1827, and that there were men belonging to the Corps at that time, of 20 years' service and upwards, who had never worn any other kind

APPENDIX.

of Cap; and I have no doubt the same pattern has been used by the Cameronians ever since they were raised in the year 1689, it being national, and denoting the origin of the Corps. There are no letters or general orders with the service companies of the Regiment of an older date than September, 1843.

Under these circumstances, I trust His Royal Highness the General Commanding-in-Chief may be pleased to sanction the continuance of a Cap, the pattern of which has been of such very long standing in the Regiment.

I have, &c.,
A. T. HEMPHILL, *Colonel,*
Lt.-Col. Commanding 26*th Cameronians.*

The Adjutant-General of the Forces,
Horse Guards, London.

Horse Guards,
31*st March,* 1858.

SIR,—With reference to your letter of the 24th ultimo, I have it in command to intimate to you, that the General Commanding-in-Chief is pleased to sanction the continuance of the present pattern Forage Cap in the Regiment under your command.

I have, &c.,
T. TROUBRIDGE,
D.-A.-G.

The Officer Commanding
26*th Regiment, Bermuda.*

W. O. Mitchell, Printer, 39, Charing Cross, S.W.

www.ingramcontent.com/pod-product-compliance
Lightning Source LLC
Chambersburg PA
CBHW052057300426
44117CB00013B/2168